ADVANCE PRAISE FOR
THE MIGRATION-DEVELOPMENT REGIME

"The subject of Indian emigration needed a great book, and this is it. Agarwala gives us a meticulous history of Indian emigration and a novel framework for understanding the role the state plays in shaping emigration. In doing so, she not only shows how class differences have been at the heart of all India's emigration regimes, but also reveals the dynamic link between emigration, political legitimacy and global economic transformations. *The Migration-Development Regime* is bold, beautifully argued, and guaranteed to change how we think of migration and development."

—**Patrick Heller**, Professor of Sociology and
International Affairs, Brown University

"For more than a century, India has sent migrants abroad to work; today, remittances from overseas workers make up one of the country's largest sources of foreign exchange. Yet, as Rina Agarwala points out in her remarkable new work, discussions of India's economic growth rarely acknowledge migrants' contributions, nor do they explore the way national and state policies continue to shape migrants' options, from Silicon Valley's highly-educated computer scientists, to construction workers packed into migrant hostels in the Middle East. Especially as she lays out the changing dynamics that have produced India's circular migration patterns over the past few decades, Agarwala's carefully-researched, insightful analysis will change the way we think about India's diaspora, provoke new questions about how sending countries could protect workers abroad, and ensure their communities benefit from the 'development' that the migrants are supporting."

—**Gay Seidman**, Martindale Bascom Professor of Sociology,
University of Wisconsin-Madison

The Migration-Development Regime

How Class Shapes Indian Emigration

RINA AGARWALA

OXFORD
UNIVERSITY PRESS

OXFORD
UNIVERSITY PRESS

Oxford University Press is a department of the University of Oxford. It furthers
the University's objective of excellence in research, scholarship, and education
by publishing worldwide. Oxford is a registered trade mark of Oxford University
Press in the UK and certain other countries.

Published in the United States of America by Oxford University Press
198 Madison Avenue, New York, NY 10016, United States of America.

Library of Congress Cataloging-in-Publication Data
Names: Agarwala, Rina, 1973– author.
Title: The migration-development regime :
how class shapes Indian emigration / Rina Agarwala.
Description: New York, NY : Oxford University Press, [2022] |
Series: Modern South Asia | Includes bibliographical references and index.
Identifiers: LCCN 2022010900 (print) | LCCN 2022010901 (ebook) |
ISBN 9780197586396 (hardback) | ISBN 9780197586402 (paperback) |
ISBN 9780197586426 (epub)
Subjects: LCSH: Social classes—India. | Emigrant remittances—India. |
East Indian diaspora. | India—Emigration and immigration—History. |
India—Emigration and immigration—Government policy. |
India—Emigration and immigration—Economic aspects.
Classification: LCC JV8501 .G43 2022 (print) | LCC JV8501 (ebook) |
DDC 304.80954—dc23/eng/20220701
LC record available at https://lccn.loc.gov/2022010900
LC ebook record available at https://lccn.loc.gov/2022010901

DOI: 10.1093/oso/9780197586396.001.0001

1 3 5 7 9 8 6 4 2

Paperback printed by Lakeside Book Company, United States of America
Hardback printed by Bridgeport National Bindery, Inc., United States of America

To Ramgopal and Bimala Agarwala
And to Carsten, Nadia and Felix
Treasured companions on the journey

CONTENTS

ACKNOWLEDGMENTS

Writing this book has been a journey of its own—long and full of unexpected twists and turns. What began with a generous, but bounded, invitation to contribute one chapter on Indian immigrants in the United States to a larger multi-country study led me to wonder about the mass population of Indian immigrants in the Gulf. This led me to wonder about the connections between Indian migrants in the United States and the Gulf and those left behind in India. Once I was back in India, I began to wonder about the role of the Indian state (at the national and sub-national levels), migrants' families, migrant recruiters, the Indian NGOs with whom Indian emigrants partnered, and the migrants themselves who had landed back in India either voluntarily or by force. And my discussions with these groups led me to wonder about India's past patterns of emigration dating back to the 1800s. As I moved through new spaces and time zones, I was forced to migrate into new literatures, academic networks, classes, methodologies, theoretical traditions, cultures, organizations, occupational settings, political contexts, and subject matters. At times I felt like a foreign guest looking in from the outside, but at other times I felt I had earned my citizenship as an insider. Like most migration journeys, parts of this journey have been exhilarating. But parts have been debilitating and full of anguish. My learning curve has been steep. I have been exhausted, confused, and (very often) frustrated. I have questioned my decision to go further and further away from my origin. And I have reminisced about simpler moments in time and dreamed of a simpler future.

But now that I am bringing this project to a close, I am most of all feeling extremely grateful for all the guides and teachers I met along the way who urged and encouraged and carried me to this point. First and foremost are the hundreds of migrants, government officials, and recruiters who shared their time, insights, experiences, and emotions with me. This book would not exist without them. I have tried my best to accurately reflect their words. For the first time in my academic career, some of my interviewees requested I anonymize their contribution in order to protect their willingness to speak openly with me. I have done so. I have also concealed the names of organizations in Chapters 8 and 9.

Margery Daniels, Patricia Fernandez-Kelly, Alejandro Portes, and Min Zhou introduced me to the world of immigration in the United States. Lingxin Hao continued this education and even agreed to coteach a class on migration and development with me, so we could learn from one another—an experience that turned out to be so enjoyable we repeated it. Ruth Milkman not only helped deepen my understanding of the historical and contemporary patterns of US immigration and introduced me to more literature on the subject; she read my entire manuscript and gave me her perfect blend of warm praise and sharp critique—both of which I will forever remember and appreciate. Chris Tilly also generously read the entire manuscript, sharing with me his insights on US immigration, his encouragement, and his excellent suggestions for improvement. On the Middle East, I am grateful to May Aldabbagh, Swethaa Ballakrishnen, Anver Emon, and Natasha Iskander for their honest insights on the region, their assistance with basics (like the politics of terminology!), and their help with data. And on Africa, I thank Gay Seidman for her insights, her literature suggestions, her phone calls, her personal stories, for reading the entire manuscript, and, most of all, for finding the flaws and the gems in the argument at a moment when I was having trouble seeing either. On Indian emigration, I continued my journey of learning. Binod Khadria, Irudya Rajan, and Daniel Naujoks provided their help and patience, sharing with me their data, contacts, reports, and research. Devesh Kapur generously shared with me his data, his attention to detail, his references to other works, and his deep knowledge on the subject. He, too, read the entire manuscript and shared with me his insightful and sharp criticisms, for which I am extremely grateful.

Outside the world of migration and back in my more familiar territory of development, Joel Andreas, Erin Chung, Ron Herring, and Michael Levien all took the time to read all or parts of the manuscript. I am extremely grateful for their time, their insights, and their suggestions, all of which helped me strengthen the book. Patrick Heller went above and beyond with his support. He read countless drafts, told me "Name it!," shared with me his infectious enthusiasm for the project, gave me unending encouragement, and always managed to not only home in on exactly what was missing but also suggest how to fix it. Patrick, Ruth, Gay, Devesh, and Chris all provided me with exemplars for advising that I can only hope to one day emulate.

Ann-Marie Livingstone, Smriti Upadhyay, Alex Rakow, Swati Goel, and Caroline West provided exceptional research assistance. David McBride served as the most supportive and responsive editor one could ask for, reading drafts, providing suggestions, and introducing me to other great books on migration.

Research grants from the MacArthur Foundation and the Mellon Foundation provided generous funding that allowed me to conduct this research. Ann Morning, Natasha Iskander, May Aldabbagh, and Gayatri Menon of the AW collective gave me light at the end of this long tunnel with their example, encouragement, and wise advice to "leave the home!"

More than anyone else, I must thank my family—my personal transporters and my constant cheerleaders. My parents remained my foundational supporters, housing me, feeding me, helping me with child care, reading drafts, and always listening as I bounced ideas around. Carsten, Nadia, and Felix offered me my scaffolding. They were dragged into this journey without absolutely any say or vote. They followed me back and forth and forth and back to India. They were left on their own so I could work. And they listened as I subjected them to my ups and downs. Throughout the journey they never complained. Not even once. Rather, they offered to read my work, edit my pages, brainstorm titles, draw my cover, and finally, in the end, reminded me to "just get it done." Thanks to them, that is what I have done. As I promised Felix, I dedicate this book to all of them for embodying migration physically and mentally and making my world whole. To M&D, for moving to give me my life; to Carsten, Nadia, and Felix, for moving to join my life with yours. Thank you forever.

1

Introduction

"Let me make one thing clear," Dr. Singh began. "We are not standing with begging bowls asking for diaspora investments. Absolutely not! This is the biggest misconception among the diaspora, that we want their money. We are just as happy if they want to invest their money elsewhere."[1] Dr. Singh's words were crystal clear: the Indian government, whom Dr. Singh represented, did not rely on money from its "diaspora" or Indians living outside India. His tone, which was full of pride, passion, and a hint of irritation, was understandable given the Indian government's postcolonial tradition of showcasing its self-sufficiency.

While Dr. Singh's tone was understandable, the context was confusing. Dr. Singh said these words while sitting at his impressive office desk, where he served as secretary, or chief bureaucrat, in charge of the Ministry of Overseas Indian Affairs (MOIA) in the government of India—the very ministry responsible for bridging India's relations with its diaspora. Other sending countries, including China, the Philippines, Mexico, and Morocco, had been building similar bridges with their respective diasporas for decades. Such bridges, in turn, promised to bring foreign capital into sending countries in the form of remittances (wages that emigrants earn abroad and send to their home country), as well as foreign investments (that emigrants residing abroad make in their home country). Indeed, by 2018, officially recorded annual remittances to low- and middle-income countries had reached a record high of US$529 billion, a figure that far exceeded overseas development aid (ODA) and came close to the level of foreign direct investment (FDI) that year (Ratha 2019). And sending countries such as China had become well-known for their extraordinary success in attracting foreign investments from their overseas emigrants (Ye 2014). As a result, the World Bank and other development institutions were promoting

---

[1] Interview, January 19, 2011.

The Migration-Development Regime. Rina Agarwala, Oxford University Press. © Oxford University Press 2022.
DOI: 10.1093/oso/9780197586396.003.0001

emigration as the third leg of the globalization triad, alongside free trade and finance—a trend that some have called "the new development mantra" (Kapur 2005).

Within this context, India seemed well-positioned to be a poster child for the newfound migration-development mantra. By the early 2000s, India had joined other sending countries in establishing new awards and citizenship options that recognized and celebrated its overseas emigrants. It had also instituted a battery of new government programs designed to tap its overseas emigrants for their financial, social, and political contributions. In 2004, India became one of a handful of countries to promote diaspora issues to a cabinet level by establishing the MOIA. As a result of its efforts, India had become the world's largest migrant exporter and largest recipient of financial remittances—a trend that is still going strong today. In 2019, India had approximately 30 million overseas residents (17.5 million of whom are Indian citizens), and it received a whopping *US$76 billion* (roughly 3% of India's gross domestic product) from them in remittances (Ministry of External Affairs 2020; Reserve Bank of India 2021; United Nations 2019).[2] For decades India's annual remittances have exceeded the combined annual amount the country receives from ODA and FDI, as well as from foreign portfolio investments (FPI) and bank deposits made by Indian emigrants abroad (Reserve Bank of India 2018).[3]

But clearly Dr. Singh was in no mood to chant new mantras. His defiance toward overseas Indians' money reflects the complicated nature of international human migration, not just for receiving countries but also for sending countries. Despite the high financial returns emigration promises to bring to sending states, emigration also raises multiple challenges for sending countries, including labor shortages, undermined political legitimacy, geopolitical tensions, and questions around state responsibility for citizens abroad.

[2] The overseas Indian population figure from India's Ministry of External Affairs is the most recent one available at the time of writing. It draws on the 2015 estimate of Indian citizens living abroad (known in India as Non-Resident Indians or NRIs) and foreign-born Indians or those with Indian heritage (known in India as Persons of Indian Origin or PIOs). The United Nations migrant population figure delineates NRIs. I have drawn on the 2019 population and remittance figures given the extraordinary circumstances of 2020 due to the COVID-19 pandemic. In 2019, Mexico had 11.8 million emigrants abroad; China had 10.7 million; and Russia had 10.5 million (United Nations 2019). In 2019, migrant remittances to all developing countries totaled US$448 billion. The steady rise in global remittances since the 1990s can be attributed to the rise in international migration, improved data collection, lower transaction costs, and the depreciation of the US dollar. In 2019, the total remittances to India was followed by Mexico (US$36 billion), Philippines (US$26 billion), and China (US$4 billion) (World Bank n.d.).

[3] In 2019–2020, FDI was US$43 billion; FPI was US$1.4 billion; ODA was US$3.8 billion; and NRI deposits were US$8.6 billion (Reserve Bank of India 2018).

Dr. Singh's words also reflect a central and more understudied claim of this book: that underlying the complicated nature of emigration is an important *class story*. Labor shortages resulting from emigration, for example, may involve a shortage of formally trained professionals (known as a "brain drain") or a dearth of manual labor (known as a "brawn drain"), each of which creates very different consequences within sending countries. As well, different classes of emigrants have been found to send different financial flows and demands to sending states. An important subtext of Dr. Singh's statement, therefore, is that the term "diaspora investments" refers to inflows received from elite emigrants. Such diaspora investments have been surprisingly low in India, especially relative to the widely celebrated exemplar of its neighbor China. In contrast, almost all Indian government officials I spoke with credited India's poorest emigrants, not its wealthy emigrants, for sending the vast majority of the country's extraordinarily high level of remittances. This raised for me an important question: What exactly was it that Dr. Singh was defying? Was it elite Indian emigrants (who have come to be known as "the diaspora")? Or was it their investments in particular? And how does he feel about India's poor emigrants and their remittances?

In other words, a key question that motivates this book is: What is the relationship between the Indian state and its different classes of emigrants? To examine this question, I conducted an archival analysis of parliamentary debates (1920s–present); analyzed the annual reports of the Ministry of Overseas Indian Affairs (2004–14), the Ministry of External Affairs (2000–2020), and the Reserve Bank of India (1970–2020); compiled an original database of over 600 transnational Indian migrant organizations; and held over 200 interviews with Indian government officials (at the national and subnational levels), poor Indian emigrant workers in the Gulf region of the Middle East, elite Indian emigrants in the United States, and private migrant recruiters in India. The next chapter provides further detail on this book's data and methodology. Before turning to that, let me briefly summarize this book's main findings.

The Migration State and the Management of Class Inequality

Why should class matter in migration? A look at the discussions on the flip side of emigration (i.e., immigration) provides some clues. Specifically, immigration produces benefits and challenges for receiving states; to manage this tension, receiving states have an uncontested right to differentially treat, regulate, and protect migrants according to their class, thereby exacerbating class inequalities among migrants.

In contrast to the development mantra that frames contemporary emigration as a simple boon to sending countries, contemporary immigration into wealthy receiving countries is routinely depicted in public discourse as a flash point for state leaders—"the biggest wedge in American politics," "the greatest challenge European leaders have faced since the debt crisis," a critical test of our "commitment to human rights," and "a defining issue of this century" (Betts 2015; Park 2015; Thompson 2018). Although for centuries people have moved their families in search of better lives, the number of people migrating today is indeed unprecedented (Dimock 2016). In 2019, the growth rate of the world's population of migrants was higher than that of the world population (United Nations 2019). In 2020, 3.5% of the world's population lived outside their country of origin (International Organization for Migration 2020). That this surge in immigration levels has coincided with slumping economies and strained welfare programs in receiving countries, especially in the Global North, has stoked tensions along racial, ethnic, and cultural differences between native and foreign-born populations and catalyzed countless xenophobic and mass nationalist movements. Although migration has always involved cultural clashes, the contemporary wave is unique in also threatening populations that are economically and culturally dominant at the global level.

Threaded through the angst around contemporary immigration's size and racial/cultural tensions in receiving countries is an equally important, albeit less often highlighted set of class-based tensions. Although immigrants are sometimes superficially depicted as a homogeneous population in class terms, they obviously represent diverse class positions with diverse interests and diverse impacts on receiving countries. For example, most of the tensions arising from migration's size and racial diversity in the Global North focus on low-wage immigrant workers, leaving the growing mass of professional immigrant workers relatively unscathed, in some cases even celebrated by native populations. Similarly, the opposition to migration often comes from low-wage native workers who feel their livelihoods and lifestyles are threatened by low-wage immigrant workers, whereas native employers who rely on low-wage immigrant labor for their profitability support immigration. In contexts of generous state welfare, it is the native working classes who have become most anti-immigrant, claiming that poor immigrants are using up local welfare without contributing enough labor. Meanwhile, native employers argue that existing welfare programs are unsustainable irrespective of immigration and that poor immigrants without state welfare should fill growing labor demands in countries with aging populations.

Framing these class-based tensions around immigration is a general consensus that states have the right to regulate human mobility, even if they don't always have the capacity to do so. James Hollifield (2004) famously expanded this right into a duty with his term "the migration state," when he argued that the need for states to manage the tensions catalyzed by immigration is as important as the need for states to manage violence or trade. While overtly regulating immigration according to race or culture is no longer viewed as legitimate in the global arena, most states (whether authoritarian or liberal democratic) continue to have an uncontested right to differentially regulate human mobility according to class. State leaders in the United States, Canada, Australia, and the European Union therefore attempt to balance (or, at the very least, address) the opposing class interests of their own citizens by enacting different immigration policies for different classes of immigrants. In some cases, such as the United States, receiving countries have enabled a convenient mismatch between their anti-immigration rhetoric (to appease native workers) and lax implementation of labor and immigration laws (to appease native employers). In other cases, such as Canada and Denmark, receiving countries have enacted overtly discriminatory regulations that distinguish which migrants can and cannot enter based on their class characteristics, such as ownership of assets and human capital or "skill." In all cases, the state's right and duty to discriminate according to an immigrant's class is rarely questioned.

Of course, state immigration policies (like all policies) are messy, contingent on multiple actors, and full of unintended consequences. For example, some immigration scholars have rightly noted that employers hold as much (if not more) power as states to regulate who does and does not enter a country's borders (Jacobs 2020; Milkman, Bhargava, and Lewis 2021). And others have astutely highlighted the power of unregulated recruiters and "human supply chains" that operate largely outside the state's legal arm (Gordon 2017). Nevertheless, receiving states remain responsible for managing the class-based tensions that arise from immigration, and class-differentiated immigration policies (in their presence and their conspicuous absence) remain powerful vectors through which nations (and their corresponding class structures) are defined.

In short, the "migration state" in receiving countries helps structure class inequalities.

The Migration State in Sending Countries

Such trends in receiving countries raise an important question: How are *sending country* governments and populations managing and experiencing the multiple classes of their emigrating citizens?

Some readers may argue that sending states operate within the constraints of wealthy receiving countries' migrant demands and do not, therefore, have any power to manage their emigrants. But, as elaborated in the next chapter, scholars have detailed how sending states, such as India, Mexico, China, Morocco, and the Philippines, have actively (and sometimes unintentionally) used emigration to fit their own economic and political interests (Iskander 2010; Kapur 2010; Portes and Fernandez-Kelly 2015; Rodriguez 2010; Ye 2020). In other words, despite the global power hierarchies within which sending countries operate, they are not mere pawns of receiving countries' interests and thus do exert some agency in terms of emigration practices.

Some readers may also assume that sending countries will not restrict emigration, let alone regulate emigration by class. There is a practical reason to permit all emigration, since controlling who leaves and who stays inside a country is costly and requires more fine-tuned levers than controlling who enters and who does not. There are also strategic reasons to permit all emigration, since emigration enables sending-country citizens to tap higher wages abroad and relieve employment pressures and political discontent at home. Nevertheless, sending countries have long enacted different emigration regulations for different classes of their emigrants, and they continue to do so today.[4] As in receiving countries, the most common measure of class used by sending countries to manage emigration has been emigrants' "skill level," which has been (rather arbitrarily) defined by the emigrants' number of years of formal education or type of formal education and/or vocational certifications. Under Indian law, for example, emigrants are explicitly divided into two groups based on their number of years of formal education. Those with less education are subjected to different regulations, restrictions, and treatment compared to those with more education.[5] In other words, despite the costs, sending countries do invoke the right and duty to serve as a "migration state" that differentiates emigrants by class. In the process, they manage and often reproduce class inequalities. As this book exposes, India has been doing so since the 1830s.

Still other readers may assume sending countries would encourage the emigration of their poor workers to relieve domestic unemployment while preventing the emigration of elite workers to retain their skills for domestic modernization. Indeed, this was what many European sending states did in the 19th century (Bartlett 2010). And at first glance, this argument could explain Dr. Singh's stand against elite emigrants' diaspora investments.

---

[4] In addition to differentially controlling who leaves a country according to class, sending states have differentially regulated emigrants by class while they are abroad and imposed class-differentiated terms of emigrant return.

[5] Although India's education cut-off line for emigration has always been at the secondary school level (between 10th and 12th grades), it is worth noting that until the 1990s, India's central bank, the Reserve Bank of India, forbade foreign exchange for undergraduate tertiary education abroad except to Oxford, Cambridge, and Harvard.

But, in fact, India has done the opposite. As detailed in Chapter 4, India *legally prohibited* the emigration of its poorest workers (defined by number of years of education received) from 1947 until the early 1980s, while *simultaneously permitting* elite exit. As detailed in Chapters 5 and 6, India still *restricts* the emigration of its poor but has recently begun to *celebrate* its elite emigrants abroad with partnerships and glamorous awards. Therefore, the question of exactly how sending states manage the different classes of their emigrants cannot be presumed; it must be empirically investigated for different sending-country contexts.

Importantly, sending states' class-based emigration practices have shifted over time. Earlier, sending states' class distinctions were overt. For example, Algeria in the 1970s, Libya in the 1950s and 1960s, and India from the 1950s to 1980s (as I elaborate in Chapter 4) forbade emigration by denying their citizens a passport stamp, monitoring documentation at points of embarkation (such as the airport or port), and employing police enforcement, surveillance technologies, and physical barriers along their national borders. But in all these cases, elite emigrants were given exceptions. In India, students and educated professionals were legally permitted to move abroad; in some cases, the state gave them settlement packages and subsidized airfare. Similarly, Libya granted exit visas to students, invested in specialized schools to improve their foreign-language skills, and granted scholarships to citizens intending to study abroad (Tsourapas 2019).

But in recent years, sending states' class-based emigration distinctions have become subtler. As elaborated in Chapters 5 and 6, during the early 1980s India legalized emigration across classes, which created the appearance of consistency in treatment. But in practice, the state still restricts poor emigrants' mobility by subjecting them to a dizzying array of regulations, requirements, and fees that are not applied to elite emigrants. Moreover, the Indian state still legally forbids the emigration of poor women to certain countries. To implement these restrictions, the Indian government's Protectorate General of Emigrants has the power to prevent certain poor citizens from legally exiting India's borders by denying them the coveted government-issued "emigration clearance" stamp in their passport (a stamp that is required only for poor workers). Meanwhile, the Indian government facilitates shiny fast-track visa services for Indian students planning to study abroad and institutes no emigration restrictions against Indians graduating from India's high-quality, publicly financed education system. In the Philippines, the state allows home communities to shame lower-middle-class women who emigrate to work as domestic workers and entertainers (calling them "sexually immoral" or "bad mothers"), while celebrating the emigration of educated youth (Parrenas 2004). And Mexico and Morocco legitimize local emigration industries that enable their poor citizens to enter receiving countries through illicit pathways (and even engage those emigrants on local development programs), while ensuring their elite emigrants follow legal entry channels (Iskander 2010). Moreover, sending states today regularly help some emigrants return home, while encouraging others to stay abroad (Goldring 1998; Smith 1998).

These historically contingent patterns of sending countries' class-based emigration practices call on us to ask: How and why do states enact class-based regulations (despite their costs), and how and why do states change their practices over time?

As in receiving countries, sending states' emigration practices, like all statecraft, is contingent on multiple forces and actors. Therefore, to answer the first question, we must identify which forces and actors shape sending states' class-differentiated emigration practices. Some emigration scholars have highlighted the forces "from above" that shape sending states' emigration practices. These scholars argue that northern countries, and the international development institutions they control, determine the global market constraints and development ideologies within which sending countries must operate. Specifically, these scholars credit the ideology of "neoliberal globalization" for forcing sending states to encourage and celebrate emigration (Bakker 2015b; Castles and Wise 2007). Other scholars spotlight the forces "from below" that shape sending states' emigration patterns. These scholars argue that emigrants themselves have organized to make demands on sending states (Delgado Wise and Ramírez 2001; Portes, Escobar, and Radford 2007) and that emigrants have reshaped sending-country actions through the so-called social and political remittances they send home (Kapur and McHale 2005; Levitt 1999; Pessar and Mahler 2003; Portes and Zhou 2012). The next chapter offers a more detailed discussion of the strengths and weaknesses of these studies. Here, let me simply underscore that none of them offers insights on the forces and actors shaping sending states' class-based emigration patterns. They do not, for example, explain how, when, and why states differentially use elite versus poor emigrants within the norms of neoliberal globalization. Nor do they shed light on how different classes of emigrants differentially experience, resist, and reshape sending states' emigration practices over time.

To answer the second question, on changing emigration practices over time, we must understand the long arc of sending states' class-based emigration practices before and after the start of neoliberal globalization. As elaborated in the next chapter, the recent emigration literature focuses almost exclusively on the contemporary era of neoliberal globalization. This presents an ahistoric understanding of human migration, which we know began long before neoliberalism. It also cripples our ability to understand how and why we got to this present moment of neoliberal globalization in the first place. A robust literature (examined in the next chapter) on 19th-century emigration patterns from Europe and European colonies reminds us that large-scale international migration is a function of capitalism, not neoliberal globalization (Bartlett 2010; Hobsbawm 1975). Therefore, it is reasonable to assume that sending-state emigration practices have changed and will continue to change alongside the shifting political and economic structures of capitalism over time.

Finally, underlying the global migration literature is an assumption that "the migration state" (in receiving and sending countries) manages international migration to further the state's economic agenda. But can the arrow also point the other way? In other words, can sending-state emigration practices, and emigrants themselves, *alter* sending states' economic development agendas at different points in time?

This book seeks to address these questions using the case of India.

The "Invisibles" of Indian Emigration

Understanding the Indian state's relationship to its diverse classes of emigrants proved to be a more elusive task than I expected. Despite the millions of Indians who rely on emigration to survive, and the tremendous financial contribution that emigration has made to India's coffers, the state's emigration practices remain oddly invisible. In fact, according to India's foremost emigration scholars, the country has never even had a formal emigration policy (Kumar and Rajan 2014). The government's data on its different classes of emigrants is also oddly imbalanced. Although state emigration authorities collect data on poor Indian emigrants, they do not collect any on elite Indian emigrants.[6] In an unfortunate twist of words (as per global accounting custom), remittances (which are heavily influenced by India's poor emigrants) and the export of software services (which are heavily influenced by India's elite emigrants) are classified in India's balance of payments as "invisibles" (referring to the trade of physically intangible items between countries). What makes this term especially ironic is that remittances and the export of software services constitute the largest foreign inflows in India's balance-of-payment accounts. In other words, it is the net export of India's services from emigrants, not India's manufacturing exports, that has yielded a surplus in recent years. Yet Indian emigration rarely features as a hot-button issue in Indian domestic political campaigns, and academic studies on Indian emigration

[6] While the Indian Intelligence Bureau keeps data on all cross-border traffic, data on educated emigrants who do not require government clearance is not kept (and thus not publicly reported) by any Indian emigration office.

are limited in number.[7] In my own interviews with state officials, I repeatedly heard statements similar to Dr. Singh's that underplayed statecraft in emigration. This invisibility of the Indian state's emigration practices, and of Indian emigrants' contributions to the country's balance of payments, is particularly striking in the contemporary era, when a nation's balance of payments (which in India have been unquestionably strengthened by its emigrants) signals sovereign worth in the global arena. It is also unique relative to other large emigrant-sending countries, such as Mexico, China, and the Philippines.

Equally striking is how easily Indian emigration is divorced from public and academic discussions on Indian development. Despite the heated debates around class within India, such debates are never extended to examine the state's differential treatment of its poor versus elite emigrants. Discussions of domestic elites rarely connect to discussions about elite emigrants abroad. Similarly, Indian development scholars and labor unions focus exclusively on poor workers operating within India, while ignoring poor Indian workers abroad. Even when highlighting the vulnerabilities faced by migrant workers, an unquestioned distinction is made between domestic and international migrants. These silos were prominently displayed in the months following the 2020 outbreak of COVID-19, when countless newspaper articles, blogs, and workshops (in India and globally) critiqued the Indian government's sudden lockdown and its disastrous effects on poor Indian migrant laborers. Yet only a handful of newspaper articles (in Indian and foreign papers) discussed how the lockdown affected poor Indian emigrant laborers, who faced equally crippling consequences as they were forced to leave their jobs abroad and return to India.[8]

Given the massive numbers of Indians who rely on emigration for their survival, the enormous influx of money the Indian state receives from its emigrants, and the state's long history of regulating its emigrants differentially by class, the invisibility of India's migration state is deeply problematic for any study of Indian development and class inequality. India thus provides an ideal case with which to begin an inquiry into the class politics of sending-country emigration.

First, India's long emigration history enables us to examine its emigration practices before and after the contemporary era of neoliberal globalization. Indian emigration was alive and well long before neoliberal globalization. Evidence of ancient Indian influences has been found in present-day Malaysia and Burma from AD 110. From the 9th to the 15th century, the spice route

---

[7] Devesh Kapur's work on professional Indian emigrants in the United States and Irudya Rajan's work on poor Indian emigrants to the Gulf provide the most robust work available on Indian emigration to date.

[8] In my review of English-language news articles in this period, I found only four that featured emigrant workers.

offered a way for Indian traders and banished princes to travel, trade, spread religion, and eventually settle in Southeast Asia and the Middle East (Jaiswal 2018). And (as detailed in Chapter 3) during the 18th and 19th centuries, under the British Empire, poor and elite Indians embarked on mass migrations across the Indian Ocean, Southeast Asia, Africa, the Caribbean, the Middle East, and even North America (Amrith 2013; Vora 2013). During the postcolonial era, from 1947 to the late 1970s (as detailed in Chapter 4), although the Indian government officially discouraged emigration, elite emigration continued during this period. This history calls on us to examine the ancestral lineage of India's contemporary emigration patterns in order to better understand their strikingly solid foundation.

Second, unlike in many sending countries where emigration provides a ready release valve from political and social turmoil, Indian emigrants today are almost uniformly motivated by prospects for economic betterment. The 1947 partition of British India, when over 7 million Muslims moved from present-day India to present-day Pakistan, marked a dramatic moment of Indian emigration motivated by nationalizing imperatives. But since then, despite the great political and social strife that Indians bear each day, conflicts in Kashmir and the Northeast, and secession movements, India has remained a formally stable democracy, and relatively few emigrants leave as political refugees (in contrast to Cubans and Moroccans). For the most part, Indians are economic migrants, enabling us to home in on the class basis of the country's emigration practices.[9]

Third, India's emigrants have always been among the world's most diverse in class terms. During the British Empire, Indian emigrants included middle-class merchants, farmers, and indentured laborers. Today the vast majority of Indian emigrants are poor workers. For reasons that deserve further study, the Indian government has never followed Mexico's strategy of allowing poor workers to meet US employers' labor needs by entering the United States extralegally. Instead, India's poor emigrants in the postcolonial era have mainly flocked to the Persian Gulf region of the Middle East, constituting approximately 33% of labor migrants in those countries, reaching 50% in some countries.[10] But India is also the world's largest exporter of tertiary-educated, professional emigrants, of which there were 2.2 million in 2011 (World Bank 2016). India's large share of emigrants in professional occupations stems from its disproportionate public

---

[9] Unlike so many sending countries in Latin America, the Middle East, and North Africa, India does not border a rich, migrant-receiving country that provides an obvious (albeit risky) chance for economic betterment. Therefore, India's economic migrants move far distances and to a range of receiving countries.

[10] Estimate is drawn from various databases on Gulf migration collected by the Gulf Labor Markets and Migration website, https://gulfmigration.org/.

expenditure on tertiary education, which is unique among most developing countries. As well, Indian emigrants come from rural, semi-urban, and urban settings; this differs from European sending countries of the past and contemporary sending countries in Latin America and other parts of Asia. This class diversity allows us to compare a single state's use of different classes of emigrant workers, as well as emigrants' class-varying responses to sending-state emigration practices.

Fourth, as already indicated, India has long enacted different regulations over the different classes of its emigrants, enabling us to examine how, when, and why such state practices do and do not change over time. In general, India's changing emigration practices have not neatly followed global patterns or common scholarly assumptions, and they, therefore, raise several important puzzles.

For example, in contrast to much of the recent literature that depicts contemporary emigration practices as "new," Chapter 3 details how India's current legalized class distinctions for emigrants, emigration institutions, and emigration processes stem from those the British colonial government first instituted in the early 1900s. This continuity of institutionalized class-based distinctions between emigrants calls on us to examine why and how India's postcolonial government has legitimized and sustained them, especially given its commitment to a democratic system that purports to treat all citizens equally under the law.

The recent emigration literature is also insufficient in explaining India's discontinuities with earlier eras. After years of legally forbidding emigration, India began to slowly liberalize some of its policies in the late 1970s and has increasingly recognized some of its emigrants abroad since then. Recent studies credit similar changes in other countries to dictates from northern-led development institutions, a herd effect among fellow developing countries, and the power of neoliberal ideologies (Bakker 2015b; Itzigsohn 2000; Turcu and Urbatsch 2015). But unlike most other sending countries, India is still resisting full liberalization of its emigration policies and has retained many of its restrictions on poor workers' mobility. To the extent that India liberalized some of its emigration practices, it did so decades after Turkey, Morocco, Mexico, China, and the Philippines had already recognized emigration as a useful way to export surplus labor, increase foreign exchange reserves, and control political dissidence.

While we might assume India's delayed and uneven liberalization of emigration simply reflects the similarly delayed and uneven liberalization of its broader economy, a closer look shows India's liberalization of poor workers' emigration and its celebration of elite emigrants came over a decade *before* its government officially launched its domestic liberalization reforms on finance, goods, and services in 1991. Therefore, the recent changes to the Indian government's class-based emigration policies cannot be explained with simple nods to "neoliberalism," "northern powers," or "herd effects." Rather they call on us to also examine who (within India) pushed for these changes and who is resisting further change, who benefited and who lost from the changes, how the government has sustained consent for these changes (despite the losers), and how these changes in emigration may have shaped India's liberalization efforts rather than the other way around.

The invisibility of the Indian government's interactions with its different classes of emigrants also calls on us to examine why, despite the development community's excitement over emigrants' remittances and the flood of remittances that India receives every year, the government has remained reluctant to celebrate or even recognize these flows, especially relative to other countries, such as Mexico, Morocco, and the Philippines. Notably, the Indian government has been reluctant to overtly celebrate the financial contributions of both poor and elite emigrants. Poor emigrants and their remittances are rarely mentioned in national-level political campaigns, parliamentary discussions, or development debates. Yet, as detailed in Chapter 6, the government has managed to continue drawing poor emigrants' financial contributions, while successfully undermining their organizing efforts for recognition, welfare, and support. These trends force us to ask exactly how the Indian state has managed to do so while still retaining its political and electoral legitimacy among poor emigrants.

Similarly, the Indian government rarely acknowledges or celebrates elite emigrants' financial inflows—again a sharp contrast to China and sending countries in Latin America (Tsai 2010). Echoes of this could be heard in Dr. Singh's remarks at the start of this chapter. Some have highlighted that elite Indian emigrants' investments are low relative to other countries, such as China (Ye 2014). While elite emigrants' cumulative bank deposits and bonds have helped India access more foreign debt, their annual contributions are indeed less than the annual remittance inflow.[11] Others have argued the Indian government undercounts elite emigrants' financial contributions (Kapur 2018). The government's data on FDI from elite emigrants is imperfect, and FPI from elite emigrants is not even counted. As noted, the Indian government's migration offices do not maintain any data on elite emigrants (although they do maintain data on poor emigrants, who must receive approval to emigrate). This raises an obvious question as to why the Indian government downplays (or fails to attract) its elite emigrants' financial contributions.

In contrast to its reluctance to acknowledge its emigrants' financial contributions, the Indian government has recently invested heavily in celebrating its wealthy emigrants' social, political, and ideological contributions; the same cannot be said for its poor emigrants' social, political, and ideological

[11] See Reserve Bank of India 2021.

contributions. In 2003, the government inaugurated an annual conference, Pravasi Bharatiya Divas, or "Overseas Indian Day," a high-level, glossy event designed to foster state relationships with emigrants abroad. The event has also become known for marking the annual Pravasi Bharatiya Samman Awards that the president of India bestows upon emigrants in recognition of their technical, social, and political contributions to the country. It is notable that these awards are not given for financial contributions, and at first they did not include a category for poor workers.[12] In 2006, the government launched the Overseas Citizenship of India (OCI) status to provide citizens of other countries who can prove Indian heritage a pathway to Indian citizenship, visas facilitating their entry to India, improved rights to property investments in India, favorable bank accounts, and a bill to enable them to vote in India. At first, the OCI applied only to emigrants living in countries of the Global North, most of whom are middle- and upper-class professionals.[13] These trends call on us to examine what the Indian government attains from such recognition and how elite emigrants are reacting.

The Argument and Structure of the Book

This book seeks to bring Indian emigration out of the shadows and into the spotlight to expose the vital role that the Indian state, as well as its poor and elite emigrants, have long played in forging and legitimizing class inequalities within the country through the management of international emigration patterns.

To unpack the dynamic story of the causes and consequences of India's ever-shifting emigration practices over time, this book introduces a new analytical framework that I call "Migration-Development Regimes" (MDRs). MDRs capture the full set of emigration practices and policies that (among other forces) enable sending countries to ensure domestic capital accumulation and their own political legitimacy at the global and domestic levels. They expose the class inequities that this fine balance rests on.

MDRs capture the ideological, economic, and political structures that help shape sending states' emigration practices "from above." After all, sending countries' actions are constrained by global employers' labor demands and receiving

---

[12] Contributions eligible for the award include support to India's causes and concerns in a tangible way; building closer links between India, the overseas Indian community, and emigrants' country of residence; social and humanitarian causes in India or abroad; welfare of the local Indian community; philanthropic and charitable work; eminence in one's field or outstanding work which has enhanced India's prestige in the country of residence/work.

[13] The OCI still omits citizens of Bangladesh and Pakistan.

states' immigration policies—both of which hold undeniable power to shape the rules and norms of the global migration game. But MDRs also shed light on the competing interests of the domestic actors—including subnational governments, domestic elites and workers, and elite and poor emigrant citizens—who reshape statecraft "from below." MDRs help us identify when and why emigrants consent to particular emigration practices, and when and why they resist them.

MDRs are partly rational, especially for some, and often yield unintended consequences. While they may appear coherent, they are full of contradictions and contingencies. As a result, they rise and fall and shift over time. Depending on a sending country's size, migrant resource base, and geopolitical power, its MDRs sometimes reproduce, but other times reshape, domestic development ideologies and thus the very rules of the international migration game.

Drawing from this framework, this book divides India's emigration practices into three MDRs, spanning nearly two centuries: the Coolie MDR (1834–1947), the Nationalist MDR (1947–77), and the CEO MDR (1977–present). The Coolie MDR covers the period under British colonial rule. The Nationalist MDR covers the first postcolonial emigration regime in India, under Prime Minister Jawaharlal Nehru and then Prime Minister Indira Gandhi. The CEO MDR covers the contemporary period of neoliberal globalization, which has spanned several prime ministers and ruling political parties.

Within each MDR, I compare the Indian state's emigration practices toward poor versus elite emigrants (at the national and subnational levels), as well as poor and elite emigrants' differential responses to each MDR. Across MDRs, I examine the constraints and contradictions that provoke them to transform over time. Although constantly changing, MDRs remain linked to one another through this history. Understanding this ancestral lineage, this book argues, is vital to deepening our understanding of the present moment and exposing what is truly novel about it.

By taking this long view of India's changing MDRs, this book reveals a simple fact that is too easily glossed over in contemporary studies on emigration: India's MDRs have *always* sought economic growth and domestic political legitimacy at the cost of deepening class-based inequalities. Since the early 1900s and continuing to this day, Indian emigrants have been legally divided into two categories, based on a crude and arbitrary boundary defined by the number of years of formal schooling.[14] Although the boundary is arbitrary, the consequences have been very real. Those with little schooling are

---

[14] As I elaborate in the next chapter, these two groups are commonly referred to in Indian emigration parlance as "high-skilled" and "low-skilled." But given the loaded and detrimental effects of these terms, I instead use "elite" and "poor" to denominate these emigrants.

subjected to a battery of state regulations that restrict and control their international mobility; those with more schooling are not. In recent decades, those with little schooling have been invited to send their wages earned abroad back to India; in return they receive little welfare or recognition. Those with more schooling have been invited to send their investments, skills, and ideas back to India; in return they receive favorable financial terms, partnership opportunities among India's domestic elite, awards, and recognition. Across time and through different economic paradigms, political parties, and globally sanctioned moral norms, India's emigration practices have not only reflected already existing class inequalities; they have also *actively accentuated such class inequities* across time—all while remaining strikingly invisible within Indian debates on development.

This finding helps redefine the central problem of sending states' emigration practices. The primary question featured in most development debates around emigration is whether sending states should deter or promote emigration. But as the following chapters illustrate, the Indian state has tried both options, and both options have hurt poor workers and favored elite workers, thereby exacerbating class inequalities. Therefore, this book argues, *the key problem with Indian emigration is not its quantity, but rather the discriminatory regulations, restrictions, and treatment the state enacts over its emigrants based on their class.* It is this unequal treatment of emigrants that the state must rectify to create a more just development agenda.

Second, this book's long view of MDRs exposes the precise economic benefits the Indian state has long attained from its different classes of emigrants. Under the Coolie MDR, the British Raj used poor and elite emigrants to serve as racialized coolies for the empire, advancing economic accumulation in the colonies and ultimately in the United Kingdom. Under the Nationalist MDR, the state shifted tack to forbid poor Indians from emigrating so it could retain their labor for its domestic industrializing agenda. Meanwhile, it allowed elites to emigrate, but gave up the chance to use their labor to further India's economy.

As detailed in Chapters 5 and 6, under the CEO MDR, the Indian state shifted tack once again. Unlike in earlier MDRs, the state is now attaining extraordinary *financial returns from its poor emigrants.* In addition, it is now tapping its *elite emigrants for their social and ideological returns* for the first time. To this end, elite Indian emigrants residing in the United States have helped valorize the Indian government's current embrace of privatization, voluntarism, and self-sufficiency. Moreover, these chapters illustrate how the financial and ideological remittances that both poor and elite emigrants have brought to India under the CEO MDR offered an important pilot phase for the country's later acceptance of globalization and liberalization in other parts of the economy. In other words, the global movement of people presaged Indians' recent consent to the global movement of goods and services, not the other way around.

This finding reminds us that *emigration's economic impact on sending countries is both material and ideological.* Emigration is more than just the pathway to foreign finances that the new development mantra celebrates. It also serves as a quiet but crucial ideological vector (similar to education and the media) that enables sending states to cement domestic consent for new economic development agendas. In the case of India, poor emigrants' financial remittances offered an important first step in attaining consent within India for tapping foreign capital. In addition, although elite emigrants' ideological remittances are rarely featured in policy discussions or the critical scholarship on development ideologies, this book argues they have had a much larger impact than their financial remittances on building domestic consent for India's contemporary economic framework of liberalization, self-sufficiency, and privatization.

Third, by exposing the connection between India's international emigration practices and its domestic class inequalities, this book forces us to examine exactly how the Indian state has balanced the contradiction inherent in furthering domestic economic growth using class-differentiated emigration, while retaining its electoral and political legitimacy in a democratic context where all classes can, and indeed do, vote.

The Indian state has consistently legitimized its practices toward poor emigrants by promising *"paternalist protection" as opposed to rights-based protection.* Across time, paternalist protection has increased state control over poor workers and deflected attention away from the severe exploitation they face. Under the Coolie MDR, the colonial state instituted India's first emigration regulations to justify its export of poor Indians by certifying their consent to emigrate and thus protecting their right to be "free" laborers. Under the Nationalist MDR, the Indian state justified its restrictions over poor emigrants' mobility by claiming to protect them against racist and exploitative foreign employers (in contrast to the prior colonial state). Under the CEO MDR, the state has justified its reliance on poor workers' foreign earnings by underscoring workers' demands for free mobility, maintaining restrictions over some workers (including female migrants), and offering return migrants some welfare. As well, the state has recently offered to help poor return emigrants join a newly emerging, mostly male category of "migrant entrepreneurs." In all these cases, poor emigrants are disempowered.

In contrast, the state's political justification for its lack of control over elite emigrants has shifted over time. Under the Coolie MDR, the colonial state tried to resist regulations over elite emigrants by (ironically) insisting on the equal treatment of Indian and British emigrants' cross-border mobility. Under the Nationalist MDR, the state claimed independence from its elite emigrants to bolster its global image as a self-sufficient, modernizing nation.

But under the CEO MDR, the state has shifted to building *"an elite pact"* with its elite emigrants, joining forces with domestic business leaders and elite, mostly male emigrants for the first time, while still keeping poor emigrants at bay. Because elite Indian emigrants reside in wealthy receiving countries in the North, this finding disrupts our understanding of power hierarchies rooted only in race or simple North-South dynamics. Instead it exposes *how class inequalities operate across country contexts, empowering elite emigrants (even when they come from the global South) over poor emigrants.*

These findings on sending states' need to politically justify their class-based emigration practices also remind us of MDRs' potential weaknesses, thereby underscoring why emigration is such a complicated matter for sending states. In India, state promises to protect poor emigrants must eventually be fulfilled in order to retain any heft. And promises to partner with elite emigrants need to ward against power grabs.

This brings us to a final finding: this book's long view exposes how, when, and why, at certain moments, Indian *emigrants have resisted the state's emigration practices* and successfully pressured the state to enact new ones. Despite the Indian state's differential use of emigrants by class, poor and elite emigrants have often joined forces to resist state practices in unexpected ways. For example, as detailed in Chapter 3, poor and elite emigrants joined to resist colonial rule in the 1930s and 1940s and fought against the use of Indian emigrants for economic accumulation at home. And, as detailed in Chapter 4, poor and elite emigrants joined to resist authoritarian rule in India in the 1970s (in the context of the Emergency) and demand the liberalization of emigration and emigrants' capital flows. Chapters 7 and 8 detail how poor and elite emigrants in the contemporary era are organizing to make various demands on the Indian state.

This finding reveals how sending countries' emigration and development practices are mutually constitutive. At times development agendas shape emigration practices, but at other times emigrants reshape those agendas. This provides an important corrective to common assumptions that the contemporary liberalization of emigration policies (and their capital flows) is simply a page torn from a northern-imposed development script on neoliberal globalization. India's liberalization of emigration is, in fact, also a product of elite and poor Indian emigrants' demands. This finding exposes the extraordinarily solid foundation of India's current MDR despite its deleterious consequences for poor emigrants. But it also raises questions as to whether or not poor and elite emigrants might eventually join forces to resist India's current MDR—a question I begin to address in the final chapter.

The Chapters to Follow

Before we can reflect on the demise of India's contemporary CEO MDR, we must deepen our understanding of its strengths and weaknesses. To this end, this book is organized into three empirical sections. Chapters 3 and 4 examine the MDRs preceding the contemporary era and thus cover the Coolie MDR and Nationalist MDR. Chapters 5 and 6 examine the CEO MDR from the perspective of the Indian state. And Chapters 7 and 8 examine the CEO MDR from the perspective of poor and elite emigrants' organizations.

Chapter 2 explains this book's methodological approach and its analytical framework of MDRs. To do so, it draws on the global literature on emigration to identify four sets of forces and actors that shape sending-state emigration practices. These include northern-imposed development ideologies/norms, sending-state agency, emigrants' agency and their transnational organizations, and the role of history.

Chapter 3 details the rise and fall of the Coolie MDR (1834–1947). Contrary to claims that sending-state governments have only recently started to use emigrants to meet domestic development needs, this chapter shows that emigration has been an important state subject in India since the colonial era. The Coolie MDR instituted a racialized development model, whereby the state exploited poor and nonpoor Indian emigrants to serve as "coolies" for the British Empire, advancing economic accumulation in the colonies and ultimately in the United Kingdom. The Coolie MDR also inaugurated India's first migration state, gradually building a regulatory framework that empowered the state to not only use, but also control, the global mobility of "free" (as opposed to enslaved) commodified human workers. Underlying this framework was a class-based distinction of Indian emigrants. This regulatory framework was so successful that it continues to guide Indian emigration today. Despite the resilience of its regulatory infrastructure, however, the Coolie MDR's racist model of accumulation eventually mobilized cross-class solidarity among Indian emigrants, who joined forces with Indian independent leaders to resist global racism, British colonialism, and, ultimately, the Coolie MDR itself.

Chapter 4 details the rise and fall of India's first postcolonial MDR, the Nationalist MDR (1947–77). Although the Nationalist MDR retained the Coolie MDR's class-based regulatory infrastructure, it instituted a new development model defined by the nation's new geographic boundaries. To support its domestic image as a protector of vulnerable Indians, and its global image as a self-sufficient, modernizing nation, the new Indian state legally forbade emigration. But it only applied these restrictions to poor workers, thereby legitimizing state control over them and ensuring their availability to service India's domestic industrialization. Meanwhile, the state permitted elites to emigrate, but distanced them (at least in public) from India's development agenda. This approach broke the cross-class solidarity among emigrants that had arisen to resist the Coolie MDR, and it bred new resentments. The state's promises to protect the poor, while laudable, failed to deliver and thus mobilized poor workers to demand the liberalization of their emigration. The state's dismissive stance toward elite emigrants mobilized them to join India's anti-Emergency movement for global democracy and against the Nationalist MDR. This chapter thus exposes how both elite and poor Indians were instrumental in fomenting India's subsequent and contemporary MDR

Chapters 5 and 6 detail the CEO MDR (1977–present), which is progressively liberalizing emigration and is differentially using poor and elite emigrants to fuel Indian development while widening class inequalities. While the CEO MDR echoes parts of the Coolie and Nationalist MDRs, it has instituted a new development model in India that valorizes global markets (for people and capital), privatization, and self-sufficiency and entrepreneurship for both elite and poor emigrants. By tracing the origin of the CEO MDR to the late 1970s, these chapters expose the vital but understudied role that the Indian state and emigrants themselves have played in securing consent within India for this new development model.

Chapter 5 details how the CEO MDR has used poor and elite emigrants' financial contributions from abroad (in the form of remittances, savings accounts, investments, and bonds), thereby reframing emigrants as a resource for India (rather than an embarrassment, as in the Nationalist MDR) and building consent for foreign capital inflows. To cement its political legitimacy, especially among domestic resisters to globalization, the state has emphasized poor workers' demands for mobility, maintained some restrictions (especially over female emigrants), and provided some welfare upon return. Toward elite emigrants, the state has appealed to shared racial and ethnic solidarity bonds between domestic Indians and emigrants (a practice first initiated during the Independence movement) and offered material incentives in return for their financial contributions. These attempts have yielded uneven results. While poor emigrants' financial remittances have been astounding, elite emigrants' financial contributions have been costly, volatile, and meager given their salary base.

Chapter 6 exposes how the CEO MDR has forged an elite class pact of "global Indians" that includes India's state officials, domestic business leaders, and elites abroad. This celebrated group dominates Indian development and attains material wealth and status in the process. To seal this class pact, the CEO MDR has tapped elite emigrants' social and ideological contributions to development (in the form of their ideas, ideals, tastes, networks, and technical expertise). It has invited elite emigrants to forge partnerships with Indian businesses, reshape India's voluntary sector, invest in Indian real estate, and serve in elite policy

positions within the government. And it has framed Indian Americans, in particular, as successful, hard-working, private-sector professionals and entrepreneurs
whom domestic Indians should emulate. The CEO MDR has not, however,
tapped poor emigrants for their social and ideological remittances. Rather, it
has tried to cement their consent to elite ideals of privatization, self-sufficiency,
and entrepreneurship upon their return. Thus, the CEO MDR has reframed
poor emigrants' identity as members of a cross-class category of "migrant
entrepreneurs," thereby occluding their class differences with elite emigrants
and deflecting attention away from wage labor and its underlying structures of
exploitation.

Chapters 7 and 8 turn our analytical gaze downward to examine how poor
and elite emigrants are experiencing and organizing to cement, resist, and reshape the CEO MDR. An important unintended consequence of the CEO
MDR was that it created the conditions for the growth of migrant organizations.

Chapter 7 analyzes the strategies and demands of poor emigrants' organizations and migrant recruiters. Poor Indian emigrants have drawn on their
structural power as voters and "protectors of the nation's foreign exchange" to
demand the liberalization of emigration, "rights-based" (as opposed to paternalist) welfare, increased data, and recognition. But the partisan and cross-class
nature of their organizations have de-radicalized them, especially compared to
domestic labor organizations. The CEO MDR has ironically undermined the
private recruiter, a class actor that the CEO MDR legitimized and legalized in
the first place. Under the CEO MDR, small and medium-size private recruiters
have become bankrupt, have shut down, or have returned to extralegal business
operations, while large private recruitment businesses have prospered.

Chapter 8 analyzes the strategies and demands of elite emigrants' transnational organizations with a focus on the United States. Indian American
transnational organizations embrace, rather than critique, the CEO MDR's
development ideals of privatization, voluntarism, and self-sufficiency. In fact,
they helped cement these ideals by enthusiastically participating in the national
government's call for their ideological remittances. To channel these ideological remittances, Indian Americans have built hundreds of transnational diaspora organizations that promote private education, private philanthropy for
poverty alleviation, and private business development. Almost none addresses
social inequities based on class, caste, or gender. Although diverse, these organizations reflect exactly the portrait of the elite global Indian that the CEO MDR
idealizes. Doing so not only empowers Indian Americans to help shape India's
future; it also valorizes their own status within the United States and India and
thus affords them material and symbolic benefits in the process.

Chapter 9 explores the future prospects of the CEO MDR by underscoring its
contradictions and emerging weaknesses. First, the promise of entrepreneurship

has been (unsurprisingly) limited in uplifting poor emigrants. State welfare programs for emigrants have also failed to deliver. Second, given most private recruiters' class position as small and medium-size entrepreneurs, their current discontent exposes a fallacy in the CEO MDR's claims to promote this very line of labor. Finally, elite emigrants' call for privatization and their underlying distrust of the government's ability to deliver on development are fomenting fault lines in their relationship with Indian NGOs and the Indian state—a tension that could be heard in Dr. Singh's remarks. If history is any guide, the CEO MDR will eventually fall. This final chapter thus explores the potential for the CEO MDR's weaknesses to mobilize resistance.

As this book details, although sending states' emigration practices sometimes reflect and reproduce the rules of the game that are determined by receiving countries, emigrants also sometimes reshape domestic regimes of capital accumulation and thus the rules of the global migration game. So the question this book leaves us with is this: How can we ensure that India's next MDR addresses and mitigates, rather than exacerbates, class inequities? Can poor and elite emigrants be mobilized to bring forth a moral compass in India's development trajectories—one that understands, empathizes, and even alleviates the personal anguish that is always attached to human migration?

2

Migration-Development Regimes

This chapter explains the methodological and analytical framework of Migration-Development Regimes (MDRs) that structures this book. As noted in Chapter 1, although migration is a global phenomenon, we know shockingly little about the class politics of emigration from the perspective of the source: sending countries. MDRs, I argue, offer an analytical framework with which we can deepen our understanding of the class politics of sending-state emigration. But before explaining MDRs, let me first outline the global literature on sending-state emigration. Although this literature does not directly address the class basis of emigration, it provides a useful starting point from which to build the framework of MDRs.

The Forces and Actors Shaping the Migration-Development Nexus

Although in the Global North, the migration literature has focused almost entirely on receiving states and immigrant reception, a few scholars in recent years have begun to examine the causes and effects of sending countries' increasingly overt focus on emigration. These studies reflect the rise of the development mantra, which celebrates emigration as a development panacea, alongside its critics, who expose the development disasters undergirding emigration. They focus on contemporary emigration in the neoliberal era and mostly draw upon the experiences of sending countries in Latin America and East and Southeast Asia and receiving countries in the Global North, especially the United States. The few sociological examinations of historical emigration patterns tend to feature emigrants going from the sending states of Europe to the receiving country of the United States starting in the 17th century. Most existing studies on emigration do not address migrants' class at all; those that do, focus on one class

The Migration-Development Regime. Rina Agarwala, Oxford University Press. © Oxford University Press 2022.
DOI: 10.1093/oso/9780197586396.003.0002

of emigrants at a time rather than comparing emigrants across classes. Despite these limitations, the small subset of studies on emigration usefully highlights four sets of forces and actors that shape sending countries' class-based emigration practices.

Northern-Imposed Development Ideologies

The overwhelming focus on receiving countries in the contemporary migration literature may lead many readers to assume receiving countries determine sending countries' class-based emigration controls. After all, receiving countries define global labor demand and have the power to determine who does and does not enter their borders.

A growing literature by sociologists critical of neoliberal globalization has added an additional dimension to this argument that emphasizes the role of economic development ideologies on sending countries' emigration patterns. In the contemporary era, wealthy receiving countries of the Global North, so the argument goes, have written and imposed the development ideology of neoliberal globalization on sending countries, and a key component of this ideology is that it valorizes and encourages emigration. Sending countries, in turn, have abided in order to signal their "modernity" in the global arena, thereby creating a herd effect (Turcu and Urbatsch 2015). Importantly, these scholars emphasize that through international institutions, northern states press southern states to enact emigration policies that ultimately favor the North (Al-Ali, Black, and Koser 2001; de la Garza et al. 2000; Guarnizo 1998; Itzigsohn 2000; Louie 2000; Mahler 2000). Sending states' emigration practices are mediated by their low structural positions in the global economy but justified by their consent to the development ideology of neoliberal globalization, which further perpetuates their low structural position.

As evidence for this line of argument, these scholars highlight the recent efforts by international donors and commercial financial institutions to count, celebrate, and promote emigrants' remittances as an economic development panacea for sending countries (Bakker 2015b; Castles and Wise 2007). At the turn of the millennium, following requests by the Group of 8 countries, the United Nations Security Council, the World Bank, the International Monetary Fund, and the Inter-American Development Bank established an international working group, the Technical Sub-Group on the Movement of Persons, to improve global remittance statistics (United Nations 2010). As well, development institutions during this time celebrated remittances for providing a steady source of foreign exchange with which sending countries can repay debts, finance foreign trade deficits, improve their balance of payments, and sustain their integration in the global market. In other words, international institutions have equated the benefits of exporting workers to the benefits of exporting goods—never questioning the human costs of such exports. Since remittances are paid directly to emigrants' families at home, international institutions also celebrate them for relieving sending states of public welfare burdens, while still assisting with household maintenance and consumer goods purchases among the poor, providing social protection and social clout to dependent household members left behind, and financing local community events and projects (Cohen and Rodriguez 2005; Eckstein 2010; Orozco 2006). Interestingly, development institutions have also promoted remittances as an ideal, countercyclical "stabilization fund" against the failures of neoliberal globalization (Al-Assaf and Al-Malki 2014; World Bank 2015).[1] During the 2008 financial crisis, for example, representatives of the World Bank argued, "It is best to think of migration and remittance practices as the outcomes of the failures of national economic policy to address public needs" (Sirkeci, Cohen, and Ratha 2012: 16).

But critical sociologists have countered development institutions' feverish praise for remittances by exposing the considerable costs that also underlie emigration. For example, remittances have been found to increase inequalities between migrant and nonmigrant families, as well as between genders within emigrant households, in sending regions (Walton-Roberts 2012; Zachariah and Rajan 2009). In addition, remittances have been shown to provide more short-term fixes on market failures than long-term economic investments (Durand et al. 1996; Taylor 1999). Remittances increase developing countries' dependence on foreign markets to include not only foreign capital and foreign consumers but also incomes earned abroad (Itzigsohn 2000). Maintaining the steady rate of remittances in the face of economic downturns forces migrants to make severe sacrifices, as shown by Indian workers in the Middle East who incurred wage cuts in 2008 and thus lowered their consumption, shared accommodations with fellow workers, and worked illegally in lower-paying jobs to remain abroad (Malkani 2009). Finally, critics argue emigration is costly to sending countries. In India, the indirect tax yields from remittances are far less than the earnings lost due to the emigration of Indian professionals (Desai et al. 2009). In addition, the recent emigration of mothers who work as nurses, teachers, cooks, domestic workers, and entertainers has led to a "care drain" in sending countries,

[1] The development of export-oriented economies in the Global South has relied on assembly manufacturing, nontraditional agricultural products, services and labor as the main income generators. Trade surpluses in these countries, however, have been elusive, and given the inability of these states to tax the wealthy sectors, public deficits are recurrent. Additionally, the abandonment of a development model that could rely on a domestic market has increased internal social polarization.

which in turn has provoked further out-migration (Keely and Tran 1989; Lipton 1980; Reichert 1981; Rubenstein 1992; Valiani 2012).

Given these costs, why would development institutions continue to celebrate and promote remittances? Scholars highlighting the power of development ideologies argue they do so to legitimize the concepts of decentralization and marketization, build consent for neoliberal development ideologies, and defuse social conflict arising from the failures of neoliberalism (Bakker 2007). Remittances offer to sustain the private sector as the main engine of economic growth (and a partner in development projects), the financial industry as the main focal point for growth, and markets as a key mechanism (Mawdsley 2015). Remittances also offer an ideal market-driven "financial flow" by individual migrant entrepreneurs, and they force sending countries to initiate market-based policies, such as increasing competition among remittance-transfer service providers and securitizing remittances as a "future-flow receivable" (Bakker 2015a; Ketkar and Dilip 2007). Individual migrants complement the increasing role of private firms in a prescribed shift away from government-sponsored foreign aid and toward "blended" finance instruments that use privatized forms of foreign income (Adelman 2009; Moyo 2009). As Matt Bakker (2015a: 24) caustically notes, "The R-2-D [remittances-to-development] agenda is then, undoubtedly, a form of global neoliberal policymaking, an effort to incorporate migrants' money into global financial markets."

Within this literature, sending states' recent celebration of emigration is simply a page torn from a "neoliberal ideology" script that works in the North's favor. Specifically, capital in receiving countries is vested in accessing an unregulated and unprotected labor force from across the world, and international management organizations facilitate this access (Georgi 2010). The celebration of remittances for development is simply a hegemonic tool that northern countries use to entice sending countries to coordinate their emigration practices with receiving-country interests and to control and assist their emigrants when needed so receiving countries don't have to (Bakker 2015b; Castles and Wise 2007). This was exemplified by the 2006 International Organization for Migration annual meeting in Bellagio, which articulated sending-state responsibilities for mitigating harm to emigrants.

Some scholars in this line of argument highlight the material basis of northern interests, arguing that while development institutions are encouraging sending-country emigration to foster neoliberal development (through remittances), northern states and capital are simultaneously framing immigrants as a "security threat" to spur a profitable migration industry (Glick Schiller 2012). The migration industry is said to open new employment options for agents, recruiters, guards, and document certification attainers, counterfeiters, and verifiers on the backs of immigrants who take on increased risk and debt (Sørensen 2012).

As evidence of this claim, these scholars point to the high-level dialogue on international migration and development that the UN initiated in 2006 and that spurred a subindustry of international migration "governance." The resulting annual Global Forum on Migration and Development, a government-led meeting, now provides a marketplace for diaspora policies, consultations on lessons learned, and platforms for best practices to help sending and receiving countries better "manage" international migration.

A related trend that is less emphasized by the development ideology scholars, but is especially relevant to this study, is the increasing reliance on and celebration of circular or temporary migration for both poor and educated workers. In India, the vast majority of poor workers emigrate on temporary labor visas to the Gulf region of the Middle East, and an increasing share of its educated emigrants are traveling to the United States on the temporary H1-B visa. From the perspective of receiving states, temporary immigration enables employers to tap global labor supply while assuaging the native population's xenophobic fears of racial, ethnic, and cultural dilution. In the United States, for example, employers have handled the 65% decline in undocumented immigration (and the corresponding low-wage labor supply) by sponsoring legal temporary low-wage immigrant workers (Gordon 2017). While this benefits US companies, as well as US politicians seeking public approval for enforced immigration restrictions, it has catalyzed what Jennifer Gordon (2017: 445) calls a "human supply chain," a transnational network of labor intermediaries "whose operation undermines the rule of law in the workplace . . . placing temporary migrant workers in situations of severe subordination." In addition to hurting migrant workers, temporary migration also shifts the burden of migrant care to sending governments (while emigrants are in receiving countries and upon their return home to sending countries). Following the logic of the development ideology literature, we should not be surprised that international norms have pressed sending countries to absorb the costs and responsibility of regulating migrant intermediaries and that sending countries (including India) have taken on such responsibilities and even celebrated circular migration for ensuring more remittances and reversing the "brain drain" to a "brain gain." Unfortunately, however, such efforts have not been found to be successful in protecting migrant workers (a topic I will revisit in Chapter 7).

The development ideology literature underscores the power that receiving countries, and especially employers, have in structuring global migration. It also usefully exposes the vital role that ideologies and the institutions that purport them play (alongside material structures) in shaping sending-state emigration practices. In addition to examining the economic determinants of global emigration practices, therefore, this book takes seriously the role of economic development ideologies in shaping sending countries' class-based emigration practices.

But the development ideology literature also raises three important questions that deserve further inquiry. First, these studies are limited by their exclusive focus on the contemporary era, creating a false impression that sending-state management of emigration is uniquely new and exclusively tied to neoliberal globalization. But as I show in the next chapter, India has been managing emigration to fuel domestic development since the early 1900s. This raises the question: How have other development ideologies in prior eras affected sending-state emigration practices and policies? And what is truly unique about the contemporary era? I will return to this question of history in the final section of this review of emigration studies.

A second question these studies raise is: How and why (if at all) are sending countries consenting to these ideological imports from abroad, especially when they yield such minimal material benefits at home? By focusing exclusively on northern interests in global migration, these studies falsely depict sending countries as unidimensional, passive victims trapped in a transnational capitalist system that is perpetually rigged against them. But this depiction contrasts with Dr. Singh's defiance of the contemporary development hype around emigration. It also belies what we know about capitalist systems (at the national and global levels): they are mired with contradictions that give even the most vulnerable actors (such as sending states) opportunities to exert agency. Hegemony and dominance are real but never absolute, always subject to complex negotiations and struggles (Gramsci 1971). Moreover, we know that such struggles and negotiations are always mediated by class and that sending states are far from unidimensional in class terms. This raises additional questions as to who within sending states or even among emigrants may also be promoting these ideologies.

Finally, underlying these studies is a common misperception that is also found in the development literature, namely, that migration practices simply reflect existing development ideologies (de Haas 2010). But in reality, political parties (on the left and right, in receiving and sending countries) oftentimes reverse the directional arrow and use migration practices, and migrants themselves, to resist and alter development ideologies. In North America and Europe, right-wing parties have defeated pro-market elites by vilifying immigrants and passing anti-immigration polices (Freeman 1995). In Brazil and Mexico, left-wing parties have heroicized and supported emigrants to oppose the ruling state's neoliberal authoritarianism, exclusion, and failure to incorporate productive sectors of society (Levitt and de la Dehesa 2003). In Turkey and El Salvador, right-wing parties (often religious and nationalist) have fostered connections with emigrants to overturn contemporary attempts to globalize (Itzigsohn 2000; Østergaard-Nielsen 2003). As I demonstrate in this book, India has a long tradition of mobilizing emigrants to resist ruling parties and alter reigning development ideologies. This raises an important question for our inquiry: When do development ideologies shape emigration practices, and when do emigration practices (and emigrants themselves) reshape development ideologies? The answer to this question will help us understand when and if emigrants might mobilize to resist contemporary emigration practices and alter contemporary development ideologies in the process.

To answer these questions, we must open the black box of sending states to examine how, when, and why sending states sometimes attain consent for northern-imposed development ideologies and sometimes resist and even reshape these ideologies.

Sending-State Agency, Economic Growth, and Political Legitimacy

A second set of studies usefully helps us open the black box of sending states. These studies stem from the economic and economic-sociology literature on development. Unlike the development ideology scholars, these scholars emphasize the agency that sending states exert within the constraints of the contemporary global economy and emphasize the material and political gains that sending states seek through emigration. These studies underscore that sending states are not just pawns of the Global North; they also shape contemporary global migration to fit their own economic and political interests. Although not explicit, these studies offer a counterclaim to the northern-imposed development ideology literature by highlighting that sending states' emigration practices help define (and sometimes redefine) global development ideologies.

The sending-state agency literature usefully exposes when and why some sending countries have resisted dominant development ideologies imposed from abroad. Some have pointed to sending states' economic calculations of the benefits of engaging their emigrants abroad against their capacities to absorb the costs involved (Levitt and de la Dehesa 2003; Pearlman 2014). Others have pointed to sending states' differing political calculations. For example, while Morocco's government in the 1970s followed global recommendations to increase remittance statistics in order to bolster its own political legitimacy, the Mexican government avoided doing so, also to bolster its political legitimacy in the domestic sphere (Iskander 2010).

Sending-state agency studies have also noted how sending states use emigration to capitalize on the rules of the game. International migration as a function of global capitalism no doubt binds countries into interdependent relationships that rely on economic and political inequality across nations. But some scholars rightly note that in today's rapidly globalizing world, emigrants' remittances offer one of the few existing mechanisms of capital redistribution between developed and developing economies (Walton-Roberts 2004: 56). Others point out that emigration (especially when permanent) is one of the only ways that individuals from the Global South can secure a life out of poverty (Korzeniewicz and Moran 2009). Still others have described emigration among poor workers as a form of class struggle. Vladimir Lenin (1956) famously argued that migration widens the mental horizon of poor laboring migrants who do not own their own means of production by exposing them to a more advanced and dynamic economic system. Similarly, Peter Linebough and Marcus Rediker (2000) showed in their celebrated work, *The Many-Headed Hydra*, that migration creates a highly class-conscious stratum of workers that constantly struggles against the ruling classes and the state (be it a sending or receiving state). Indeed, global capitalism has given migrants some structural power. In a world where the volume of a nation's capital inflows is used to measure that nation's legitimacy, prestige, and potential, sending states keen to ensure domestic accumulation cannot afford to ignore emigrants as one important source of foreign capital.

Finally, sending-state agency studies usefully highlight how sending governments have sometimes reshaped emigration edicts stemming from international institutions. For example, it was sending states that realized the need to recognize emigrants themselves and not just emigration's role in economic growth or poverty alleviation. The World Trade Organization, the International Organization for Migration, and the controversial Commission on Global Governance all addressed migration as a mere movement of commodities divorced from the human actors who embody the commodity (Georgi 2010; Ghosh 1995). The General Agreement on Trade in Services (GATS), the foremost legally enforceable global agreement to expand trade, delineates "the cross-border movement of people" as one of four modes of "trade in services." And as the World Trade Organization, the parent body for GATS, notes, "The GATS is not a migration agreement. Its focus on migration is incidental, as migration under the GATS is not an end per se, but rather a means to the end of trading services."[2]

In contrast to international institutions, the sending states of India, Mexico, China, Morocco, and the Philippines recognized, celebrated, and built relations with their emigrants abroad (Iskander 2010; Kapur 2010; Portes and Fernandez-Kelly 2015; Rodriguez 2010; Ye 2020). In doing so, they forced international institutions to recognize that humans do not merely facilitate the goods and services afforded through migration (as they do in trade and finance); they *are* the goods and services facilitated by migration. Sending states

---

[2] United Nations (n.d.), "International Migration and Development: A Perspective from the World Trade Organization," https://www.un.org/development/desa/pd/sites/www.un.org.development.desa.pd/files/unpd-cm7-2008-11_p13_wto.pdf.

thus taught international institutions how to maximize the economic benefits from emigration by fueling migrants' loyalty to their home countries, which increases remittances and investments through bureaucratic reforms, investment policies, political rights for emigrants, state services abroad, and symbolic politics (Itzigsohn 2000; Levitt 2001; Levitt and de la Dehesa 2003; Østergaard-Nielsen 2003). The Filipino government, which Robyn Rodriguez (2010: xix) calls the "quintessentially neoliberal" "labor brokerage state," has "heroicized" migrants to retain their ideational connection to the Philippines, built a massive state bureaucracy to manage migrants' movements and remittances, and researched global immigration laws to facilitate bilateral agreements that secure niche opportunities for its citizens. The Moroccan and Mexican governments first engaged their emigrants to grapple with domestic political crises, and after decades of what Natasha Iskander (2010: 12) calls "interpretive engagement" between a "creative," powerful state and active emigrants, these countries experienced significant but unintended economic development. The Indian government has created the Overseas Citizenship of India (OCI) status in an attempt to increase emigrants' financial contributions to India through what Daniel Naujoks (2013) calls "rights" and "identity" effects.[3]

By underscoring sending states as agents in and for themselves—striving to ensure domestic material accumulation, political legitimacy, and material redistribution at the global level—these studies usefully complement the development ideology literature that spotlights the role of wealthy receiving countries. As well, by offering detailed empirical cases of different sending states' emigration technologies, the sending-state agency literature offers an important corrective to the development ideology literature. Specifically, these studies remind us that neoliberal globalization (like all hegemonic ideologies) does not have universal consequences; it impacts different states in diverse ways (Ong 2006).

Following these studies, this book views sending states as agents in themselves that differentially manage the constraints imposed on them by receiving countries and sometimes reshape development ideologies in the process. This is not to deny the power that receiving countries clearly have in determining sending states' class-based emigration patterns, but rather to nuance our understanding of the multiple forces at play. Also, by combining the sending-state agency literature with the northern-imposed development ideology literature, this book argues that emigration practices and development ideologies are mutually constitutive. In other words, although development ideologies sometimes shape emigration practices, sending countries sometimes use emigration

---

[3] For a detailed analysis of OCI's impact on remittances, diaspora investments, return migration, and philanthropy, see Naujoks (2013).

practices to redefine development ideologies. Which way the arrow points is an empirical question that deserves our attention.

But these studies do not provide us with much insight on how states differentiate their emigrants by class, if they recognize and celebrate some classes more than others, or how different classes of emigrants differentially relate to the state. To attain insights on this topic, we must look deeper down the analytical tree to examine the migrants themselves.

Migrant Agency and the Transnational Sphere

The third set of studies on sending countries' recent investments in emigration emphasizes the emigrants themselves as a political force "from below" that can shape sending states' emigration practices and policies (Portes 2001, 2003; Portes, Escobar, and Radford 2007; Portes, Haller, and Guarnizo 2002; Delgado Wise and Ramírez 2001; Kearney 1991). These studies stand out as the only ones to highlight the class heterogeneity of emigrants, although none has examined multiple classes in relation to one another and most focus on poor emigrants. Contrary to expectation, these studies show that even the poorest, most vulnerable migrants have organized to assert their power on sending states and development institutions. Drawing from these studies, this book argues that emigration is not only class-differentiated; it is also contingent, contested, and thus ever-changing across time.

In the 1990s, a group of studies known as the "new economic literature on migration" (NELM) highlighted migrant families as agents in themselves. NELM argued that people move across borders not just for higher wages but also to attain short-term security during the disruptive processes of capitalist transition; in developing economies these include imperfect credit, capital, futures, and risk markets (Massey et al. 1993; Stark 1991). Like the sending-state agency literature, these studies emphasize the material reality undergirding the recent optimism around emigration's impact on economic growth (rather than framing the optimism as a simple cloak of deception imposed by the North). Unlike the sending-state agency literature, these studies argue that the call for emigration is migrant-driven. Long before the development ideology scholars addressed emigration, NELM scholars called attention to expectations, power relations, and norms that operate outside the control of an individual. But similar to classical economic arguments on migration, NELM scholars infused the decision to emigrate with a rational, economic cost-benefit calculation (albeit at the household rather than the individual level). NELM scholars depicted remittances, for example, as part of the social contract between emigrants and the families they left behind: families invest in sending certain members abroad with the expectation of remittance returns; emigrants send remittances home with the expectation of inheritance and recognition. NELM scholars also pointed to the important multiplier effects that remittances have, even when used for conspicuous consumption. For example, remittances used to reconstruct a family house in a sending village spur local construction employment and raw material suppliers (Massey et al. 2008).

Although NELM highlighted emigrant agency, it did not address emigrants' relationship with sending states. A separate literature on "transnationalism," which emerged at the same time as NELM, did highlight emigrants' relationships to their communities of origin (sometimes including sending states). These studies emerged to contest claims that migrants are bounded by state processes that define territorially bounded societies (Waldinger and Fitzgerald 2004). Transnationalism scholars argued that a small but significant subset of emigrants maintain relations with their home countries through a transnational sphere––a unique space that is "neither here nor there" (Portes 2001). Rather than migrants physically moving back to the home country, the transnational sphere enables them to influence their communities of origin while remaining permanently in their host country. This happens through frequent visits and constant communication with their home, as well as transnational networks and organizations that foster emigrants' attachments, loyalties, identities, and obligations to communities of origin. These scholars argue that emigrants have used transnational spaces to force sending states to increase their recognition of emigrant contributions and to extend citizenship rights in emigrants' countries of origin and reception.

Emigrants' transnational contributions to sending states cover a wide range. In addition to financial remittances (such as capital transfers and philanthropic donations), migrants send what scholars have dubbed "social remittances," in the form of ideas, ideals, skills, networks, and know-how (Levitt 1999). Transnational scholars have also exposed emigrants' "political remittances," arguing that the emigrants who engage with sending countries are the most assimilated in receiving countries and thus offer sending countries a pathway to strengthening bilateral relations with receiving countries (Kapur 2010; Portes and Zhou 2012).[4] Finally, emigrants have been shown to transfer ideologies back to sending countries, ranging from new gender norms to neoliberal economic policies (Kapur and McHale 2005; Pessar and Mahler 2003). In this book, I call these transfers "ideological remittances."

---

[4] Drawing on a 2008 report (Vigdor 2008), Devesh Kapur (2010: 194) notes that Indian Americans show above-average levels of economic assimilation but high degrees of cultural distinction from native-born Americans.

Migrants' financial, social, political, and ideological remittances, trans-national scholars argue, have built a new center of power that can rival the ability of sending states and international capital to unilaterally define social transformations. Such powers have been most profoundly illustrated in studies showcasing emigrants' ability to shatter traditional notions of nation-bound cit-izenship and redefine citizenship as a dynamic institution that is increasingly extending beyond national borders (Somers 1993). Emigrants have forced many sending states to decouple residence from national membership, thereby enabling emigrants to participate in sending-state development from afar (Levitt and de la Dehesa 2003). In 2013, the UN found that 53% of its 195 members allowed their nationals to retain citizenship when naturalizing in another country; 19% recognized dual citizenship under certain conditions; and only 28% did not allow any form of dual citizenship (Naujoks 2013).

But emigrants' ability to make demands on sending states raises important questions as to what structural power emigrants hold over sending states, and whether such powers (and their corresponding remittances) differ by emigrants' class. Although the transnational literature has not compared different classes with one another, it has provided useful evidence showing that emigrants' interactions with their sending countries do indeed differ by class.

For example, scholars have noted that poor emigrants send different forms of financial flows back to their sending states compared to wealthy emigrants. Poor emigrants send wage-based remittances, such as a portion of the wages they earn in receiving countries (Sirkeci, Cohen, and Ratha 2012: 16). Such wage-based remittances are sent directly to emigrants' family members residing in sending countries and are mostly used for immediate consumption purposes (rather than long-term investments). Remittances are reflected in the current accounts of a country's balance of payments and are thus considered a secure source of financial inflow. It is worth noting that the current account captures the interna-tional trade or inflow and outflow of goods and services in an economy, thereby reiterating the conceptualization of poor emigrants as an "export." Wealthy emigrants, in contrast, are most commonly known to send "foreign investments" since this financial flow assumes daily consumption needs are being met. Foreign investments are reflected in a country's capital accounts and can thus be a potential outflow.[5] Foreign investments from emigrants can be equity-based or debt-based flows. Equity-based investments include foreign direct investments (FDI), which are the investments made by emigrants residing outside their home country into business interests located in their home country, as well as foreign

---

[5] The capital account captures the international inflow and outflow of capital in an economy, made by public and private entities.

portfolio investments (FPI), which are the investments made by a firm or individual in one country in the stocks of a business in another country.[6] Debt-based foreign investments include emigrant-purchased bonds and emigrant deposits in sending-country bank accounts. Emigrant bank deposits can be withdrawn at any time. Therefore, emigrant bonds and bank deposits comprise a portion of a sending country's foreign debt.

Scholars have also shown class-based differences in emigrants' collective interactions with sending states. One set of studies, for example, examines poor emigrants who move from rural villages and small towns in their home countries to urban centers in the United States. These emigrants organize into hometown associations (HTAs) to pool individual financial donations and fund roads, hospitals, schools, temples, churches, and ornate gateways in their hometowns and villages. Most of these studies feature Latin American migrants.[7] Scholars credit HTAs for fueling service economies in agrarian centers, providing a democratizing influence in authoritarian regimes, and fostering an aspirational class among youth. Perhaps the most famous illustration of HTAs' success is the Mexican state's 1998 Three-for-One program that offered state grants to match HTA contributions. Today, Three-for-One supports migrant-organized initiatives that promote development through educational programs, social infrastructure, and community service projects (Gobierno de México, Secretaría de Bienestar 2017). Significantly, scholars note that HTAs showcase poor emigrants' penchant for public-oriented initiatives (Iskander 2010; Levitt 2001; Portes and Zhou 2012).

The HTA scholarship contrasts with other studies that argue wealthy emigrants tend to be suspicious of community-based efforts and thus prefer individual, philanthropic donations to their home countries (Sidel 2008). Studies on wealthy emigrants offer a rare reminder that sending-country emigrants are not homogeneous in class terms. But because these studies focus on wealthy emigrants in the United States, they feature different populations than the HTA literature, such as Indians, Chinese, and Filipinos. These studies often feature wealthy emigrants' social remittances and credit the decentralized structure of the information technology (IT) industry in the United States for facilitating "brain circulation" (as opposed to a "brain drain") between wealthy emigrants and sending countries (Yatsko 1995). The US IT industry, scholars argue, thrived on networks of immigrant scientists

[6] Although the vast majority of FDI is still sent to developed economies, the share of FDI going from wealthy emigrants to developing countries has increased, especially since the 1990s. FPI is not commonly connected to emigrants in the literature, because data on FPI by ethnic origin is not yet widespread.

[7] Zhou, Wang, and Lee's (2010) study on Chinese HTAs offers a useful exception.

and engineers, who transferred technology, skill, and know-how from Silicon Valley to their home countries faster and more flexibly than most corporations did (Saxenian 2002, 2005). By 2000, over half of Silicon Valley's scientists and engineers were foreign-born. Indian and Chinese immigrants alone accounted for one-quarter of the region's scientists and engineers, or approximately 20,000 Indian, 5,000 Taiwanese, and 15,000 Chinese engineers (Saxenian 2005). Clearly, for these emigrants the dominant ideologies of neoliberal globalization have been beneficial. These studies push us to ask how wealthy emigrants have related to their sending countries.

Perhaps the most important study of this subset is Devesh Kapur's (2010) examination of how elite Indian emigrants to the United States have impacted India's development and democracy. Unlike most contemporary studies on emigration, Kapur offers insights on Indians' emigration trajectories over time. Like other studies on migrant agency, Kapur pushes our understanding of elite emigrants' contributions beyond the financial realm to also illuminate their social, political, and ideational impact on India's political economy. Drawing from a unique database of "elite decision makers" in Indian politics, bureaucracy, science, and business, Kapur shows how such individuals have long imported new ideas into India after studying abroad. After 1991, Kapur argues, the sons and daughters of Indian elites imported new ideas back to India after studying abroad. As Kapur (2010: 127) writes, "Elite circulatory migration and the US-based diaspora in particular have reshaped the preferences of Indian elites." In addition to examining the narrow slice of elite Indians who return to India, Kapur shows how elite emigrants permanently residing in the United States have helped bridge bilateral relations between the two countries and bolstered the global reputation of Indian technology businesses.

While the migrant agency and transnationalism literature has usefully highlighted the class heterogeneity of migrants, no study has systematically compared the class differences in emigrants' interactions with their sending countries. Part of this is due to the exclusive focus on the United States as a receiving country. The United States houses the largest share of elite Indian emigrants but not the masses of poor Indian emigrants. Therefore, to examine how sending states' relationships with elite emigrants differ from their relationship with poor emigrants, we need to expand our analysis across space to include additional receiving countries.

As well, these studies' insights on migrant agency remind us that sending-state agency and northern-imposed development ideologies are subject to resistance from below, and therefore emigration practices may change over time. This brings us back to the need to extend our analysis across time.

The Historical Trajectory of Emigration

Drawing from a fourth set of studies examining the historical trajectory of emigration, this book takes seriously the impact that the ancestral lineage of states' past actions has on contemporary state practices on emigration. To understand India's class-based emigration practices in the contemporary era, we must examine when and why India altered its emigration practices in the past. How did India react to past development ideologies and demands from different classes of emigrants? And how did India reshape its development ideologies and manage its different classes of emigrants over time?

As scholars examining emigration from Europe have long taught us, international migration is not a product of neoliberal ideology; it is a product of capitalism. Liberal capitalism relied from the start on the creation of a proletariat that was at once "free" from the encumbrances of the ownership of means of production and feudal fetters and "free" to sell their labor anywhere (Marx 1976). The ability to move (even under duress) enables labor's search for new ways of achieving economic sustenance and is therefore key to the reproduction of capitalism. International migration originated in the social, economic, and political transformations that accompanied the expansion of capitalist markets into under-marketized societies in search of profit, land, raw materials, labor, and consumer markets. Such global-level influences have always disrupted existing social and economic arrangements at the local level and brought about the widespread movement and displacement of people. In addition to offering labor an expanded space within which to seek sustenance, international migration offered capital an expanded space for accumulation.

It is no wonder, then, that mercantile capitalism during the 17th century brought the international deployment of capital and what Eric Hobsbawm (1975: 228) called "the greatest migration of peoples in history." Already a variety of nations were incorporated into the world economy as labor suppliers, and classes were differentiated at a global level by hierarchies of income, status, race, and ethnicity. During the industrial period of the 19th century, the development of Europe spurred the emigration of European workers searching for better lives in the so-called New World, as well as the emigration of colonial citizens sent to work throughout European empires. While these migrations were differentiated from those of the earlier slave trade by their "voluntary" nature, they remained a product of duress. And much like today, such outflows of poor workers from Europe offered workers who remained behind less labor market competition, relieved sending-state governments of rising unemployment and civil protest, and brought sending economies an important source of income. Between 1860 and 1880, Irish emigrants in the United States sent US$30 million home to relatives in Ireland (Bartlett 2010: 292). As a result, by the early 19th century some sending states implemented class-based regulations over emigration. For example, while the British government allowed the mass emigration of its poor workers, it restricted the emigration of its high-skilled workers by seizing their land and property if after six months from being told to return they still remained abroad (Kapur 2010: 125).

By the early 1900s, European sending countries were acknowledging, analyzing, and debating the significant impact that emigration had had on their economies. For example, emigration is said to have been "the key driver of modern Irish history" (Bartlett 2010: 291). When Ireland's middle and professional classes were prospering during the 1930s, emigration "siphoned off potential troublemakers among the lower classes, and thus reduced considerably the combustible elements in Irish society" (445). In 1948, the Irish government set up a Commission of Emigration to study and gather statistics on emigrants. That it became a subject fit for investigation at that time was, according to scholars of Ireland, "truly groundbreaking" (483). By the late 1950s, Irish emigrant remittances constituted 2% of southern Ireland's gross national income (292). Irish emigrants also founded, funded, and joined movements (sometimes violent) that supported Irish independence from afar (294).

In addition to international migration itself, the concept of extending citizenship beyond national boundaries is also not simply a product of new technologies of neoliberalism; it has long been recognized as a resilient facet of human attachment and identity. In 1870, British nationality established that "no one can renounce his country," thereby enabling British emigrants to retain their British citizenship for life.[8] This is similar to laws in Colombia, Argentina, Panama, and Venezuela today. Under Napoleon, the French Nationality Law asked French emigrants to simply express a "will to return" in order to retain their citizenship, and by 1945, the Law required all French citizens (at home or abroad) to preserve their "national state." In 1912, Italy recognized dual citizenship, and between 1958 and 1969 Spain and 12 Latin American countries established bilateral agreements to manage their dual citizens (Naujoks 2013).

Examining the long history of emigration, therefore, can help us expose what is (and is not) new about contemporary emigration patterns. To do so, this book asks not just how neoliberal ideologies shape emigration but how shifts in capitalism (before and after the start of neoliberalism) have shaped (or are shaped by) emigration. How and why do sending states alter their emigration practices and their modes of national accumulation over time? Is there any link between the two?

---

[8] Although, as I discuss in Chapter 3, this was eventually complicated for British subjects of the colonies.

Scholars of 19th-century emigration from Europe have shown how emigration and capitalist accumulation within sending countries were long intertwined in a virtuous cycle. From this we learn that emigration not only fosters sending-country economic growth; it also results from economic growth in sending countries (Martin and Taylor 2001). In an influential paper, Doug Massey (1988) illustrated how economic growth in Europe during the 19th and 20th centuries spurred increased emigration as economic transformations disrupted and displaced people from their traditional livelihoods through concentrated capital accumulation, land enclosures, and the creation of markets. Moreover, development (defined as economic growth alongside the formation of regulatory institutions designed to govern the growth) made emigration easier, cheaper, and more accessible. This remains true today as the growth in national incomes across the Global South has spurred emigration, especially from Asia and Latin America (Sassen 1988). Once in place, emigration has further assisted industrial growth and capital accumulation in these sending countries by providing an outlet for surplus labor during periods of recession and inviting social, economic, and political remittances.

But the historical trajectory of emigration and capitalism from the Global South has not been nuanced enough in the existing literature. Part of this is due to this literature's nearly exclusive focus on the experience of the United States as the receiving country of our time. Beginning with the collapse of European colonialism, scholars highlight changes to the international division of labor and the transformation of global investment flows that accompanied the shift in the locus of global hegemony from Europe to the United States (Cohen 2006; Sassen 1988). The periodization, however, is framed entirely around the shifts in immigration policies that took place in the United States (which I detail in Chapter 4). Less developed in this literature, however, are the parallel shifts that took place outside the United States. The 1970s was marked by a rise in transnational capital the world over, the economic boom in oil-producing countries, and the relocation of manufacturing capacities to Asia. These trends catalyzed new South-South migration flows that were massive and significant. By 2016, South-South migration flows exceeded South-North flows, and South-South remittances were nearly as high as North-South remittances (Castles and Miller 2009; World Bank 2011).

To truly understand the class politics of sending countries' emigration practices over time, therefore, we must extend our analytical lens across time and space—to include the periods before and after neoliberalism, as well as the massive South-South flows of migration that follow the geography of a commodity rather than a global hegemony.

To this end, let us now turn to the analytical framework I use to explain the class politics of Indian emigration over time.

An Analytical Framework: Migration-Development Regimes

Building on the small but growing literature on emigration and development, this book reframes sending states' emigration practices as a *regime*. To highlight the dynamic and robust relationship between sending-country emigration and sending-country development agendas, I call this regime a "migration-development regime." Scholars of the Regulation School famously illustrated how each phase of capitalism has a distinct regime of accumulation—a set of regularities in the economy that enable processes of capital accumulation (Jessop 1982). While in hindsight each phase might appear to add up to a seemingly coherent process of capitalist transformation, in practice each phase is full of contradictions and contingencies. Other scholars have similarly employed the concept of regimes to understand the shifting social relations of surplus labor value extraction and coercive land redistribution (Burawoy 1985; Levien 2018). Here, I define MDRs as the full set of emigration practices and policies that (among other forces) enable sending countries to ensure domestic capital accumulation as well as their own political legitimacy at the global and domestic levels.

While MDRs can be applied to receiving or sending countries, or even to subnational regions that control global migration, I use the framework here to unpack the complicated and messy web of sending-country actions, initiatives, and responses over time. Given global power structures, sending country MDRs are necessarily constrained by external conditions (such as labor demand and immigration regulations in receiving countries, as well as labor supply in competing sending countries). The degree to which a sending country's MDR is discernable from global factors therefore depends on its size, its resource base, and its geopolitical position. In the case of India, with its substantial economy, political power, and enormous population of both poor and highly educated workers, it is reasonable to assume that its MDR has a fair share of autonomy—at least enough to warrant our investigation. While I do not wish to deny the clear role that receiving countries have in shaping India's emigration practices, my focus in this book is on how India has managed the global relationship, formed a pact with its domestic polity, and (at times) helped shape global paradigms.

An MDR framework requires us to analyze the multiple forces and actors (and their motivations) that shape emigration practices. First, MDRs capture a sending state's ideological, economic, and political interests. On the ideological front, MDRs instill particular institutions, habits, and norms, or what scholars have called a *mode* of regulation within a sending country (Jessop 1982). An MDR mode (which may reflect an ideology imposed by a development institution or a set of ideas, tastes, and norms imported from different classes of emigrants) is designed to attain consent for the regime across all classes— including those that benefit from the regime as well as those subordinated by the regime. A key feature of MDR modes, I argue, is that at certain times they cement consent for existing development ideologies, but at other times they are used to attain consent to *alter* a development ideology, particularly when a previous one signals vulnerability.

On the economic front, MDRs reflect sending states' attempts to advance the economic and material structures of domestic development (through, for example, the management of receiving countries' labor demand and/or the importation of different financial flows from different classes of emigrants). Whether or not a sending state privileges ideological over economic needs in a particular MDR becomes an empirical question.

On the political front, MDRs reflect the sending state's attempts to retain its own legitimacy by grappling with domestic actors' competing political interests. These may stem from within the state itself (across branches of the government, ministries of the bureaucracy, political parties, and national versus subnational levels of the state). But they may also stem from outside the state to include demands by receiving countries, global powers, and the different classes of a sending state's own citizen base.

Second, MDRs point our analytical gaze downward to examine the emigrants themselves. After all, MDRs represent a site of struggle and are thus contingent on resistance from below. Such resistance emerges from different classes of actors with necessarily different interests. Over time, statecraft from above and class-differentiated resistance from below interact to create the rise and fall of various MDRs.

This rise and fall leads MDRs to shift over time. Underlying this shift is the reality that all regimes are undergirded by contradictions and constraints, which eventually lead to their downfall. An MDR framework enables us to define, compare, and contrast sending states' changing emigration practices across different regimes over time and helps us empirically answer if, when, and how emigrants alter a sending country's development ideology *versus* when development ideologies shape emigration.

Such analyses, I argue, help deepen our understanding of past and contemporary emigration practices. But most important, they help us expose the ever-changing class basis of global migration—illuminating moments when certain classes of emigrants exert power over sending states, other moments when states exert power over certain classes of emigrants, and still other moments when states enact class pacts and compromises across different migrant interests. Understanding this class basis enables us to more robustly analyze the consequences of the class inequalities emanating from global migration.

Unpacking the State

In the context of India, some scholars have posited the state as a "third class," with interests distinct from those of capitalists and working classes (Bardhan 1984), while others have framed the state as an expression of the ruling capitalist class (Chibber 2003). In both instances, however, the state is conceived as the site of political society where repression is executed and dominant ideologies are built, managed, cemented, and transmitted (Gramsci 1971). Even in the contemporary neoliberal context replete with calls for reduced state involvement in the economy, the Indian state remains the unquestioned shepherd of economic development and provider of welfare. Moreover, in India's democratic context, the state is as much motivated by ensuring economic growth as it is by ensuring its own legitimacy among all classes of the electorate. Therefore, drawing on the MDR framework, this book centers the Indian state as an active agent of global migration, and emigration as a proactive vector that it employs to meet its ideological, economic, and political interests.

Readers may ask: How do we define "the state"? In the case of emigration, the national-level government is generally (and correctly) acknowledged as the entity formally responsible for controlling people's movement across national boundaries. It is the only entity with the power to legitimately use violence to enact such controls. And, since the French Revolution, it is the entity most empowered to define citizenship policies.[9] Social and political theories have thus assumed national governments are the natural authority over migration policies (Agnew and Corbridge 1995; Baubock 2003; Varsanyi 2006). As scholars of transnationalism have argued, the literature on migration has been marked by a "methodological nationalism" as a result of this consensus (Castells 2010; Wimmer and Glick Schiller 2002).

To examine the Indian national government, I conducted an archival analysis of all parliamentary discussions, presidential speeches, and national budgets on emigration from the 1920s to the present. I also examined the annual reports of the key government bureaucracies responsible for emigration (the Ministry of External Affairs, the Ministry of Overseas Indian Affairs, and the Reserve Bank of India). Finally, I conducted 30 interviews with national government officials responsible for emigration. These interviews took place in person in India's capital city, Delhi.[10] These sources enabled me to expose the tensions that arise over

[9] Prior to the French Revolution, this power lay with cities and religious groups.

[10] Government officials were from the Ministry of Overseas Indian Affairs, Ministry of External Affairs, Ministry of Home Affairs, and the Ministry of Minority Affairs in Delhi; the Department of Industries and Commerce, the Overseas Manpower Company of the Department of Employment and Training, and the Special Secretary of Non-Resident Indian Affairs in Andhra Pradesh; the Non-Resident Indian Division of the Government of Gujarat, the Gujarat State Non-Resident Gujarati

time within the national state across political parties and across divisions of government (such as the Supreme Court and the Ministries of Labor, External Affairs, and Small and Medium Enterprises).

But "the state," especially in India, also comprises the subnational level. Subnational state actors, depending on their electorate and their legislative powers, might have competing interests, which could force them to resist national-level emigration policies and practices. While subnational variation in migration approaches has been less highlighted in sending states, a few studies in the receiving-country context of the United States have offered useful insights on how "sanctuary cities" have resisted national-level integration policies (Hoye 2020). In India's federalist structure, states are the subnational unit of interest since they shape emigrants' linguistic and cultural identities, are responsible for their citizens' welfare, and have exhibited varied outreach to their emigrant populations. Subnational state actors in India have sometimes represented working-class emigrants and at other times represented professional emigrants, depending on the state's particular electorate.

Therefore, in addition to analyzing India's national-level state actors, this book also examines how India's subnational states have sometimes resisted and sometimes inspired national-level emigration policies. I conducted interviews with government officials in three Indian states that have significant emigrant populations: Kerala, Andhra Pradesh, and Gujarat. I selected these three based on my qualitative interviews that indicated they have the largest and longest emigrant streams, as well as the most active subnational government efforts on emigration. These state government interviews were vital because the national government does not maintain detailed data on emigration by state (despite consistent demands to collect such data).

Interestingly, unlike at the national level, India's state-level emigration efforts focus on one class of emigrants, thereby reflecting their respective electorates. The Kerala government, which has shifted between the Communist Party of India–Marxist and the Congress Party, has long supported its massive voter base of poor emigrant workers to demand from the national government the right to emigrate, recognition for their economic returns, increased protections, and welfare benefits. Kerala was one of the first states in India to facilitate the export of poor emigrant workers, even before it was legal at the national level. Still today, Kerala is one of the largest state exporters of poor emigrants in India,

Foundation, the Gujarat Chamber of Commerce and Industry in Gujarat; chief minister of Kerala, minister of rural development and planning and culture in Kerala, minister of Kerala's Non-Resident Keralite Association (NORKA), finance manager of NORKA, present and previous CEOs of NORKA, and head of NORKA Welfare Board.

and the state's income is highly dependent on the economic earnings of these emigrants.[11]

The Gujarat government, in contrast, has invested in building cultural bonds with its large middle-class, entrepreneurial, and family-based emigrant population, exemplifying for the national government how states can encourage ethnic identities to draw greater returns from their wealthy emigrants. As well, the Gujarat government has enacted programs to draw investments from the large overseas Gujarati business community and is one of the few states in India to use HTAs. In 2000, the Gujarati population in the United States was 150,000, about one-third of the Indian immigrant population in that country (Ministry of External Affairs 2000). A large percentage of Gujarati Americans are business owners. Today, 65 percent of budget motels and 40 percent of all motels in the United States are run by a subsect of Gujaratis (known as "Patels") (Assar 2000). Thus, Gujarati Americans tend to be permanent immigrants who have recently increased their interest in strengthening relations with their home state. From 1995 to 2014, Gujarat was ruled by then Chief Minister and now Prime Minister Narendra Modi of the Hindu nationalist party the Bharatiya Janata Party. Overseas Gujaratis support Modi and draw enormous pride from the state's recent economic success, Modi's conservative social tendencies, and his attention to Indians living overseas.

The government of Andhra Pradesh has focused on connecting with its more recent, temporary, professional emigrant population, illustrating how states may try (but fail) to draw investments from elite emigrants. The architect of the emigration surge from Andhra Pradesh was Chief Minister Chandrababu Naidu (of the local Telugu Desam Party), who ruled the state from 1994 to 2004. Naidu's migration-development approach earned substantial praise in the West, although it faced opposition at home.[12] During his rule, Naidu hosted visits by Tony Blair, Bill Clinton, and Bill Gates, earned a "Naidu Day" by the governor of Illinois, and won numerous awards, including South Asian of the Year from *Time Asia* (Monbiot 2004; Singh 1999). Underlying the West's praise

---

[11] In recent years, Uttar Pradesh, Bihar, Tamil Nadu, West Bengal, and Rajasthan have surpassed Kerala in terms of total emigrant population, especially among poor workers. These states have larger populations than Kerala and represent a new stream of emigration. But I focus on Kerala since it has had the longest running history of poor workers' emigration, the most active mobilization of poor emigrants, and the most advanced governing structures around emigration. These features make it a fitting case for this study. Moreover, Kerala remains a major emigrant-exporting state today.

[12] Unlike Gujarat, politics in Andhra Pradesh have not been dominated by elite Hindus or national-level parties. Muslims have long retained a large presence and dominated the police and military services; local ethnic parties have attained electoral success; and ethnic separatist movements and a strong Maoist insurgency have challenged mainstream power. In this context, public-sector unions and the rural poor in Andhra Pradesh opposed Naidu for ignoring their needs.

for Naidu were his investments in the IT sector and private colleges, which were recognized by Western employers as a secure source for IT professionals (Xiang 2002). In 1995, Naidu created the Hyderabad Information Technology Engineering Consultancy City, where he provided investors with exemptions from statutory power cuts and labor inspections and permission for three-shift operations. Under Naidu, Microsoft chose the state's capital, Hyderabad, for its first foreign research and development center. Naidu was also the first Indian chief minister to digitize state government activities and maintain a state government web portal.

Within the Indian American software professional community, Telugus (as natives of the state are named) have become a majority group as a result of Naidu's approach. Telugus represent 23 percent of Indian IT professionals worldwide (Xiang 2002). Unlike Gujaratis, most Telugu Americans hold temporary visas. In the early 2000s, Andhra Pradesh drew the largest relative share of FDI from its emigrants abroad compared to other Indian states (Kapur 2010). Although the Andhra Pradesh government continues to create software technology parks to draw overseas Indian IT entrepreneurs to invest in local start-ups or return to India to work, it is now less active than the Gujarat government. Moreover, Andhra Pradesh's investments in education and IT, combined with its countermovement history, have made Telugu Americans' transnational activities more diverse than those of Gujaratis.

Unpacking Emigrants by Class: Transnational Organizations

To unpack the class basis of India's MDR, I examine two groups of Indian emigrants: highly educated Indian emigrants in the United States (who occupy middle- and upper-class positions and work as professionals or business owners) and poor emigrant workers in the Gulf region of the Middle East (who work as masons, carpenters, and general laborers). While at first glance this bifurcation may seem crude, especially since it masks substantive within-class heterogeneities, in the Indian context it is meaningful because it follows India's legal demarcation of emigrants. Under Indian law, those with greater than 10 years of formal schooling are subjected to far fewer emigration restrictions and regulations than those with less than 10 years of formal schooling.[13] In Indian emigration parlance, these two groups are referred to as "high-skilled"

---

[13] Restrictions are enforced through the passport, the document required to legally exit India. Those with greater than 10 years of formal schooling are eligible for what is known as an ECNR (Emigration Check Not Required) passport, while those with less than 10 years of formal schooling can only receive an ECR (Emigration Check Required) passport.

and "low-skilled," respectively. Given the loaded and detrimental effects of these terms, I avoid using them in this book and instead use the terms "elite" and "poor."[14]

The Middle East and North America represent the two largest recipient regions of India's economic emigrants. Within the Middle East, the Gulf Cooperation Council countries of Saudi Arabia, United Arab Emirates, Kuwait, Qatar, Oman, and Bahrain are the top six receiving countries of poor Indian emigrants.[15] Current estimates show the Gulf countries today host more than 6 million Indian emigrant workers (with masons, carpenters, and general laborers being the top occupations).[16] Within North America, the United States is the largest receiving country of Indians, 96% of whom are educated.[17] Each class grouping represents the majority of the Indian emigrants in its respective region.

This approach of examining different class actors in India's emigration industry within a single theoretical frame is unique in contemporary studies of emigration. In the course of my research on poor Indian emigrants, I also folded in another group of actors who are integral to Indian emigration but are largely invisible in existing studies of emigration: migrant recruiters. In India, this population occupies a middle class of small and medium-size business owners.

To unearth the role that different classes of emigrants have played in shaping, cementing, and changing India's MDRs over time, I use migrant organizations (rather than individual migrants) as my unit of analysis. As we know, organizations are more than and different from the mere sum of their individual members (Dimaggio and Powell 1983). Organizations operate at the level of

[14] It is widely known that the vast majority of international emigrant workers are not the poorest of the poor; indeed, they need a baseline of resources to emigrate in the first place. Still, few would deny the basic fact that relative to India's highly educated, professionally employed emigrants, its poor emigrant laborers occupy subordinate class positions—with none to little ownership of capital and usually in debt, and with minimal assets, income, education, and political or social power. For a beautiful discussion on terminology around skill and its consequences on migrant laborers in the Middle East, see Iskander (2021).

[15] Although migrant data in the Gulf Cooperation Council is harder to tabulate, most estimates show working-class Indians comprise the largest share of Indian immigrants. There has, however, been a rise in semiskilled and skilled jobs in recent years (including drivers, mechanics, and building tradesmen), as well as professionals (including engineers, nurses, medical practitioners, managers, and technical posts). The most recent estimates for the Indian population in these countries is Saudi Arabia (2017) 3.2 million, UAE (2015) 2.6 million, Kuwait (2018) 1 million, Oman (2018) 766,735, Qatar (2017) 650,000, and Bahrain (2018) 316,784 (https://gulfmigration.grc.net/; accessed July 22, 2021).

[16] See the website of the Gulf Labour Markets and Migration, https://gulfmigration.org/.

[17] In the United States, working-class Indian immigrants represent less than 6% of the Indian immigrant population.

"civil society," a sphere Antonio Gramsci (1971) famously described as the key sphere through which the state can transmit its dominant ideology and economic imperatives to attain universal consent. But Gramsci also showed us that civil society can just as easily represent the sphere where alternative hegemonies arise. Migrant organizations thus serve as key intermediary actors that sit between the state and individual migrants. Such organizations reflect the conscious political choices of their members "for themselves" that may or may not represent the population's structural realities "in themselves" (Marx and Engels 1965). Therefore, examining migrant organizations enables me to capture emigrants' overt, sustained, group-based expressions of migrant identities and interactions with the Indian state.

Modern organizations have also been said to reflect the myths of their institutional environments rather than the actual demands of their work's activities, because doing so is more likely to ensure the organizations' ability to attain legitimacy, resources, and stability and even secure its survival (Meyer and Rowan 1977). Therefore, in addition to providing insights into individual migrants' political expressions of collective identity, they also shed light on the constructed (at times mythicized) understandings of the state and of development agendas. A cross-class comparative examination of migrant organizations thus provides important insights into how different migrants interpret the state's actions and represent themselves to the state, and why some groups attain visibility and power while others do not. In other words, migrant organizations offer a key to understanding migrants' civil society.

Within emigrant organizations, I interviewed organization leaders for two reasons. First, leaders provide official articulations of the discursive elements of organizations' collective efforts, thereby highlighting how different groups (not individuals) publicly interpret and assign meaning to their own identities. Second, leaders are often the key conduits in transnational interactions between actors in the United States and those in India, and they thus provide the most insights into how their organizations translate their identities into development goals in India. By limiting my interviews to organizational leaders, I was able to control for intra-organizational politics and difference, which is not my focus. I found that these leaders were eager to participate in the interviews as a way to increase the visibility of their organization's goals, activities, and achievements; only one person declined the invitation to participate.[18]

Among poor emigrants, I interviewed 20 leaders of return migrant organizations in the state of Kerala. Given the tight regulatory control over Indian

---

[18] In the early phases, I encountered skepticism from leaders of Christian and Sikh organizations. This was overcome by my employing kinship networks and introductions from within-group informants.

emigrants in the Gulf region of the Middle East and the lack of formal migrant organizations in those countries, I accessed poor emigrants upon their return to India. The nature of Gulf migration is by definition temporary and circular, so many of these organizations represent migrants who have either completed their migration cycle or are in the midst of it.

To supplement my migrant workers' organization interviews, I conducted 20 interviews with registered recruiters based in Delhi. These recruiters work with migrants from across India, and their agencies have branch offices in several states. All 20 of them were the managing directors of their recruiting agencies. Most were the founders of the agency (or the son of the founder). And since the agencies were relatively small, all the interviewees were deeply involved in the day-to-day process of recruitment. Two of the agencies were government-based, and the remainder were private. While my recruiter interviewees were randomly selected based on the list of registered recruiting agencies published on the Indian government's website, these interviews were not designed to be representative, but rather illustrative of a third set of actors that sit between migrants and the Indian state in the emigration process.

To analyze middle- and upper-class Indian emigrants in the United States, I compiled a unique inventory of 647 Indian transnational organizations that operate nationally, virtually, and in the four metropolitan statistical areas where over 55% of the Indian American population resides.[19] This was necessary because the Indian government (unlike other sending countries, such as China) does not maintain a database on transnational Indian migrant organizations abroad. All organizations in the inventory began before 2009, have had at least one project in India since 2005, and are founded and led by a person of Indian origin. Therefore, the inventory reflects sustained transnational efforts motivated by immigrant logics rather than those of multilateral organizations staffed by Indian Americans. This inventory is the first of its kind for the US-based Indian population. Data for the inventory was collected using online databases, Indian business directories, websites, Indian American newspapers, and advertisements for the India Day Parade. Organizations were categorized based on their self-identified "type" since this is where I found significant variation.

---

[19] These are New York City (and northern New Jersey, Long Island, and parts of Connecticut and Pennsylvania); Washington, DC and Baltimore (and parts of Virginia, West Virginia, and Maryland); Chicago (and Gary and Kenosha); and San Francisco (and Oakland and San Jose). Other significant metropolitan statistical areas of Indians not included in the study are Los Angeles, Philadelphia, and Houston. This information was drawn from my analysis of the US Census and the Integrated Public Use Microdata Series. A national-level census would yield an even more complete picture of the hundreds of additional Indian diaspora organizations that exist in the United States. Such a study census should be conducted and maintained by Indian embassies in receiving countries.

I then conducted 75 semistructured interviews with leaders of Indian transnational organizations in the United States (located in four metropolitan areas: Washington, DC; New York; Chicago; and San Francisco) and 71 interviews with leaders of partner organizations in India (located in Delhi, Kerala, Gujarat, and Ahmedabad). Most of these interviews were held in person (at the interviewee's office or home, or in a neutral location such as a restaurant); some US interviews were conducted over the phone. All interviews lasted one to four hours.

To select interviewees, I first drew from my inventory to identify the principal organizations in each category. Principal organizations were defined as those that represent a significant portion of the community (be it an ethnic, professional, or religious group) and have a voice that is recognized by individuals, other organizations, and government officials in the United States and India. I then narrowed the list of principal organizations using a snowball technique based on interviews with scholars, activists, and other key informants knowledgeable about Indian diaspora affairs in the United States. Because the network of Indian transnational organizations in the United States is relatively close and heavily influenced by the "major" organizations, this purposeful sampling technique offered more useful insights on general patterns than a random sampling approach (Neuman 2011). The final list of principal organizations roughly represented the inventory distribution of organizations by type.[20] The principal organizations also varied in terms of membership size and budget, enabling me to control for resource-based explanations.

Interviews and site visits in India were conducted in Delhi to capture the national level, and in the states of Gujarat and Andhra Pradesh to capture the subnational level. These states represent the largest exporters of middle- and upper-class emigrants to the United States. Both states are prosperous, have embraced liberalization and globalization, and have pursued their diasporas as a development resource. Politically and socially, however, they differ in ways that have shaped their transnational connections. Finally, I supplemented my interviews with government officials and emigrants in India with additional interviews with Indian migration scholars, union officials, and migration activists.

This multipronged methodological approach enabled me to uncover the social processes and mechanisms that often remain hidden in survey data. As with most qualitative studies, the findings in this study do not purport to be generalizable to all emigrants. Rather, they provide an important and underexamined,

---

[20] My interviews oversampled "religious combination" organizations because they yield important insights into the transnational politics and identities of Indian immigrants, and professional/alumni organizations because they represent a primary focus of the Indian government.

historically informed contribution to our understanding of one sending government's transnational practices, as well as different classes of emigrants' collective transnational identities. Moreover, qualitative methods have long asserted that the "process of discovery" is as much a part of the "process of justification" as is the "process of verification" (Burawoy 1991: 8). To this end, I argue that the findings detailed in this book expand our understanding of the class basis for the processes and actors involved in the migration-development nexus.

The MDR framework unpacks the complicated and messy web of global and domestic forces that the Indian state has always had to grapple with in order to achieve economic growth, political legitimacy, and class inequalities at once. Armed with this framework of MDRs, let us now begin with this book's first MDR, the Coolie MDR of 1834.

3

The Coolie MDR (1834–1947)

Racializing Emigrants' Class Exploitation

Using the MDR framework described in the previous chapter, this chapter and the next examine India's shifting MDRs in the period *preceding* India's contemporary liberalization reforms. This chapter traces the rise and fall of what I call the Coolie MDR, which ran from 1834 to 1947 under British colonial rule. The next chapter traces the rise and fall of what I call the Nationalist MDR, India's first postcolonial MDR, which ran from 1947 to 1977. As noted in the previous chapter, sending-country emigration practices reflect a complex web of forces emanating from labor demand and development ideologies in receiving countries, labor supply and political-economy needs in sending countries, and migrants' class-varied interests and motivations. The MDR framework helps us home in on exactly which forces and which actors shape and undermine sending countries' class-based emigration practices over time. In addition, the MDR framework helps us expose how different classes of emigrants themselves help shape evolving domestic ideologies. The MDR framework thus exposes the processes through which migration and development become *mutually constitutive*.

In this chapter (and the next), I illustrate how the Indian colonial state (and subsequently the postcolonial sovereign state) grappled with political-economy forces from abroad and within to justify a set of emigration practices that would ensure domestic accumulation and its own continued political legitimacy at the global and domestic levels while simultaneously institutionalizing class inequalities between emigrants. Each chapter also unveils the contradictions within each MDR, which eventually led to the demise of the MDR. Together, this chapter and the next make two central points. First, MDRs rise, fall, and shift over time—thereby reflecting and shaping ever-changing global and domestic forces. Although constantly shifting, MDRs remain linked to one another

The Migration-Development Regime. Rina Agarwala, Oxford University Press. © Oxford University Press 2022.
DOI: 10.1093/oso/9780197586396.003.0003

through this history. The constraints and contradictions of India's earlier MDRs likewise have shaped India's contemporary MDR. And understanding this ancestral lineage, I argue, is vital to deepening our understanding of the present moment. Second, since the colonial era, the subject of emigration and different classes of emigrants have differentially played an important role in resisting a reigning MDR (and its underlying development ideology) and transitioning the nation to a new one. In addition to exposing the understudied role of emigrants in shaping national development agendas, this historical legacy raises important questions of whether and how emigrants might resist India's contemporary MDR.

Contrary to claims that sending-state governments throughout the world (including India) have only recently started to use emigrants to meet domestic development needs, this chapter shows that emigration has been an important state subject in India since the colonial era. But unlike India's subsequent postcolonial MDRs, the Coolie MDR instituted an overtly racialized development model, whereby the colonial state exploited poor and middle-class Indian emigrants to serve as coolies for the British Empire, advancing economic accumulation in the colonies and ultimately in the United Kingdom. The Coolie MDR therefore represented the only MDR in India's recent history that overtly promoted the emigration of all classes of Indian workers, thereby bringing Indians to the colonies of Africa and Southeast Asia, as well as to Australia, Canada, and the United States.

The Coolie MDR also inaugurated India's first migration state. In response to public pressures from local citizens and receiving contexts, the colonial government was forced to gradually build a regulatory framework that empowered the state to not only use, but also control, the global mobility of "free" (as opposed to enslaved) commodified human workers. At times, the state had to forgo the economic benefits of emigration to retain its political legitimacy. Underlying this framework was a class-based distinction of Indian emigrants. So successful was this approach that many of the regulations and institutions born during the Coolie MDR continue to guide India's class-based emigration infrastructure to this day.

Eventually, however, the Coolie MDR crumbled. Its racist model of accumulation mobilized cross-class solidarity among Indian emigrants who resisted global racism, British colonialism, and, ultimately, the Coolie MDR itself.

A Liberal Experiment

Underlying the Coolie MDR's class-based emigration infrastructure was an important and complex experiment for the modern migration state—an experiment that remains oddly pertinent today. The Coolie MDR emerged in the wake of the global ban on enslaved labor. Ideologically, therefore, the Coolie MDR had to buttress the then-burgeoning development paradigm of Liberal capitalism, whereby all humans (i.e., Indian and British) were deemed (1) "free," commodified, wage workers (i.e., not enslaved) and (2) equal at birth (i.e., not measured by family lineage). At the material level, however, the Coolie MDR needed to ensure continued capitalist accumulation within the British Empire and thus needed "coolies" to develop the empire's rural and urban productive sectors.

Linking the Liberal ideological paradigm to the sending (and receiving) British state's capitalist material goals required an important ingredient: a migration state that could draw on and control "free" Indian emigrants, thereby distinguishing them from British workers by race and class. The catch was that the British state had to do all this without appearing to do so, since states no longer had the right to distinguish human bodies by race.

Under the Coolie MDR, therefore, the colonial state encouraged poor Indian workers to emigrate to service plantations across the empire. It also encouraged a smaller group of middle-class Indian emigrants to emigrate abroad to manage manual workers in other colonies; work as traders, clerks, and shopkeepers; or study to eventually work in the British civil service. The Coolie MDR's early promotion of Indians' emigration across classes was, of course, facilitated by the unique contours of the empire, where the British state controlled and benefited from both sending and receiving contexts.

But such encouragement required political justification, which over time resulted in successive layers of new regulations. At first, the colonial state justified the Coolie MDR's race- and class-based exploitation of Indian emigrants by enacting a narrow band of formal regulations designed to officially certify that Indian indentured laborers were, in fact, "free" rather than enslaved. At the same time, the Coolie MDR left a far larger, unregulated, informal sphere of emigration open for the remaining poor and middle-class Indian workers to continue emigrating uninhibited. These porous borders that encouraged the mobility of Indians across the empire were consistent with the prevailing emigration patterns from other European countries, as well as the dominant development ideology that promoted liberal markets and the free movement of capital, finance, and people.

Eventually, however, resistance from below forced the colonial state to enact additional regulations and controls over Indian emigrants. The first demands for such regulations emerged from white settlers in wealthy receiving colonies, who feared the racial dissolution of white Europeans as well as labor competition and thus wanted to restrict the influx of Indian immigrants. To meet their demands, the British government introduced the modern passport in 1917. But the next, more damning set of complaints emerged from a cross-class coalition of Indians (including emigrants) who condemned the British state's racist exploitation of Indian emigrants (across classes) and demanded independence from British colonial rule. In a desperate grasp at renewed legitimacy, the British banned indentured servitude in 1917 and enacted a new Emigration Act restricting Indians' emigration in 1922.

Together, the newly established passport and the ban on indentured servitude established a race-based double standard in global migration whereby Europeans retained the right to free movement, while the British sending state micromanaged the emigration of all Indians—whether indentured, unindentured, or middle class. To implement these regulations, the British state established an intricate bureaucracy, complete with new legislation, personnel, departments, and procedures all designed to monitor and control the movement of Indian emigrants. Although the Coolie MDR was officially disbanded when India gained independence in 1947, it yielded the blueprint for the institutions, legislation, infrastructure, and practices that still govern India's emigration to this day.

The significance of the Coolie MDR is that the experiment it launched over a century ago (i.e., exploiting international emigrants for domestic accumulation while simultaneously claiming to protect them) continued to rear its head in the postcolonial context. By ultimately restricting Indians' emigration, particularly that of poor indentured workers, despite the economic benefits such emigration could bring the colonial regime, the Coolie MDR piloted a new development agenda based on closed borders, state protection of Indian workers, and national self-sufficiency. Little did the architects of these restrictions know at the time that it was this development agenda that would soon be extended to goods and services and govern India for the next half-century (the subject of Chapter 4).

Establishing State Control of Human Mobility by Class (1834–1922)

From 1834 to 1922, the Coolie MDR slowly built India's first regulatory infrastructure that enabled the state to not only encourage but also differentially manage Indian emigrants' mobility by race and class. The colonial state enacted such race- and class-based regulations in order to retain its political legitimacy in the face of mounting public pressure.

Exporting Poor Emigrants

Under the Coolie MDR, the British state capitalized on the labor of poor Indian emigrants to ensure accumulation throughout the empire.[1] The British colonial government made considerable investments in facilitating the one-way export of laborers, such as offering subsidies to Indian shipping companies that carried Indian workers and building extensive infrastructure and communication networks (Jaiswal 2018; Slezkine 2006). Over time, the British state was also forced to institute regulatory oversight and control over these laborers. The resulting system was at once clear and messy and relied on a distinction between formally regulated indentured labor and informally regulated nonindentured contract workers. Whether formal or informal, the Coolie MDR's emigration regulations allowed for the continued export of poor Indian laborers to service the material and economic needs of the British Empire. By one estimate, four-fifths of the 3 million Indians who emigrated between 1800 and 1945 were poor agricultural laborers with little to no education (Madhavan 1985).

Throughout this period, the colonial government of India (much like today) kept state emigration efforts in the shadows, never directly promoting emigration, rarely raising the issue in public debate, and framing recruitment as a commercial transaction that did not require too much government intervention. In doing so, the government profited from emigrant labor but absolved itself of responsibility for labor abuses, as well as some sending regions' concerns of labor scarcity.

Formally Regulated Indentured Labor

Probably the most well-known basis of the Coolie MDR was its reliance on the emigration of millions of poor Indian laborers, who served as indentured plantation workers in other British colonies for a contractual period of five years. In total, the indentured labor system is estimated to have transported

---

[1] Prior to the export of "free" laborers across the empire, the British government exported Indian convicts to penal settlements in the colonies (such as the Andaman Islands, Mauritius, Ceylon, present-day Malaysia, Singapore, and Burma). Transport was by sea and considered a worse punishment than death, since crossing the *kalapani* (black water) was believed to alter one's caste purity. Upon arrival, convicts were forced into hard labor—clearing jungles and constructing roads, canals, bridges, and buildings—in order to build the early colonial infrastructure. This practice brought tens of thousands of Indians across the Indian Ocean and Southeast Asia from the late 1700s to the mid-1800s. This practice eventually tapered as British officials in receiving colonies refused to accept more convict migrants, fearing their own security. Since this labor was not legally "free," I do not detail it here. For a more detailed analysis of this practice throughout colonial regimes, see Anderson (2018).

over 1.4 million Indians across the globe (Lal 2006). Indentured labor offered British colonial rulers and plantation owners across the empire a ready labor fix in the wake of the 1833 Slavery Abolition Act that gradually banned slave labor throughout most of the empire.[2] Indian laborers were abundant in numbers, and the coercive power of the colonial state could force Indian workers to emigrate to work for minimal wages. As Radhika Mongia (1999: 22) notes in her history of British migration controls, "Lord Stanley, Secretary of State for the Colonies, [was clear] in his dispatch: free labor could be as effective and advantageous to the capitalist as slave labor." The shift from slave to indentured labor was swift. Before the ink on the ban on the use of African slaves had even dried, anxious plantation owners in Mauritius and the Caribbean quickly pivoted to using Indian indentured laborers instead. According to Mongia (1999: 25), on the very day that the emancipation of slaves came into effect, the ship *Sarah* sailed into the harbor at Mauritius carrying 39 indentured Indian migrants.

For a few years, indentured laborers emigrated unencumbered by any state regulations on human mobility. But public pressure in the wake of the recent worldwide antislavery movement, and reports of the abuse and neglect of indentured labor, soon forced the British government to intervene on private labor contracts and formally prove the difference between indentured and slave labor. To do so, the British government under the Coolie MDR established the first regulations over the movement of "free" laborers. In 1835 the Court of Directors of the East India Company, the primary administrative body of British colonial rule in India, enacted new state mechanisms to monitor and control indentured Indian labor emigrants, and by 1837 the British Parliament had ratified its first act to regulate the mass movement of "free" human labor (Mongia 1999). The purpose of these regulations was not to prevent or even discourage the movement of indentured laborers. Rather, they were designed to offer legal proof that the state was exporting "free" (rather than enslaved) labor and to claim some semblance of state oversight and protection against abuse. In short, state legislation aimed to certify the commodification of Indian emigrants' labor, and not their bodies. Therefore, all indentured Indian laborers thereafter were required to appear before a district magistrate to declare their voluntary migration in an agreement known as *girmit*.

Not surprisingly, plantation owners resisted the Coolie MDR's new regulations over indentured labor. Many questioned the legality of state monitoring of the movement of free and peaceful laborers; after all, European emigrants were not monitored or controlled by sending (or receiving) states, so long as they did

---

[2] For some years, planters could use ex-slave labor as "apprentices," although this practice also died by 1838, since most ex-slaves refused the system.

not prove a political threat.[3] Moreover, there was no precedence for state legis-lation to hinder capital's labor demand, and plantation owners questioned the British government's right to undermine capital's right to import free labor. Such regulations were accused of undermining the very notion of "liberty."

But the British government defended the Coolie MDR's (albeit minimal) regulations by claiming to "protect the security and well-being" of poor Indians who wanted to emigrate for work, especially given their "ignorance."[4] As well, the British government relied on the widely accepted practice of "colonial ex-ception," which justified different rules for white Europeans and colonial natives, despite their shared label as "British subjects" (Mongia 1999). Together these defenses underscored the need for British colonial rulers to "civilize" Indian natives.

After years of intense parliamentary debate over the legality of state regula-tion of labor mobility and a volley of prohibitions and subsequent resumption of indentured labor between 1939 and 1842, the Coolie MDR ultimately deemed *consent to a contract* as the primary proof of "free" labor. The contract specified the duration, type, and pay of the work (which usually included food, clothing, medical facilities, and sometimes an optional free return passage to India at the end of the contract). Indentured labor was thus permitted so long as such consent to a contract existed, and the state was given authority to certify such consent and oversee the terms of the contracts (although planters were rarely held accountable for breach of contract after a laborer gave consent). To do this work, the Coolie MDR birthed a new regulatory infrastructure within the state, which included a series of new acts; a new department, the Protectorate General of Emigrants (PGE), which still exists today; new salaried emigration officials at multiple levels of the bureaucracy located in both the sending and receiving regions; new registration systems; new licenses for recruiters; and countless new technologies of surveillance and record-keeping—all designed to certify indentured laborers' consent to emigrate for work abroad.[5] This new regulatory infrastructure echoed the general trend of expanding the colonial state apparatus in India during the late 19th century. Over the second half of the 1800s, the government repeatedly expanded the regulatory infrastructure of emigration and intermittently tried to streamline it and remove its dizzying inconsistencies and contradictions. These efforts ended with the Emigration Act XXII of 1882,

---

[3] Although England had exercised exceptional powers to monitor the entry of Jacobins after the French Revolution in 1792, that was justified on the grounds of political threat.

[4] Edward Lawford (solicitor to the East-India Company) to David Hill, June 12, 1838, *Papers Respecting the East India Labourers' Bill* (London: J. L. Cox and Sons, 1838), 2–3, India Office Library and Records, London, V/27/820/4, quoted in Mongia (1999: 530).

[5] The creation of the Protectorate of Emigrants was detailed in the 1864 Emigration Act XII.

which became the definitive regulation on indentured emigration until its abolition in 1917. But lack of enforcement and the speed at which the system needed to constantly expand (to include new terms and new destinations) demanded continuous modifications in the law, each of which in turn maintained the regime's messiness.[6]

Despite its lumpy texture, the Coolie MDR clearly established India's first regulatory infrastructure through which the state could govern global emigration. It established concrete criteria that could justify the migration of indentured Indian labor as "free" and "just," it established precedence for the state to monitor and control such human movement, and it established a state machine to implement the new regulations. Most important, the Coolie MDR's governance system took on the responsibility of managing the delicate balance between ensuring public legitimacy on one hand and capital accumulation on the other. Specifically, it offered just enough regulation to appease public disapproval and enable the bulk of government-approved exploitation to occur behind the curtain of public scrutiny. As I indicate throughout this book, it is this very system established during the Coolie MDR that continued to shape India's postcolonial MDRs.

With the governing system in place, the Coolie MDR's state-controlled indentured labor system grew exponentially over the next decades, reaching far beyond the original agricultural needs of sugar plantation owners in Mauritius. By the early 1900s, poor Indian indentured laborers had been sent to service a wide variety of plantation crops (including coffee, cocoa, tobacco, cotton, tea, rubber, and rice) in colonies as far-reaching as the West Indies (including present-day Guyana, Trinidad, Jamaica), the smaller islands of the Caribbean (including present-day Grenada, St. Lucia, and St. Vincent), Fiji, Africa (Tanzania, Kenya, Uganda, and South Africa), Burma (present-day Myanmar), Malaysia, and Ceylon (present-day Sri Lanka) (D'Souza 2000). While many remained abroad after the completion of their contract, a sizable number returned to India with some earnings from abroad.

Informally Regulated, Nonindentured Labor

Two important features of the Coolie MDR were that its state-regulated indentured labor system was not the only pathway for poor workers' emigration and that the other pathways were only informally regulated. From the late 1800s to 1937, poor Indian laborers also emigrated abroad through *kangani* and *maistry* systems, which echo the systems still used to export poor Indian

[6] For example, a minor modification was made in 1908.

emigrants today (see Chapter 5).[7] *Kanganis* and *maistries,* who themselves were Indian emigrants, were responsible for recruiting and supervising groups of 10 to 30 Indian laborers, who were not indentured. *Kanganis* and *maistries* usually shared kinship links with the nonindentured laborers. Most came from middle castes, although some worked their way "up" the migration chain from lower castes. They worked through hierarchical chains that usually ended with the direct supervision of a British employer in the colonies. The precise role, pay, and power of *kanganis* and *maistries* differed across colonies and time, but in all cases, they absorbed the brunt of Indian workers' resentment and anger, deflecting attention away from the British rulers. By the late 1800s, many nonindentured laborers were encouraged to emigrate with their families to increase the permanency of their emigration. The share of nonindentured laborers emigrating under the *kangani/maistry* systems is estimated to have reached over 6 million, a far larger share of Indian emigrants than were indentured laborers (Jaiswal 2018; Madhavan 1985; Singha 2013).

Alongside the Coolie MDR's public efforts to formally regulate and protect indentured labor, therefore, was an alternative realm for the undocumented, unregulated, and unrestricted movement of nonindentured Indian laborers to continue. The British government argued that these workers did not need state protection or oversight because they were traveling to destinations that were closer to India and could thus learn on their own about the work conditions and manage their own return home. The vast majority went to Ceylon, Malaya, and Burma, although some went further, to East Africa. As with indentured workers, the government argued that nonindentured emigration would help low-caste Indians escape the punitive rules and restrictions of the Hindu caste system and thus improve their social status.[8]

Because poor Indian workers who migrated under the *kangani* and *maistry* systems were recruited through informal kinship networks, they were depicted as "free" by definition. In reality, however, they were kept bonded through an advanced loan used to cover family expenses and transport, as well as a promissory note or contract demanding work in return for debt repayment. The bondage was justified by the promissory notes that the British state actively enforced with acts such as the 1869 Workmen's Breach of Contract Act, which empowered a magistrate in Burma to imprison a worker for up to three months or impose a fine for refusing to fulfill his contract with the *maistry*. Recruiters were also

[7] The *maistry* system was used to recruit Indian labor to Burma and, although similar to the *kangani* system, was even more notorious for the chain hierarchy of middle-men employers and abuses to laborers.

[8] *Report of the Committee on Emigration from India to the Crown Colonies and Protectorates,* 1910, cited in Singha (2013).

technically licensed. But the British did not apply any protective regulatory mechanism or oversight over nonindentured emigrant laborers.

Because they operated largely outside the regulatory arm of the state, nonindentured emigrant laborers recruited by *kanganis/maistries* were able to go to more destinations and work in more diverse areas than indentured laborers. In addition to cultivation, these laborers were employed to pack, load, and transport produce. They helped build the infrastructure underlying the colonial regime's export-oriented production, including railways in Uganda, Tanzania, and Kenya, as well as the roads, ports, and sewage systems in Burma. Eventually they also helped build nonagricultural export industries, such as chemicals, oil, and timber, and worked in mills and factories.

In most cases, these workers' debt bondage, combined with the dearth of employment opportunities in India, prevented them from permanently returning to India. According to some reports, many nonindentured emigrant laborers did return due to the harrowing work conditions abroad and near absence of female emigrants. And already, they were sending remittances home to sending communities and returning with substantial savings (Jaiswal 2018).[9] But there is little evidence indicating the British government invested in helping return migrants find employment or recognized their skills or earnings after their return. Rather, most return migrants failed to find adequate employment, and under the heavy weight of debt had to emigrate again in search of more work abroad. In some cases, as in Fiji, nonindentured Indian emigrant workers eventually comprised a majority of the population, and a small minority even moved into the middle classes as small business owners and elected politicians (Larson and Aminzade 2007). But, as I illustrate later in this chapter, poor Indian emigrants who remained abroad retained few ties to India after the demise of the Coolie MDR (until recently).

Exporting Middle-Class Emigrants

In addition to exporting poor laborers, British colonial law under the Coolie MDR facilitated the emigration of nonlaboring, middle-class Indians to serve as merchants, traders, shopkeepers, accountants, labor supervisors, and clerks, as well as soldiers, police officers, and seamen, throughout the empire. Like their poor laboring counterparts working in colonial plantations and mills, this group of middle-class Indian emigrants served as "coolies" to the British Empire, recruiting, transporting, feeding, and overseeing Indian laborers; managing the

[9] See also Kapur (2010).

packaging, transport, and financing of exports; and servicing the financial and administrative needs of plantation owners and other employers.

On one hand, this group of Indians represented a heterogeneous group. While some came from low-caste peasant backgrounds, most came from lower-middle to middle-class backgrounds. In some cases, as in Burma, the first batch arrived as members of the colonial troops, or sepoys, that conquered the colony. In other cases, they arrived in the colonies as escaped or abandoned workers, or lascars, on British ships that were transporting indentured laborers or goods for trade. Some were, in fact, re-migrants who had first left India as poor laborers (either under the indentured labor system or through a *kangani*) and had completed their contracts. In still other cases, middle-class Indians emigrated to help meet a rising demand for middle-class services in the colonies. Some left as independent entrepreneurs trying to sell Indian medicines, carpets, and spiritual traditions in new lands; others drew on family networks that had been established in the Gulf states as early as the ninth century. In many colonies, British policies cemented a racial division of labor that prevented native populations from attaining credit, trading licenses, and training. Instead, Indians were exported to serve as commercial intermediaries, traders, shopkeepers, moneylenders, and even some professionals, earning them the title of "middleman minority." In Rangoon, middle-class Indians constituted 83% of bankers and moneylenders by the early 1930s (Jaiswal 2018).

But despite this heterogeneity, the colonial state distinguished this group of emigrants from the laboring poor in terms of emigration regulation and oversight. First, they did not require the same proof of consent and other state-sanctioned documents that poor laborers needed to depart India. In fact, they were not even classified as "emigrants" until 1922. This was in large part due to their smaller share of all Indian emigrants. While there are almost no official records of this stream of emigrants, estimates range from a half-million to one million by the time of independence (Lal 2006). They represented a more privileged population relative to Indian labor emigrants; most were endowed with some initial capital, and many had some level of education, information, and networks to draw on. Given their relatively small numbers and more privileged backgrounds, they were subjected to far less public scrutiny for their protection than were poor emigrant laborers.

Second, they did not emigrate under a labor contract or the direct supervision of a recruiter or employer in the receiving colony (although those who left India as seamen were expected to return). Rather, this group of Indian emigrants moved under the empire's allowance for the free movement of "respectable temporary sojourners," even though many opted not to return to India (Lal 2006). Therefore, they could largely choose their destination. Moreover, after emigration they were not required to work as manual laborers (although some did, and some were even captured and forced to work as indentured laborers against their will).

In receiving contexts that had a large share of poor Indian emigrant laborers (such as in Africa, the Caribbean, Southeast Asia, and the Middle East), these emigrants maintained social, residential, and political distance from poor Indian (and native) laborers while abroad. And in receiving contexts with large white settler populations (such as the United States, Canada, Australia, and parts of Africa), they were forced to maintain social, residential, and political distance from whites. In several colonies, these communities brought family members and established local cultural and religious institutions.

The colonial state's initially lax regulation over middle-class Indian emigrants caused them to become highly visible and often resented fixtures abroad (Larson and Aminzade 2007). This eventually spurred outcry from native populations in East and South Africa, as well as white settler populations in the dominions. In response, the colonial state eventually regulated middle-class Indian emigrants as well.

Regulating Nonlaboring Emigrants

Although the British government initially resisted regulations over nonlaboring emigrants, the Coolie MDR eventually gave birth to the first set of state regulations over this population in order to assuage public pressure from citizens in receiving locales. The result was the formation of the modern, universalized passport, which gives both sending and receiving states the uncontested power to determine who leaves and enters their national borders. According to some scholars, the impetus for modern passports first emerged to restrict the immigration of Indians into North America (see Mongia 1999).

Resisting Pressures to Regulate

By the late 1800s, some Indians had managed to push the open passages underlying the Coolie MDR to emigrate to the more prosperous and semi-independent parts of the empire with Dominion status (such as Canada and Australia), as well as to the neighboring and sovereign nation of the United States. European settlers had originally staked out these lands for whites. But the Coolie MDR had unexpectedly enabled a unique group of Indian farmers and ex-soldiers to arrive on the shores of these lands. Unlike Indian indentured or *maistry* laborers, these emigrants did not arrive with a labor contract explicitly designed to fulfill a receiving employer's needs. Most of these emigrants also came from slightly more privileged backgrounds than indentured or *maistry* laborers. Unlike the other streams of poor and middle-class Indian emigrants, they did not serve the

British Empire upon arrival in the receiving country. Rather, they benefited the empire by relieving surplus farm labor within colonial India.

Although their departure benefited the sending context, their arrival in the receiving context elicited strong and explicit race-based resistance from white middle- and working-class settlers. Some feared the racial dilution and degradation of their newly emerging dominions; others feared for their jobs. This resistance from receiving contexts created new challenges for the British Raj.

While the British government was keen to maintain sound relations with its dominions, it was, at first, reluctant to institute explicit race-based restrictions on labor mobility within the empire. Such restrictions would undermine the material basis of the Coolie MDR that relied on facile labor mobility for accumulation within the empire (Singha 2013). Moreover, such restrictions threatened to undermine the British colonial regime's claim of the universal and equal "British subject" (Mongia 1999). Therefore, for decades the British refused to prohibit Indians' emigration abroad. At the same time, the British government also refused to protect Indian migrants who faced resistance upon arrival in receiving regions.[10]

By the turn of the century, despite British calls against restrictions, Australian authorities instituted the first race- and class-based restrictions to affect Indian emigration. Specifically, they insisted that short-term migration to Australia be limited to "respectable" migrants, which would be measured by education level (Singha 2013). To this end, the 1901 Australian Emigration Restriction Act instituted a dictation test in English or some other European language, which was explicitly expected to exclude Asian settlers. In 1904, the Act's class basis was made more explicit by allowing Indian merchants, students, and tourists to enter and stay for up to a year without the dictation test (provided they attained documentation from the sending British Government of India certifying their identity and the purpose and duration of their travel). Lord Ampthill, the acting viceroy of India, was said to be effusive that "the Australian government had acknowledged the standing of educated Indians in the Empire" (quoted in Singha 2013: 295).[11]

Although on the surface, the British government accepted Australia's new immigration restrictions, in practice it did little to help implement them from the sending side, arguing that Indian emigration law did not formally authorize the British to prevent poor Indian laborers from emigrating within the empire or

---

[10] Similar resistance against Indian immigrants was also occurring in East and South Africa at the time, from both Africans and European settlers. For the purposes of space and my focus on elite emigrants in the United States, I detail only the context of North America.

[11] Governor-General India to Governor-General Australia, October 17, 1904, Foreign, General, B, February 1905, 23–25, National Archives of India, Delhi.

punish them for doing so. The only formal preventative mechanism the British government had at its disposal was to claim an Indian emigrant was not "free" but was actually being exploited against his will to serve as an indentured laborer in a restricted destination. Such claims were no doubt made, even in cases where emigrants had their own means to travel. But, in general, British officials allowed many Indians to emigrate without the necessary documentation.

As for elite "respectable" Indian emigrants, the British Raj maintained its already existing controls over them. The colonial state had long allowed a minority of educated Indians to emigrate abroad to deliver lectures or to study in elite Western schools. This practice was framed as part of the "civilizing mission" of colonialism. More important, it yielded a ready supply of civil service leaders the British government could employ to administer the colonial regime. But the British government closely watched these elite emigrants in case they become too radicalized during their studies (which, of course, they did). In fact, by the eve of World War I in 1914, the English press was reporting the British regime's growing anxieties around the population of Indian student emigrants in the West. Excepting these students from the new and more complicated documentation requirements of the Australian Emigration Act enabled the government to continue its simpler (and already extant) surveillance techniques, which relied on easily attainable certificates of identity attested at the district level (by a district magistrate or police) and, in the case of students, by a headmaster (Singha 2013).

The Rise of the Modern Passport

In was in this context that a group of male Muslim and Sikh Punjabi Indians made their way to North America during the late 1800s and early 1900s, thereby sparking the "first wave" of Indians to arrive in the United States and, eventually, the first wave of regulations over nonlaboring Indian emigrants.

These Indian immigrants stemmed from a community of farmers, and nearly half were ex-soldiers who had served in the British army. They were escaping recurrent famines plaguing the capitalist transformation of Indian agriculture, as well as the British government's new Criminal Sedition Act of 1908, which was designed to repress the mounting resistance to colonial rule in India. Taking advantage of the relatively free mobility within the empire at the time, these immigrants first arrived in Canada; in 1907 alone, 2,623 Indians arrived.

Although they did not necessarily stem from the poorest classes in India, they attained jobs constructing railways, bridges, and tunnels and working in mines. And despite their contributions, they faced substantial anti-Asian sentiment and violent attacks by white settlers. Many thus fled across the border into the United States, where they once again found jobs in the lumber industry and in railroad construction on the Northwest, Canadian Pacific, and South and Western Pacific lines. By 1900, there were 2,031 Indians in the United States.[12] In 1910, additional Indian immigrants arrived directly into the United States at the Seattle harbor via the Philippines (a US territory) by appealing to the right to mobility held within empires.[13] By 1910, the number of Indians in the United States had more than doubled, to 4,664.[14]

At first, US employers welcomed them. Their numbers were relatively small, and employers needed low-wage labor since the 1882 Chinese Exclusion Act had decreased Chinese immigration. But soon Indian immigrants in the United States faced the same severe anti-Asian attacks that their brothers in Canada had faced from local white communities. Eventually, these Indian immigrants also faced increased repression by US authorities suspicious of their growing political radicalism (Leonard 2007; Sohi 2011).

As a result of the anti-Indian sentiment, nativists in Canada and the United States clamored, even cooperated, to impose government restrictions to prevent the further influx of Indian (and other nonwhite) immigrants (Sohi 2011; Yang 2020). As a member of the Commonwealth, Canada lobbied the British government to assist with such restrictions.

But, as in the case of Australia, the British government refused to implement restrictions on labor mobility based on race and held to their claims that the empire was "civilized," that the British state was "liberal," and that all British subjects were equal. Racialized restrictions on labor mobility within the empire, the government argued, threatened to undermine the very notion of the "British subject," as well as the material basis of the empire's Coolie MDR. For years, therefore, the British government allowed Canada to enact only minor Australian-style barriers to entry, based on "respectability" measured by linguistic skill or monetary payments. On the sending end, the British government refused to prohibit emigration from India and merely offered to inform Indians of the potential restrictions they might face in receiving regions.

After some years, Canada made a more drastic, alternative demand to the British government—to issue a universal and standardized system of passports to *all* emigrants leaving India. Motivating the proposal was still a desire to ensure that sending countries take responsibility for allowing only "desirable" and "respectable" migrants to leave their shores. But the passport system would also empower receiving countries to formally control who did and did not enter their borders (Mongia 1999; Singha 2013).

---

[12] Drawn from US Census data in Gibson and Jung (2006).

[13] These Indians also were not excludable under the US 1975 Page Act that prohibited the entry of forced labor from Asia, Asian women who would engage in prostitution, and escaping convicts.

[14] This number is drawn from US Census data in Gibson and Jung (2006).

For years, the British government declined this request for state-based power to restrict certain British subjects' mobility within the empire. But in 1913, the British government accepted the proposal, ironically, to control elite emigrants, not poor emigrants. Indians in the United States and Canada were showing signs of joining the growing anticolonial movement. In response, S. H. Slater of the British Government of India slashed the concept of free mobility within the empire and instead allowed states the right to differentially restrict human mobility across their borders (Mongia 1999). Standardized passports for all British subjects offered the guise of equality across citizens and nation-states, requiring every citizen to hold a passport and every nation to restrict entry as it so wished.[15] As well, they enabled the state to legitimately control the mobility of poor and elite Indians. As Mongia (1999: 539) writes, "What the seemingly insignificant migration of Indians to Canada instigated was the eruption and use of a variety of mechanisms for generating, obtaining, and collating knowledge on every aspect of the movement of Indians."

By 1917 all Indian migrants were required by the Defense of India Rules to obtain a passport. This act made entry into or exit from any port by sea in British India without a passport a criminal offense. By 1919, the British government was effectively using the passport to restrict the reentry of thousands of Indian emigrants it deemed "seditious by reason of their revolutionary political views e.g. Bolshevist, Sinn Feiners, members of I.W.W., or the revolutionary party in Egypt," and on the grounds they would "injure the safety, interests, or tranquility of the [British colonial] State" (quoted in Singha 2013: 311).[16] It also enabled the state to deny reentry to Indian men who married white women, "which damaged colonial prestige" (quoted in Singha 2013: 309).[17] At first, the law exempted populations whose mobility had already been regulated through other channels (such as indentured labor going to Ceylon and Malay, naval and military forces, crews of overseas vessels, or religious pilgrims). But over time, the law included all Indian emigrants.

Impact on the First Wave of Indian Americans

These trends within the British colonial regime had a direct impact on the United States, where Congress was also working hard to legally restrict the further influx of nonwhite immigrants. Local hostility toward Chinese and

---

[15] Distinctions in citizenship rights between European and Indian subjects were reflected in the passports.

[16] Ordinance V of 1914, National Archive of India, Delhi.

[17] W. H. Vincent, Home member, Viceroy's Council, December 18, 1919, Home, War, A, June 1920, 55–59, National Archives of India, Delhi.

Japanese immigrants was already high, so extending the discussion to include Indians did not require much effort. Moreover, Britain's legalization of the use of state power to restrict human mobility had set an important precedence for other nations to follow. For years, the United States had resisted restrictions on Indian immigrants for fear of disrupting its diplomatic relations with the sending state of Great Britain (a similar challenge that it faced with Japan and Japanese immigrants) (Ngai 2014). So US nativists, welcomed the British government's newfound interest in discouraging Indian emigration to the United States for fear that Indians would find sympathy there for the growing anticolonial movement. In other words, the British sending state's new distaste for Indian migration to (and from) the United States enabled the US government to pursue avenues to restrict the free movement of Indians (and other Asians) into its national boundaries.

At the heart of US immigration restrictions was legislation on citizenship. The US Nationality Act of 1790 had already barred Indians from becoming citizens by restricting naturalization to "free white persons of good moral character." As a result, the Punjabi Indians who had already entered the United States were forbidden to vote. As noncitizens, Indians were also forbidden to own or lease land under the 1913 Alien Land Law (which was amended in 1920–21). This racialized definition of citizenship, which held important consequences for the representational and material lives of countless immigrants, was contested for years, with many arguing that it was antithetical to US founding principles of equality (Yang 2020). Indian immigrants in the United States formed organizations, such as the India Welfare League and the India League of America, to fight for citizenship and other rights. Although some did manage to become naturalized citizens, the landmark case of *United States v. Bhagat Singh Thind* in 1923 established that Indians were not white and thus ineligible for citizenship. Many Indians who had already been naturalized and owned land were stripped of both, anti-Asian riots erupted, and the Asian Exclusion League agitations drove Indians out of most urban areas. Unlike Chinese and Japanese immigrants in the United States, Indian immigrants received little to no support from their sending state (the British colonial regime). This lack of support not only drove Indians out of US cities to pursue opportunities in remote rural areas; it also eventually drove them into the heart of the anti-imperial movement against the British.

Despite the resistance movements, the debates, and the clear inconsistencies with American ideals, the race-based definition of citizenship eligibility continued to define US restrictions around immigration. In 1917, the very same year that the British colonial government enacted the passport rules for India, the US Congress defined a "barred Asiatic zone" that prevented more Asians (including Indians) from immigrating As in Canada, the advent of the passport facilitated such exclusions by offering a civic document that drew attention away from overt racial discrimination and pointed instead to an invented notion of the nation-state. And in 1924, the US Congress went even further and passed the Johnson-Reed Immigration Act, which explicitly restricted nonwhite immigration using a complicated system of national origin quotas. Under the law, quotas were allocated to countries in the same proportion that the American people traced their origins. Conveniently, the definition of "the American people" excluded "aliens ineligible for citizenship" (as well as descendants of slaves and American aborigines) (Ngai 2014). It was not until 1946, when President Truman signed the Luce-Cellar Act, that Indians in the United States won the right to be naturalized and regulations were expanded to allow 100 new Indians to enter every year, albeit without spouses or children (Lal 1999).

Until the mid-1900s, therefore, Indians were forbidden to enter the United States, and the community of mostly male Indian immigrants remained small and contained, reaching a high of only 5,850 in 1930.[18] Moreover, because Indians were forbidden to bring their families and legal restrictions on marriage across races prevented them from marrying most local American citizens, they married Mexican women, forming a unique and distinct community. Due to an exception in the US landowning laws for Mexicans, Indian-Mexican marriages enabled Indian migrants to indirectly own land, and many became large farmers. For the remainder of the Coolie MDR, these Indian emigrants remained largely divorced from the colonial state of India. But as I show later in this chapter, they soon became active in the anticolonial movement and were thus influential in bringing the Coolie MDR to its end.

The Fall of the Coolie MDR (1922–47): Emigrants in the Anticolonial Movement

Although the Coolie MDR helped meet many of the economic needs of the British colonial government, like most regimes it was based on layers of contradictions and suffered important vulnerabilities. It began to show signals of its demise when the British government banned indentured labor migration in 1917 and instituted a new Emigration Act in 1922 in a desperate grasp to retain legitimacy. But rather than assuring the Coolie MDR's legitimacy, these reforms merely helped India transition to the subsequent Nationalist MDR, which officially emerged in 1947, when India gained independence.

---

[18] This number is drawn from US Census data and Gibson and Jung (2006).

One of the most significant vulnerabilities of the Coolie MDR was that its clear (albeit unstated) racist logic helped catalyze a cross-class, race-based co-alition of resistance among Indians within India and abroad. This cross-class coalition, which included lower- and middle-class emigrants as well as elite emigrant intellectuals, focused on the fair treatment of *all* Indians (no matter where they lived) in order to "resolve the question of *racial* equality all over the world" (Singh 2014: 177).[19] The demise of the Coolie MDR was, of course, connected with the general demise of the British colonial regime itself. But an important, and less highlighted, aspect of this connection is the role that the subject of emigration and Indian emigrants themselves played in facilitating the demise of the colonial regime, and hence the Coolie MDR.

Establishing a Cross-Class Coalition of Emigrant Revolutionaries

From its early years, the Indian National Congress (INC) Party, which was founded in 1885 to lead the independence movement against British colonial rule, raised issues concerning the Indian emigrants scattered throughout the empire. By 1890, Jawaharlal Nehru, a key leader of the INC, said he hoped "the Indian Diaspora [emigrants] would play a significant role in bringing about de-colonisation" (Nehru 1972, quoted in Singh 2014: 172).

Perhaps the most recognized and iconic Indian emigrant to play a significant role in India's decolonial movement is Mohandas Gandhi (commonly referred to as "Mahatma," or venerable). With his astute political skills and his ability to command a mass following, Gandhi stood at the helm of the Indian independence movement until its end (and his assassination) in 1947. Gandhi retained his leadership in spite of heavy contestation from the left and right wings of India's independence movement. He was among the minority of middle-class Indians who emigrated abroad under colonialism, moving to the British colony of Natal (present-day South Africa) in 1893 to work as a lawyer. Natal had been receiving poor Indian indentured workers and middle-class Indian merchants for over 30 years prior to his arrival. And it did not take him long to witness the unjust treatment of Indians in South Africa. Just one year after arriving, Gandhi began campaigning for the rights of Indians.

Interestingly, Gandhi's focus at the start was only on the rights and disenfranchisement of wealthy Indian emigrant merchants. He did not turn his attention to the plight of Indian indentured laborers until over a decade later. Scholars have argued that Gandhi's shift from speaking disparagingly about poor

---

[19] Emphasis added by author.

Indian indentured laborers to addressing the issues they faced was strategic. His campaigns for the rights of wealthy Indian emigrants was not yielding much success. Moreover, Gandhi and the anticolonial INC soon realized that attacking the indentured labor system would drain the material basis of the colonial economy.[20] In 1906, he launched the *satyagraha* (rule of truth) campaign in South Africa, which later became the slogan of the INC and the Indian anticolonial movement. Protests were rising against the 1906 Black Act that made registration and carrying papers for Indians mandatory in South Africa. And the following year, Gandhi led the famous (and eventually successful) passive resistance campaign against a tax that had been imposed on former technically "freed" indentured laborers in South Africa. At the same time, an anti-indentured emigration league was beginning to grow in India.

A key argument of this chapter is that what enabled Gandhi's strategic decision to focus on the rights of poor indentured labor, as well as elite emigrants, was the racist overlay of the Coolie MDR, which in turn justified a cross-class solidarity among emigrants.[21] In addition to mobilizing Gandhi in South Africa, the Coolie MDR's racist class pact also mobilized a large army of young, Indian emigrant intellectuals. While many began in the United Kingdom, by the 1910s tightening British security had pushed them to other corners of the world, including Paris, New York, San Francisco, and Tokyo.[22] Although their elite status afforded them education, professional jobs, and mobility in the empire, they remained subjected to humiliating forms of racism.

While some (like Gandhi) were radicalized abroad, others were radicalized in India and moved abroad to study, form new networks, raise funds, and expand the anticolonial movement globally. Fueled by the 1905 Russian Revolution, the radical wing of the movement particularly benefited from the ability to emigrate and pursue political work in exile. These young activists were often welcomed and housed in receiving countries by religious Indian missionaries (including Swami Vivekananda in the United States) or wealthy Indians who had emigrated earlier to collaborate with the imperial establishment but had subsequently become disillusioned by British rule.

This stream of emigrant Indian revolutionaries swelling across the world represented a relatively elite intelligentsia who were deeply convinced of the

---

[20] The INC was founded in 1885.

[21] Interestingly, in addition to condemning the persistent and extreme exploitation, abuse, and malpractice of the indentured labor system, nationalist discourse also employed symbolic gestures to the "Indian woman made dishonorable through migration," an image that would haunt India's subsequent postcolonial MDRs as well (Mongia 1999).

[22] For more detail on Indian students' activism in these cities, see Fischer-Tine (2007); Ramnath (2005). For more on the 100+ Indians studying in Japan and influenced by the pan-Asian movement, see Prasad (1979).

importance of emigration for the sake of attaining a foreign education. As Shyam Krishnavarma, a pivotal figure in the transnational anti-imperialist network in the United Kingdom, wrote in the *Indian Sociologist* in 1906, "If the funds provided by Indians . . . were spent on the education of promising young Indians in Europe, America, or Japan, we feel sure that the emancipation of India would be easily achieved at no distant date" (quoted in Fischer-Tine 2007: 331).[23]

Although fundraising efforts tried to support greater numbers of student emigrants emerging from lower classes, the vast majority of those who did emigrate for higher studies came from some means, and all had already attained a high level of education before emigrating. But there were, of course, exceptions. Among the most famous Indian emigrants to study in the United States, for example, was B. R. Ambedkar, a member of the lowest caste of Dalits, who earned his doctorate at Colombia University in New York in 1916 and returned to India to author India's constitution and lead the most influential movement for Dalit rights and citizenship to take place in postcolonial India.

Over time, Indian independence fighters also included middle-class merchants, who had settled in other colonies or dominions such as South Africa, Kenya, Canada, and Australia. Middle-class Indians living throughout the empire were facing increasing resistance by native and white settler populations. They therefore welcomed Indian independence leaders' fight against racism and for migrant rights.

Just as the British colonial regime began to institute formal regulations on elite Indians' emigration, the INC increased its efforts to fight the discrimination these migrants faced within receiving regions. In 1919, at the Amritsar Congress, INC leaders spoke to an international audience against the anti-Indian agitations taking place in East Africa; in 1921, the party lobbied for Indian immigrants living in the dominions to be granted equal rights with British settlers; in 1923, it lobbied for Indians to be given the right to settle in the Kenyan highlands (which was reserved for white settlers only); in the 1930s, INC called for a boycott on the clove trade that was overtly discriminating against Indian traders in Zanzibar; in 1941, it fought a trade agreement that overtly discriminated against Indian merchants in Burma; and in 1946, INC went so far as to announce a trade boycott with South Africa due to the mistreatment of Indian immigrants there.[24]

There were also efforts to forge solidarity between elite and nonelite emigrants. This happened most profoundly in the United States, where Indian

[23] The *Indian Sociologist*, a monthly periodical launched by Krishnavarma, was a key mouthpiece for anticolonial revolutionaries in the Indian diaspora.

[24] After the First World War, India became an independent member of the League of Nations, which enabled INC to attend several international conferences (although the Indian delegation was led by non-Indians until 1929). The trade boycott against South Africa was especially significant given the large amount of exports India sent to South Africa and the share of coal that India imported from South Africa at the time.

intellectuals first began mobilizing the anticolonial movement in New York, building an important alliance with Irish nationalists (Fischer-Tine 2007). But by the 1910s, the center of activities shifted to the US West Coast, where the charismatic leader Har Dayal was explicitly sent to bridge the gap between a small group of student radicals around Berkeley and the larger base of Punjabi farmers who had earlier settled in the valley (Sohi 2011). Punjabi immigrant laborers in the United States had already formed transnational organizations, such as the famous Pacific Coast Hindi Association.[25] They had been living and cooking and eating together for some years and had thus coalesced along their shared language (Punjabi), spiritual traditions (mainly Sikh and Muslim), occupation (as farm laborers and ex-soldiers), and experiences as a second-class race in the United States. By joining forces with the intellectual and militant arms of the swelling independence movement, Punjabi American laborers' organizations helped underscore the Indian independence movement as a radical, cross-class, global fight for racial equality, which in turn gave the Indian independence movement greater global legitimacy (Naidis 1951).

The US-based anticolonial movement became known as the Ghadar movement, the movement of mutiny, uprising, or revolt. It was radical, and it was global. It had close ties with Irish, Egyptian, Pan-Asian, and Pan-Islamic anti-imperial movements, as well as to anarchists, socialists, left-wing radicals, and even religious revivalists. It launched a newspaper that became a central voice of the transnational arm of the anticolonial movement, and it raised money through subscriptions and donations. Perhaps most famously, it offered bodies, sending thousands of Indian immigrants living throughout the United States to India to physically fight British colonial rule.

Along with mobilizing the larger community of Punjabi farmers living in the Pacific Northwest, the West Coast, and the Southwest, the Ghadar movement also mobilized a group of a few hundred Bengali seamen who were working in factories and low-wage service jobs on the other side of the country. Most of these men had entered the United States through New York after World War I, when they escaped from working in the engine rooms and kitchens of British steamships (Bald 2013). Like the Punjabi farmers, they came from and represented a working-class background and sentiment.

Although the Ghadar movement organized across classes, scholars have documented that tensions between the mostly Bengali intellectuals, the Punjabi farmers, and the Bengali seamen were chronic (Ramnath 2005). By 1917, when the United States entered World War I, the government banned the movement,

[25] One of Pacific Coast Hindi Association's most famous presidents, Sohan Singh Bhakna, went on to help found one of India's key farmer parties, Kisan Sabha, as well as the Communist Party of India.

accusing its members of illegally conspiring with the Germans to deprive the British monarch of sovereignty over India. The US government's shift to intolerance toward political radicalism has been attributed to the pressure mounting from its British allies and its own ascendance as the next global hegemon (Ramnath 2005).

Despite the challenges of cross-class tensions among Indian emigrants, Indian independence leaders continued to struggle for emigrant rights and emigrant support across classes and regions. In his presidential address to INC in 1926, Srinivas Iyengar declared, "The status of Indians abroad, whether in South Africa or Kenya, in Fiji or Guinea, in Ceylon or Malaya, in America or Australia, depends inevitably upon the status of Indians in their own land; and the *swaraj* [self-rule] for India depends in its turn upon the brave and unfaltering spirit of our kith and kin across the seas."[26] And in 1929, INC set up an Overseas Department under the leadership of Jawaharlal Nehru. In addition to rallying global support for India's independence movement, the department pledged to support all Indians abroad (whether rich or poor) by staying "vigilantly aware of all the legislations and enactments that adversely or otherwise affect Indian settlers abroad" (Singh 2014: 178). During this period, the global reach of the anticolonial movement spread beyond the British colonies and dominions to extend into other spaces of radical activism. The Ghadarites, for example, studied in Moscow and China, and in the 1940s Subhash Chandra Bose, another major leader of the Indian independence movement, formed the Indian National Army based in Burma and then Indochina and Tokyo, calling on Indians overseas to take up arms to liberate the motherland.

By the mid-1940s, the Indian independence movement (involving Indians across the world) had successfully turned the Coolie MDR on its head and established solidarity among Indians across classes and across national boundaries—but in the name of a sovereign home nation. On March 18, 1946, while speaking to 10,000 Indians in Singapore, Nehru promised citizenship to all Indians abroad, stating, "When India attains independence, she would immediately decide who her nationals were, and Indians overseas would be Indian nationals unless they choose to be otherwise" (Nehru 1972, quoted in Singh 2014: 181).

The 1922 Emigration Act: A Reform and a Shift

While Indian independence, or *swaraj,* did not materialize until 1947, on March 20, 1916, Madan Mohan Malviya moved a resolution in the Indian Legislative

---

[26] Reports of Annual Session of the Indian National Congress and Proceedings of the All India Congress Committee, 1885–1947, quoted in Singh (2014: 178).

Council for the abolition of the indenture system, and the British government formally banned the system in 1917 (interestingly, the very year that the new passport rules were passed). Exceptions were made for indentured labor to Ceylon and Malaya, and the informally regulated stream of *kangani* and *maistry* laborers continued. Nevertheless, the British government's formal suspension of indentured labor in 1917 was widely considered a major concession to and thus an important victory for the anticolonial nationalists.

In MDR terms, the abolition of indentured migration signaled a regime shift, an important historical conjuncture where ideological and political resistance from below subsumed economic gains and where emigration practices helped alter the nation's paradigmatic development ideologies. To address the anticolonial movement's accusation of extreme labor exploitation, the British government enacted the Emigration Act of 1922, which underwrote the subsequent Nationalist MDR until the late 1970s.

The significance of the 1922 Emigration Act on India's MDR is substantial. First, in the wake of the formally abolished indentured labor system, the Act vested the Indian legislature with complete state control over the recruitment and mobility of all poor Indian laborers, as opposed to just indentured workers. This marked a sharp shift from the premise of the Coolie MDR, whereby the British state was reluctant to exert control over the mobility of any Indians— rich or poor—and did so only sparingly and under strong pressure.

Second, the 1922 Act held the Indian state responsible for protecting poor emigrant workers by controlling who emigrated and to which countries. Again, this marked an important shift from the Coolie MDR's penchant for begrudgingly offering some state oversight, but only to ensure the difference between indentured labor and forced slave labor. Indians serving in the colonial government celebrated the new Act as a victory for labor protection. As B. N. Sarma, Indian revenue member of the colonial government, argued, the 1922 Act protected the most vulnerable, uneducated, "ignorant" workers: "While the Government of India are solicitous . . . in securing the freedom of . . . labourers, and do not in any way desire to keep him here as a serf to serve the purposes of the capitalist classes, whether commercial or landed, there is an imperative duty that they should safeguard their interests and protect them, possibly sometimes against themselves, against their foolishly embarking upon emigration when their interests are not safe in foreign countries."[27]

Third, the 1922 Act cemented and defined the Indian state's postcolonial pattern of restricting the emigration of poor workers in the name of protection,

---

[27] Legislative Assembly Debate, Official Report, February 6, 1922, emphasis added by author. Note: Transcripts of all Indian Legislative Assembly debates are available online at: https://eparlib. nic.in/handle/123456789/7.

while leaving middle- and upper-class Indians free from such protections and thus free from restricted mobility. To make this class-based distinction, the Act categorized emigrants into two groups: those with fewer and those with greater than 12 years of formal schooling.[28]

Effectively, the 1922 Act was rarely (if ever) implemented to regulate the latter group of formally educated Indians, enabling them to emigrate abroad for higher studies or employment. Despite the British government's growing suspicion of Indians who studied abroad, by 1950 (just after India gained independence) 10% of Indian parliamentarians, 18% of Indian bureaucrats, and 60% of independent India's science and technology experts had attained an overseas education (Kapur 2010). And despite the British government's careful surveillance of "skilled" migrants upon their return to India, nearly all the top leaders of India's independence movement, as well as the chief architects of the key institutions of independent India (the Constitution, the Finance Commission, and the Planning Commission) were educated outside India.

In contrast, those with fewer than 12 years of schooling were now deemed legally and officially "unskilled" and thus "vulnerable." Unlike the Coolie MDR that sought to justify the mobility of "vulnerable" workers, the 1922 Act sought to regulate and restrict their mobility in the name of protection. Under the Act, the state controlled these poor workers' emigration by requiring them to obtain clearance to emigrate, indicated by a stamp in their (newly acquired) passport. "Skilled" emigrants did not need any such clearance to emigrate. The clearance would be attained from a newly established government office, the PGE, which served as the apex body of the local Protector of Emigrants. The PGE would determine whether to allow or prohibit Indian workers' emigration. Although the Act involved notifications for specific countries and stipulated the steps to be taken by foreign agents for the welfare of emigrants, so few were allowed to emigrate that in practice it had little to say about recruiters, foreign employers, or receiving countries (Khadria 2009). Moreover, in 1938 even *kangani* and *maistry* labor was abolished when the Indian government placed a ban on assisted labor migration. As a result of these new laws, emigration among poor Indian workers progressively declined between 1923 and 1947.

Given these sharp shifts from the premise of the Coolie MDR, India's 1922 Emigration Act stood as an anomalous and revolutionary restriction of poor workers' emigration.[29] At the material level, it is striking that the leaders of the Indian independence movement managed to force the British government to curtail the mass export of poor Indian workers, especially given the undeniable economic costs to the British. At an ideological level, these state-controlled

---

[28] This cutoff was changed to 10th grade in 2004 (see Chapter 5).

[29] As noted earlier in the chapter, restrictions on immigration were also rising at this time.

restrictions on emigration as a form of state protection contrasted with several European governments that still relied on the emigration of their unemployed poor white workers, despite emigration's high risks, because it rid their nations of potential labor discontent and disruption (Bartlett 2010).

However, Indian labor leaders criticized the 1922 Emigration Act for institutionalizing too much state power over poor emigrant workers. These leaders framed the liberalization of poor workers' emigration as a "labor right." Therefore, trade unionists and labor members, such as Narayan Malhar Joshi, argued that the Act should be revised after a few years because it curtailed the rights of laborers to leave the country. As Joshi insisted, "[A laborer] goes out to improve his economic condition, and we have no right to come in the way of his doing it. . . . [S]ometimes, people go out when they feel that they are not properly treated in this country."[30]

Joshi's critiques of the 1922 Emigration Act are significant for two reasons. First, they represent a fleeting moment in India's history when labor activists conceived of domestic and emigrant workers as a single class and thus directly engaged the state's emigration policies. As I show in subsequent chapters, this conception was short-lived.

Second, these critiques remind us to nuance contemporary debates on migration, which too often equate an ill-defined concept of "liberalization" with harm to poor workers. Starting from the demise of the Coolie MDR, the liberalization of emigration for poor workers has been a long-held demand stemming, not from the right, but from organized Indian workers themselves.

In 1947, the Coolie MDR exhaled its last breath as the British Empire was extinguished. With the end of the Coolie MDR also came the end of the racialized class pact between emigrants and the state. Indian labor, Indian emigrants, and the leaders of the independence movement were now free to launch a new MDR with a new class pact—one that would define the nation until the late 1970s.

[30] Legislative Assembly Debate, Official Report, February 6, 1922, emphasis added by author.

4

The Nationalist MDR (1947–77)

Erasing the Indian Emigrant

This chapter continues our analysis of India's MDRs before the contemporary period of neoliberalism to examine India's first postcolonial MDR, which I call the Nationalist MDR. The Nationalist MDR was launched by India's first prime minister, Jawaharlal Nehru, and then continued by his daughter Prime Minister Indira Gandhi in 1966.[1] Although the leaders of the anticolonial movement had planted the roots of the Nationalist MDR under colonialism when they forced the British to ban indentured servitude in 1922, they cemented it in full form when India gained independence from British rule in 1947. With independence, a new world order, new migration restrictions the world over, and a new domestic development agenda, the Indian state had a new set of forces to grapple with in formulating its new emigration regime.

As noted in previous chapters, this book argues that extending our historical lens back to the pre-liberalization era provides us with important insights on the current MDR's ancestral lineage, thereby deepening our understanding of what makes contemporary emigration practices strong and where the vulnerabilities are. Additionally, this historical backdrop exposes the understudied role that emigration and emigrants themselves have repeatedly played in transitioning India to new MDRs (and new development ideologies) over time and thus yields important questions about the future of India's contemporary MDR.

Despite emigrants' important role in overthrowing the exploitative and racist Coolie MDR, the subsequent Nationalist MDR forged a new class pact between the optimistic Indian state and its emigrants that erased the figure of the Indian emigrant altogether. Rather than building solidarity with emigrants along

[1] Although Indira Gandhi's ascent to prime minister is usually credited to her position as Nehru's daughter, she proved to be a strong leader and politician in her own right who led the country for 11 years, until her assassination.

The Migration-Development Regime. Rina Agarwala, Oxford University Press. © Oxford University Press 2022. DOI: 10.1093/oso/9780197586396.003.0004

racial lines, the Nationalist MDR discouraged (even forbade) emigration and distanced itself from those already residing abroad. This was surprising given that the leaders of the Nationalist MDR were the same as the leaders of the independence movement, who had worked so hard to mobilize emigrant support for India just a few years earlier. But as this chapter details, the shift can be explained by the new global and domestic pressures facing the state.

An important though underemphasized aspect of this new emigration pact was that it was entirely class-based. Specifically, the Indian state offered to protect poor workers by keeping them within the protective arms of the newly formed nation-state and legally forbidding their emigration abroad. In contrast, workers who were not poor were quietly allowed to emigrate without any state restriction or control. However, these elite emigrants no longer enjoyed Indian leaders' earlier willingness to assist them with their struggles for citizenship and other rights in receiving countries. Nor were they invited to participate in affairs of the Indian state, either in material or symbolic terms. In other words, the Indian state under the Nationalist MDR forbade poor workers' emigration, but in return offered them state protection, while it permitted wealthier workers' emigration, but pulled back its attention to and protection over them.

A key argument of this chapter is that the stark contrast between the state's approach to poor versus elite emigrants and between the state's pre- and post-Independence promises to its emigrants had important and unintended consequences, which ultimately led to the demise of the Nationalist MDR and its corresponding development ideology during the 1970s. This is not to deny the laudable objectives of the postcolonial state's protection of poor workers or the relatively small number of elite emigrants traveling during this period. But, as I show in this chapter, the Nationalist MDR cemented a class distinction between poor and wealthy emigrants that broke the cross-class coalition that had earlier motivated Indians (within India and abroad) to join forces against a common enemy: the racially and nationally defined "white Britisher."

Although poor workers were (rightly) assumed to be more vulnerable and thus in more need of state protection than wealthier workers, the state's protection offer ultimately *failed to deliver*. Moreover, it was deeply *paternalist* and thus controlling rather than rights-based. These features created an internal contradiction in the state's nationalist and protective claims. The state's failure to meet poor workers' livelihood needs within India, combined with a spike in the demand for migrant labor in the oil-rich countries of the Gulf, motivated poor workers aspiring to emigrate to fight for the liberalization of their mobility in the 1970s. As well, the Nationalist MDR's *dismissive liberalization* of educated emigrants abroad created ripe conditions for them to join the antinational movements against the Emergency that erupted in the 1970s.

Together these movements among the poor and educated elite helped topple the Nationalist MDR, as well as the Congress-led Indian government that emigrants had ironically worked so hard to put in place half a century earlier. These findings belie recent assumptions that the liberalization of emigration today is simply part of a northern-imposed neoliberal political agenda. In contrast, this chapter shows that the contemporary liberalization and celebration of poor and elite Indian emigrants emerged as a response to demands from workers themselves, as well as from left- and right-wing Indian political parties—a reality that Indian political leaders made excellent use of when building the country's contemporary MDR (the subject of Chapter 5). Understanding this basis of India's contemporary emigration practices provides important insight into the reasons for its strikingly solid foundation.

Paternalist Protection for Poor Workers and the 1922 Emigration Act

The Indian state under the Nationalist MDR offered to protect poor workers against foreign exploitation by restricting their emigration and keeping them within India's borders.

To legislate the restriction against poor workers' emigration, the Nationalist MDR retained the 1922 Emigration Act, which remained the preeminent legislation regulating emigration until the early 1980s. As noted in Chapter 3, the Act was widely viewed by Indians as a concession by the British in response to Indian independence leaders' call to end the exploitation of Indian labor through indentured servitude. To many, it thus signaled the victory of a moral compass that would prevail even if it came at the expense of economic gain. Moreover, the Act already vested the Indian state with the power to legally control who did and did not emigrate and instituted a robust system (complete with offices, personnel, procedures, and red stamps) of requirements, restrictions, and processes through which the state could exercise its power.

As per the 1922 Act, the Nationalist MDR delineated the poor from the nonpoor by using a simple bivariate measure of formal education: those with less than 12 years of education were deemed "vulnerable" and "poor" and thus subjected to different emigration restrictions than those with greater than 12 years of education, who were deemed "nonpoor" and thus "nonvulnerable."[2] As explained in Chapter 1, although this measure is crude and masks significant

---

[2] The cutoff number of years of education used to delineate the "poor" from the "nonpoor" shifted from 12 to 10 in the 1980s.

class heterogeneities, it does provide a roughly accurate proxy for class in the context of India, and it has significant material consequences since it remains enshrined in Indian emigration law to this day. Therefore, I retain this delineation in my examination of the class basis of the Nationalist MDR. Rather than using the more common and misleading labels of "unskilled/low-skilled" versus "skilled/high-skilled" to delineate the two classes, I will use the terms "poor" and "elite."

The Nationalist MDR also retained the intricate bureaucracy and government personnel that supported the 1922 Act, including the office (fittingly) known as the Protectorate General of Emigrants (PGE) under the Ministry of Labor. The PGE was held responsible for protecting poor workers, largely by denying them clearance to emigrate; without the coveted PGE clearance stamp on their passport, uneducated Indians were forbidden to pass the border controls.

With indentured servitude formally abolished in 1917, and bonded contract labor (under the *kangani/maistry* systems) formally abolished in 1938, the newly independent Indian state could use the 1922 Act, and the state machinery underlying it, to protect *all* workers (whether indentured or not) against foreign exploitation. Indian parliamentarians during the Nationalist MDR repeatedly argued that the 1922 Act was the most effective way for the state to protect vulnerable workers against exploitative employers abroad, against mercenary recruiters and false "travel agents" within India, as well as against "workers' own foolishness and ignorance."[3] The Nationalist MDR therefore expanded the original reach of the 1922 Act to forbid almost all poor workers from emigrating abroad to work.

In theory, the Nationalist MDR applied emigration restrictions on all Indians. But to underscore its protective impetus, the state enforced the 1922 Act against only the poorest workers (defined by education level). In a committee report conducted in 1980, the Ministry of Labor conceded, "The Government have never applied the provision of the Emigration Act, 1922 to Indian nationals belonging to highly educated professional categories. The provisions were being applied to the workers belonging to the unskilled, semi-skilled and skilled categories."[4] As a result, between 1947 and 1974 the share of Indian emigrant laborers among all Indian emigrants dropped to as low as 1% in some countries—a sharp reversal from the Coolie MDR (Madhavan 1985).

[3] Parliamentary Debate, Part 1 Questions and Answers, Official Report, February 14, 1950, 231.

[4] Ministry of External Affairs, Estimates Committee Report, 1980–81, 16th Report, "Overseas Indians in West Asia, Sri Lanka, Malaysia, Burma, Indonesia, and Singapore," Part 1, West Asia, 21.

Early Support for State Protection and
Emigration Restrictions

For decades, the Nationalist MDR's strong state restrictions over the mobility of poor workers enjoyed widespread acceptance in India, eliciting little to no question, study, or debate within academic or policy circles. The Nationalist MDR's emigration restrictions were mostly justified on domestic grounds, although they also enjoyed some global support from sending European nations. Following John O'Brien's sensational publication of *The Vanishing Irish* in 1953, for example, emigration entered the public domain as a "problem" for Ireland for the first time. As Bartlett (2010: 483) writes, from then on, "no Irish government could afford to ignore emigration or fail to seek ways to reduce it."

First and foremost, Indians were deeply committed to the new era of independent nations, and thus understood that protective state powers could not extend beyond national borders. Nationalist movements rippling through former British colonies in Burma, Sri Lanka, Fiji, and East Africa had sparked ethnic feuds that targeted Indian immigrants in these countries. Indians (across classes) who had emigrated and settled abroad during the Coolie MDR were now facing disenfranchisement, violent attacks, and even expulsion from their receiving countries. But the Indian state felt it was unable to assist these emigrants abroad without disrupting these receiving nations' sovereignty. As shown in the first session of the Indian Parliament, for example, Malaya banned the Indian government from examining the conditions of Indian laborers in Malaya, stating, "Such inspectorial privileges of one country in another are an anachronism."[5] Although the Indian government expressed "emphatic disapproval" of this ban, the deputy minister of external affairs, Keskar, explained that India had little power or ability to alter it and must thus respect it.[6] Similar discussions took place regarding other host countries, such as Ceylon.

Therefore, the act of closing India's borders and keeping its workers within had become an accepted form of legitimate state protection. Within India, the state also instituted new labor regulations to protect poor workers against domestic exploitation. (For more on the history of India's domestic labor regulations, see Agarwala 2019.) Although domestic protections were insufficiently enforced, the state's expressed commitment to protecting workers and the public's belief in the state's willingness to do so were key features distinguishing the Nationalist MDR from the previous Coolie MDR.

Second, the Nationalist MDR's restrictions on poor workers' emigration seamlessly interlaced with India's postcolonial development project of Fabian

[5] Parliamentary Debate, Part 1 Questions and Answers, Official Report, February 14, 1950, 231.
[6] Parliamentary Debate, Part 1 Questions and Answers, Official Report, February 14, 1950, 231.

Socialism, which expounded a deep commitment to national self-sufficiency. At its helm was a commanding state that promised to protect its citizens and grow its economy. Importantly, both its citizenship and its economy would be bounded by the nation's newly drawn geographic borders. To protect India's fledgling domestic industries from global competition, the government instituted a policy of import-substituting industrialization, closing borders to the international trade of most goods and services.[7] By this same logic, to protect India's workforce from exploitative and racist foreign employers, the government closed borders to restrict most emigration abroad. In doing so, the newly formed Indian state also ensured a ready labor force for its domestic industries.

Third, the Nationalist MDR's restrictions over poor workers supported India's pride and global image. At the time, the global environment for Indian emigration was anything but inviting. Race-based immigration restrictions still barred most Indians from entering wealthy receiving countries. And in poor receiving countries, nationalist movements were expunging Indian immigrants from their borders. India could have followed other sending states in continuing to rely on emigration as a release valve for domestic employment pressures by turning a blind eye to citizens who attempted to immigrate into receiving countries through illicit channels. But instead, Indian government officials framed restrictions over poor workers' emigration as a way to protect the dignity of India's reputation abroad. This favorable global image resonated with many members of the newly independent government. As was noted in the second session of the pre-Independence legislative debates, "When we send our labourers abroad, we get a prejudice created against ourselves as being a country of coolies or labourers."[8] Preventing poor workers' emigration thus became a way for the government to attain legitimacy within India, as well as to create a renewed, dignified, and strong national image outside India.

Finally, the Nationalist MDR's emigration restrictions were partly motivated by the bloody and historically unprecedented mass migration that had just taken place during Partition, when colonial India was divided at independence into two nations: India, which would be secular, and Pakistan, which would be an Islamic state. Muslims who had not emigrated to present-day Pakistan (either by choice or due to lack of resources) were being treated with suspicion by India's majority-Hindu population. To ensure national unity, Nehru called on the nation to use the newly drawn physical boundaries

---

[7] Import-substituting industrialization was a popular development strategy in many developing countries during the 1950s–1970s. It encouraged governments to attain self-sufficiency by nurturing local industries, preventing imports, and ending cross-country dependence. See Gereffi (1994); Hirschman (1968).

[8] Legislative Debate, Official Report, February 6, 1922, 2185.

(rather than religious affiliation or ethnic identity) to define the nebulous boundaries of national identity; emigrants residing outside India's boundaries thus lost their Indian identity.

Paternalism, Criminalization, and Surveillance

But early support for the Nationalist MDR's emigration restrictions began to wane over time, because such protections were paternalist and thus disempowered poor workers. While the state's desire to protect workers against foreign exploitation resonated with most Indians, it also stung of hypocrisy given the insufficient state protections for poor workers against domestic employers.

Moreover, the Nationalist MDR's protections were not rights-based. By retaining the 1922 Emigration Act for nearly 30 years without a single debate or revision, the Nationalist MDR ignored the warnings made by the original architects of the Act. As noted in the previous chapter, Indian labor leaders, such as Narayan Malhar Joshi, had originally emphasized emigrants' *rights*, calling for their protected, free movement. But the Nationalist MDR instead cemented a colonial-era logic that legitimized state *control* over poor workers.

Upholding this regime over time required the Indian state to maintain a policy of legislative criminalization of poor emigrants, which was supported by the power the 1922 Act vested to the government to exert repressive controls over poor workers' movement by penalizing those who tried to emigrate. Parliamentary debates during this period are peppered with reports from Prime Minister Nehru and, subsequently, Prime Minister Gandhi reporting the numbers of workers criminally convicted for attempting to emigrate to countries the government had forbidden for poor laborers, such as Ceylon, Malaya, and Canada.[9] Preventing poor labor migration to these countries held particular symbolic value for the Nationalist MDR's protective claims as the British government had long exempted these countries from earlier attempts to regulate exploitative labor emigration.

The Nationalist MDR's strong emigration restrictions also demanded increased state investments in vigilance technologies and personnel, public awareness campaigns on the risks incurred by poor emigrant workers, public shaming campaigns against those who did leave, and claims of domestic development programs designed to deter poor Indians from seeking employment abroad.[10] The national government during these years also invested in publicity campaigns using local-language newspapers and social welfare organizations to

---

[9] Multiple Parliamentary Debate reports throughout this period.
[10] Multiple Parliamentary Debate reports throughout this period.

educate poor laborers about the laws against emigration, the risks involved, and the false claims recruiters and travel agents might use to lure emigrants.

By the early 1970s, such controls began to clash with the continuing lack of employment opportunities within India and the rising demand for migrant labor in the Gulf countries. But rather than easing restrictions or promising protected mobility, the government under the Nationalist MDR held on to its commitment to closed borders. In the early 1970s, the government increased restrictions over poor workers even further, forbidding them not only from leaving India but also from taking assets out of India (except in cases of extreme hardship and when the host country required it). In 1976, the Indian government purchased new vigilance technologies to curb illicit emigration at ports; these included boats with night vision capabilities, machine guns, and wireless communication.[11]

In doing so, the Nationalist MDR further cemented a class-based distinction between poor and wealthy workers' right to mobility, which in turn exposed the paternalist strain underscoring the Nationalist MDR's protective claims.

Dismissive Liberalization for Elite Emigrants

In sharp contrast to its paternalist protection that restricted the emigration of poor workers, the Indian government under the Nationalist MDR engaged in what I call "dismissive liberalization" toward its educated, elite citizens. Despite the government's heavy emigration restrictions and its calls for closed borders and national self-sufficiency, it quietly liberalized emigration for elite citizens. However, to justify this stance in the public sphere, the government retained a dismissive stance toward its elite emigrants abroad, ignoring and sometimes even disparaging them within India. As a result, and in contrast to what we will soon see in the contemporary era, elite emigrants during the Nationalist MDR did not forge strong ties with the Indian state.

A Quiet Liberal Stream of Elite Exit

Under the Nationalist MDR, educated Indians seeking economic opportunities abroad quietly streamed out of India without any state restriction or clearance requirement. The vast majority of these educated emigrants came from middle- and upper-class families and thus occupied distinct class locations from those

---

[11] Department of Revenue and Insurance, Customs Receipts, Public Accounts Committee Report, March 1975, 5th Lok Sabha, Report No. 203.

of poor workers. In other words, the Nationalist MDR engaged in a class-based liberalization of emigration.

Parliamentary reports from this time show that elite emigrants going to and from South Africa, Canada, and North Borneo were not only permitted to move abroad; they even received favorable settlement packages that included citizenship, land holdings, and medical and educational support (either in the host country or in India upon repatriation). From 1967 to 1971, the Indian government also provided reduced fares on the national airline, Air India, to facilitate the emigration of educated Indians to Commonwealth countries.

There are many explanations for the Indian state's permission, sometimes even facilitation, of elite exit. But each reveals an imperfect claim, thereby forcing the state to keep its leniency out of the public spotlight.

First, as the Indian state itself claimed (and as the British state had earlier claimed), educated Indians were not "vulnerable" and thus did not require the state's protection. But this claim contrasted the realities of discrimination that even elite, educated emigrants continued to face in receiving countries. As well, the claim did not fit the postcolonial democratic state's commitment to equal citizenship rights among Indians.

Second, students of contemporary emigration patterns might assume the Indian government's leniency toward its educated emigrants under the Nationalist MDR reflected state efforts to draw elite emigrants' economic returns to India. But there is almost no evidence of the Indian government formally drawing on the financial contributions of elite Indians abroad during the Nationalist MDR. India's nationalist sentiments had instituted heavy restrictions on foreign exchange entering the country, making it difficult for Indian emigrants to invest in India from abroad. My review of parliamentary debates during this period reveals a few rare cases, such as during the Indo-Chinese War of 1962, when the Indian government did welcome contributions from emigrants in East Africa to help boost its defense efforts. When a foreign journalist questioned him on this point, Nehru hedged a careful answer: "Indians overseas have dual loyalty, one to their country of adoption and [an]other to their country of origin" (quoted in Singh 2014: 183). But these moments were few and far between.

A third explanation for the state's leniency toward elite exit under the Nationalist MDR is that it was a deliberate strategy that yielded personal and political benefits for state officials. Opportunities for elites' employment within India were still minimal at the time, so enabling their emigration helped state officials meet the material needs of their class brethren. Devesh Kapur (2010: 180), for example, writes that India's elite policymakers were "loathe to check the overseas opportunities available to [their] kith and kin at a time when these opportunities were diminishing within [India]." This is likely true. But the stream of elites exiting India during this time included far more people than state leaders' kith and kin. In fact, based on my interviews, almost none of the Indians who arrived in the United States during the 1960s and 1970s had any connections to Indian state leaders.

Others have convincingly argued that Indian state officials allowed the exit of elites in order to secure their own political legitimacy since elite exit curbed competition and potential unrest over scarce resources and opportunities within India (Khatkhate 1971). In fact, the political stability that resulted from opening the release valve of elite emigration was so profound that some scholars have suggested that it enabled the political ascendancy of India's numerically dominant lower castes (Chakravorty, Kapur, and Singh 2017). Again, while this explanation is likely true, it does not explain why the Indian government sacrificed this release valve with poor emigrants.

Finally, many readers may note that, relative to the mass population of poor workers in India, the pool of elite emigrants was small and thus seemingly insignificant to the state's broader development agenda. To be sure, the number of elites leaving India during this period was smaller than in other periods due to the post–World War I rise in immigration restrictions (for all classes of workers) that still applied in some receiving countries (such as the United States) and the new post–World War II restrictions that arose against Asian immigrants in other countries (in Western Europe and the USSR). These restrictions reflected receiving countries' concerns of racial homogeneity and internal security. But, as illustrated in the previous chapter, India's independence movement had shown that even the small population of intellectual elite emigrants (many of whom returned to lead the new nation's government) could be instrumental in shaping India's very existence given their access to new ideas, networks, and finances.

Moreover, many wealthy receiving countries lifted their restrictions on educated Indians' immigration over the course of the Nationalist MDR, and the Indian government did not stand in the way of educated Indians eager to meet this rising demand. As a result, the population of elite emigrants *grew* to fairly significant levels during the Nationalist MDR (Henning, Motwani, and Barot-Motwani 1989). Under the 1948 British Nationality Act, which technically retained the same mobility rules within the empire and Commonwealth that had earlier existed under colonialism, the United Kingdom (albeit reluctantly) permitted Indian immigration during the late 1940s and 1950s.[12] Although job opportunities in the United Kingdom were slim and anti-Asian sentiment was high at the time, tens of thousands of Indian soldiers and seamen (who had fought

---

[12] The 1948 British Nationality Act allowed a unifying "Citizenship of the United Kingdom and Colonies" to anyone deprived of citizenship in an independent Commonwealth country. This Act also recognized all citizens of the Commonwealth as British subjects, thereby confirming the mobility rules that existed prior to India's independence.

for the British in World War II), as well as Indians who were displaced by India's bloody partition, entered the United Kingdom just after India gained independence. By the late 1950s and 1960s, the stream of Indian immigration grew as UK employers specifically sought Indians to fill severe labor shortages; between 1955 and 1957 alone, nearly 17,500 Indians entered the United Kingdom (Lal 2006). But most important, even when the United Kingdom tightened its immigration restrictions for Commonwealth citizens in the 1960s, elite emigrants were specifically excluded from the restrictions, which led to a new stream of educated and professional immigrants from India as well as from East Africa.

Similarly, in Britain's wealthier ex-colonies and dominions, such as Canada, Australia, and the United States, immigration restrictions that were put in place in the 1920s to bar Asian immigration were beginning to crumble by the late 1950s and 1960s. The demise of the British Empire had sparked new national identity movements in these countries, which in turn motivated more inclusive, civic-oriented definitions of citizenship. These movements coincided with a growing demand for formally trained professionals (Mann 2012). As a result, by the mid-1960s these receiving countries reduced their barriers to entry for educated immigrants from India.

The Second Wave of Indian Americans

It was in this context that educated Indians catalyzed what is commonly known as the "second wave" of immigration into the United States. As noted in the previous chapter, in 1946 the United States had made a small exception to its 1924 bill blocking Asian immigrants by passing a 100-person annual quota for Indians and the right for them to naturalize. But in 1965, President Lyndon Johnson passed the monumental Immigration and Nationality Act (or Hart-Celler Act) that abolished the 1924 national-origin quota system and forever changed the racial face and class composition of the United States.[13] Rather than admitting immigrants based on their country of origin (read: race), the 1965 Act stipulated that the United States would now admit immigrants based on their familial relationship to existing immigrants and their occupational/professional skills (read: race *and* class). While at the last minute the Act prioritized family reunification (which was intended to increase the number of European immigrants), it also enabled American employers to recruit foreign professionals in industries deemed necessary for US growth (such as engineers, doctors, and professors)

---

[13] While the Act did add an annual cap, a national-level cap, and a cap from the Western Hemisphere, scholars have shown that immigration surpassed these caps in the post-1965 period (Milkman, Bhargava, and Lewis. 2021).

and to allow in more foreign students to be trained in US universities and subsequently recruited in the US labor market.

This latter allowance, designed to meet the needs of American employers for professional and high-skilled labor, sparked a new emigration wave of educated and elite Indians. As US immigration scholars have forcefully argued, "labor demand has always been the primary economic driver of immigration" (Milkman, Bhargava, and Lewis 2021: 10). Proponents of the Act celebrated it as an ideological victory that capped their 40-year fight to undo the 1924 quota system, which they viewed as antithetical to American ideals of equality and nondiscrimination (Yang 2020). But to many, the Act was instrumental—a necessary "fix" for a weakening economy that required more professionals. Even John F. Kennedy, the original architect of the Act, had noted that US immigration reform must prioritize professional immigrants—i.e., those with "the greatest ability to add to the national welfare" (quoted in Yang 2020: 224).

While neither US officials nor the public intended, or even expected, the massive influx of professional immigrants after 1965, Indian professionals stood ready to take advantage of the new laws, and the Indian state did not restrict them.[14] Relative to the world's migrant pool, educated Indians were highly proficient in English, and they had received advanced training in science and engineering. This advanced training had been publicly funded by the newly independent Indian state's commitment to domestic industrialization at the time and was instituted through bilateral cooperation with West Germany, the United States, the United Kingdom, and the Soviet Union.

Despite the Indian government's decades of legal restrictions preventing poor workers' emigration and its professed ideals of national self-sufficiency, it permitted a massive jump in elite emigration under the Nationalist MDR. Between 1960 and 1975, the Indian-born population in the United States jumped 14-fold, an annual growth rate of nearly 20%, from 12,296 to 175,000 (IOM 2019). By 1980, the number had grown to 206,087.[15] Indian government officials also allowed medical graduates to take advantage of US laws that now enabled them to take their licensing exams in India and obtain a labor visa or a green card before emigrating. Moreover, in the case of the United States, where the 1965 Act allowed for family reunification, the Indian government permitted family members of educated elites to also emigrate. Although not all family

---

[14] Historians have shown that it was the promise of minimal change in immigration numbers that helped attain ultimate support for the passing of the 1965 Act. For a detailed history of the politics behind the Act, see Yang (2020).

[15] I calculated CAGR across 15 years to account for the 1965 Immigration Act. If calculated from 1960, the CAGR is 15%. Data drawn from Gibson and Jung (2006).

members shared the high education level of the sponsoring emigrant, most did share the sponsor's elite middle- or upper-class and caste status.

The State's Dismissal of Elite Emigrants

But exposing the Indian government's strategic reasons for enabling elite emigration is not enough to understand the contours of the Nationalist MDR. We must also understand how the government politically justified its liberal approach to elite exit, which contradicted its stance toward poor emigrants and its claims to national self-sufficiency.

Alongside its leniency toward elite emigration, the nationalist state maintained (at least in the public sphere) a dismissive, defensive, and sometimes even disparaging stance toward its elite emigrants. Doing so was viewed as legitimizing the Indian state's postcolonial promise to build a proud and self-sufficient sovereign nation. Throughout this period, for example, the government argued that India did not "need" educated emigrants' skills and had enough professionals to service its national needs. The Nationalist MDR never overtly reported elite emigrants' economic returns and did not publicly acknowledge, count, or connect to its elites abroad. In fact, to this day the Indian government has never maintained any data on its educated emigrants.[16] Drawing from my review of parliamentary discussions, the elite group of educated emigrants was rarely mentioned from the 1940s till the early 1970s. In contrast to the anticolonial era, when Indian independence leaders deliberately forged relations with educated emigrants, the leaders of the postcolonial Indian government (many of whom were the same individuals who had led the independence movement) explicitly distanced themselves. As a result, little was known about the Indian state's interactions with educated Indians after they went abroad. Drawing from my interviews with Indian Americans who migrated during this time, they held few connections with the Indian state.

In addition, the state under the Nationalist MDR pulled back on its earlier efforts to support emigrants' struggles for citizenship and rights in receiving countries. Instead, the state called on Indian emigrants to pledge loyalty to their host countries rather than to India. In 1955, for example, the government passed the Indian Citizenship Act, which specified that anyone who had "voluntarily acquired the citizenship of another country should cease to be a citizen of India." This Act reversed leaders' promises to embrace and support overseas Indians

---

[16] While the Indian Intelligence Bureau keeps data on all cross-border traffic, data on educated emigrants who do not require government clearance is not kept (and thus not publicly reported) by any Indian emigration office.

upon Independence. To justify this shift, Nehru evoked diplomatic respect and goodwill toward other sovereign nations. In 1957, for example, just 11 years after his Singapore speech in which he promised citizenship to Indian emigrants, Nehru (1972: 618) famously announced, "Indians abroad always should give primary consideration to the interest of the people of those countries; they should never allow themselves to be placed in a position of exploiting the people of those countries; in fact, we have gone thus far and said, if you cannot be, and if you are not, friendly to the people of that country, come back to India and do not spoil the fair name of India."

This dismissive leniency toward elite emigration under the Nationalist MDR eventually undermined the government's promise to ensure India's self-sufficiency, launching critiques of a "brain drain" of India's human resources. In the mid-1970s, skilled emigrants were acknowledged for the first time in Indian parliamentary discussions, notably as a cost to the nation. As stated by the Estimate Committee of the 5th session of the Parliament, or Lok Sabha, "One of the main problems being faced by the country is the emigration of Indian experts in large numbers to foreign countries." This outflow of skilled labor, or brain drain, was measured in terms of a monetary loss in rupees. The Committee went on to note, "In view of the heavy cost incurred by the country on the education of these scientists and doctors etc., the country has a prior claim on the services of these persons."[17] Others have hypothesized that India's elite brain drain may have undermined domestic pressure to improve public provision of health and education (Chakravorty, Kapur, and Singh 2017).

The exposure of the brain drain in the 1970s finally forced the Indian government to publicly address the emigration of elite Indians. Some government officials suggested applying the same policies used to restrict the poor to the elite and educated. As some noted, "There should be a law enacted to prohibit such people from going out altogether. Even if it amounts to taking extra legal steps, it would be worthwhile doing so." In the early 1980s, the Ministry of Health and Family Welfare did, in fact, ban the emigration of a subsection of skilled workers, among them nurses and doctors.[18] Others suggested skilled emigrants should be held accountable for the costs they were creating for India. The Estimates Committee reported, "Those who have been trained at public expense, should

[17] Cabinet Secretariat, Department of Personnel and Administrative Reforms, Estimates Committee, 1975–76, "Deputation of Indian Experts and Officers Abroad," Lok Sabha Secretariat, New Delhi, January 1976, 45–46.

[18] Lok Sabha Debates, 6th Session, 8th Series, Vol. 19, No. 16. August 7, 1986.

compensate at least for expenditure incurred on their training by serving in the country itself or by remitting an equivalent amount."[19]

These suggestions, if they had been taken, may have helped reestablish the cross-class solidarity among Indian workers that many leaders of the postcolonial government themselves had worked to create just a few years earlier. And they could have reestablished the legitimacy of the government's commitment to national economic self-sufficiency and the improvement of public provisioning in health, sanitation, and education. After all, Nehru had just invested a massive share of public resources to train Indians through publicly funded tertiary education institutions. So keeping graduates within India would have helped fuel the nation's postcolonial domestic modernization project. Especially in the immediate aftermath of India's cross-class independence movement, when faith and trust in the new postcolonial state was exuberant, such restrictions over elite Indians' mobility might have been politically acceptable and could have yielded a more equitable development outcome.

However, despite the critiques against the brain drain and the suggestions to restrict elite emigration, the Nationalist MDR maintained its dismissive leniency toward elite emigrants. Over time, this built a well of resentment among elite emigrants (as well as poor workers within India), eventually making them an ideal population to mobilize for the antinational movement that emerged in India during the Emergency of the 1970s.

The Fall of the Nationalist MDR: Emigrant Resistance and a New Opposition Party

Despite its long tenure, the Nationalist MDR crumbled in the 1970s alongside the demise of the Congress-led postcolonial political economy of India. And just as emigrants' role in the dissolution of the British Empire is often neglected, so too is the role that existing and aspiring emigrants played in the fall of India's postcolonial Fabian-Socialist state.

By the 1970s, the looming economic and political crises bubbling in India faced a growing demand for migrant labor in the oil-rich countries of the Middle East, as well as a growing demand for professional immigrants in the West. In addition, the Congress Party's long reign was being questioned for the first time since independence, and opposition parties were beginning to gain traction

---

[19] Cabinet Secretariat, Department of Personnel and Administrative Reforms, Estimates Committee, 1975–76, "Deputation of Indian Experts and Officers Abroad," Lok Sabha Secretariat, New Delhi, January 1976, 45–46.

within India's polity. These factors helped mobilize poor workers who aspired to emigrate and eventually also elites who had already emigrated to resist the Nationalist MDR. Emigrants' opposition to the Congress-led postcolonial Indian state was ironic given their earlier role in opposing the colonial regime to make way for the Congress Party's rule. But the internal contradictions underlying the Nationalist MDR's emigration regulations ultimately undid the regime.

Resistance among Poor Workers in Kerala and the Janata Party

Poor workers' resistance to the Nationalist MDR began in the Indian state of Kerala. In fact, to this day, the Kerala government remains the strongest state advocate for poor emigrant workers in India, and Kerala's poor emigrants remain the most politically active in India. In the context of India's federalist structure, it is significant that a single state has been able to influence the national-level MDR to the extent that Kerala has.

Poor workers in Kerala began fighting against the Nationalist MDR as early as the 1960s. Their primary demand was the legalization/liberalization of their emigration. Although some workers had managed to emigrate through illicit channels, their illegal status as emigrants kept them from organizing into official migrant organizations. Instead, they drew on their citizenship rights and electoral power to lobby elected politicians for their right to pursue economic opportunities abroad. As with so much of Indian politics, their target was the state-level government.

Given Kerala's rich history of mass political activism and leftist politics, where the Communist Party of India–Marxist and a left-center Congress Party have competed for electoral power in state government, emigrants' activism in this state and the state government's responsiveness (especially relative to the rest of the country) might be expected (Heller 1999). Less often acknowledged is that the pro-worker victories in Kerala led to substantial capital flight, which ironically forced the state's economy to heavily rely on emigration as a source of employment and finance (to supplement the state's largely agrarian economy). From the start, Kerala's leftist party officials sought to supply laborers to meet the demands arising in the Gulf countries of the Middle East. Kerala's labor minister, for example, directly appealed to the national government to "relax the immigration rules to reduce the hardships to the persons going to Gulf Countries seeking employment."[20]

---

[20] Lok Sabha Debates, April 6, 1978, Vol. 13, 141.

Even at the national level, however, it was becoming painfully clear by the 1960s that, in practice, the government's approach to restricting poor emigrants under the Nationalist MDR did more to protect the nation's global image as a "non-coolie nation" than it did to protect poor Indian workers. The government had failed to provide adequate employment (or welfare) to poor workers within its borders. Therefore, through the 1950s and 1960s, the state's emigration restrictions simply pushed poor emigrants to seek jobs abroad extralegally, creating an informal market of recruiters willing to connect poor workers to foreign employers for a hefty fee. This placed the workers in positions of greater vulnerability and precarity where they were wholly dependent on private, unregulated recruiters, vulnerable to criminal prosecution by authorities in India, and denied any right to make legal demands on the Indian state for migration protections or welfare. Moreover, as noted earlier, for those who did manage to emigrate abroad, the Indian government was unwilling to protect them for fear that such efforts would be viewed as an infringement of the receiving nation's sovereignty.

In the early 1970s, the oil boom in the Gulf raised labor demand to a new high, drawing ever more poor Indian workers into the high-risk, unregulated sphere of illegal emigration. Rather than being an exception, unregulated and unprotected poor emigrant workers suddenly became a large and highly visible sensation when their volume skyrocketed to unexpected numbers. By the mid-1970s, extralegal emigration among poor workers laid bare the material drivers of labor outflows from India. Poor Indian workers were desperate for jobs, and despite its promises to protect those who remained at home, the independent Indian state had failed them. With their survival at stake, hundreds of thousands of poor Indian workers were willing to take great risks to access jobs abroad.

Poor workers' vulnerable class position within India was further exacerbated by the fact that Gulf countries allowed only "temporary" immigration. Unlike many of their wealthy counterparts, poor emigrants to the Gulf were denied a pathway to citizenship or permanent residency. They were also denied rights to homeownership or schooling in their host countries and were forbidden to bring their family members. The most they could achieve was renewable labor contracts. Therefore, while some continued to renew their visas for decades, many returned within the two- or three-year limit of a single visa. Such temporary migration has been shown to undermine emigrants' power. As one scholar notes, "Emigrants are more likely to exert an influence while they remain abroad. However, this influence wanes when they return" (Pérez-Armendáriz 2014: 10). For these poor workers, the requirement to eventually return to India made the risks of emigrating exponentially high.

Given the particular circumstances surrounding the emigration of poor workers to the Gulf, the rise in this extralegal, high-risk emigration catalyzed the very image of India that the government had for decades vowed to prevent—that of poor, vulnerable Indian workers being exported for exploitative employment abroad. It also directly contradicted the Indian government's stated promise to protect its vulnerable workers. For years, the government tried to hide this labor outflow. As Myron Weiner (1982: 3) wrote at the time, "State governments within India make no particular effort to 'capture' remittances for investment or to take emigration or return migration into account in manpower planning." When it became impossible to hide, both the Indian and Gulf country governments justified the mass outflow of Indian workers as a temporary phenomenon that would not only fix India's underemployment and contribute to its foreign exchange but would also help meet Gulf countries' labor demands only until regional labor could replace them.

But in the mid-1970s, when it was clear that the outflow of poor laborers was not waning, emigration entered the parliamentary agenda for the first time since Independence, exposing the growing tensions within the state around this topic and the resulting contradictions in the reigning MDR.[21] First, tensions arose between different branches of government. In 1976, the Ministry of Labor tried to set up a system to regulate recruiting agencies and clamp down on the rapidly growing informal industry of labor export. However, in 1979 the Supreme Court shot down the effort as extrajudicial, thereby enabling the unregulated industry to grow even more. This led to an outcry among labor leaders.

Second, tensions arose at the political party level, providing a window of opportunity for new opposition parties to expose the ruling Congress Party's failures to meet the needs of poor workers. The most direct and damning critique of the Nationalist MDR came from the Janata Party, a coalition of left- and right-wing parties that shared not only a desire to defeat Indira Gandhi, then of the Congress (I) Party, but also a commitment to "oppose all forms of colonialism, neo-colonialism, and racialism" (Kumar 1978: 589).[22] In other words, the Janata Party drew from the ideals of the independence movement but fought to enact a new ruling government within independent India. The Janata Party's interest in emigration thus underlined the fact that both left- and right-oriented politicians (who agreed on very few other issues) were unified in demanding a new MDR—one that would liberalize India's restrictive emigration policies for poor workers and (as I detail in the next section) build deeper ties with its wealthy emigrants.

Importantly, it was the Janata Party that reframed poor workers' emigration as a potential boon to the Indian economy—a frame that staged the MDR

[21] Lok Sabha Debates, December 15, 1977, 6th Series, Vol. 9, No. 22.

[22] The Janata Party was an amalgam of four disparate parties: Congress (O), the Socialist Party, Bharatiya Jana Sangh, and Bharatiya Lok Dal.

to come. In the context of India's growing balance-of-payments crisis, Janata leaders highlighted the number of poor workers emigrating to the Gulf as a way to alleviate domestic underemployment and increase India's foreign exchange reserves through the remittances they clandestinely sent back to their families.

Initial Inertia among Elite Emigrants

Unlike poor workers, educated elite emigrants did not at first organize to oppose the Nationalist MDR, despite its official dismissiveness of them. Educated emigrants' silence at the time is understandable, since those who wanted to pursue academic or economic opportunities abroad were legally free to do so. Also, in the face of growing resentment over India's brain drain, many feared that demanding more recognition or support from the government could result in the loss of their right to emigrate. Nevertheless, this absence of organized demands for more state recognition is striking since educated elite emigrants have been the biggest beneficiaries of the demise of the Nationalist MDR (as I elaborate in Chapters 5 and 6).

As noted, the second wave of elite Indian emigrants who moved to the United States in the 1960s and 1970s arrived on a permanent basis with their family members under the 1965 US Immigration Act's family reunification preferential categories. As a result, they were more assimilated in US society than the first wave of Punjabi farmers and soldiers who had emigrated half a century earlier during the Coolie MDR. In 1965, for example, Dilip Alwin Saund became the first (and, until Bobby Jindal's election in 2004, the only) Indian American to be elected to the US House of Representatives.

Upon arrival in the United States, second-wave Indians sent individual financial contributions to their family members at home. At a group level, they formed organizations to create familiar communities and facilitate their assimilation. For example, in the early 1970s umbrella organizations, such as the Association for Indians in America and the Federation of Indian Associations, emerged to define Indian Americans' diasporic identity and mobilize them to petition the US government for a new category of "Asian Indian" in the census questionnaire (a category they won for the 1980 census). By the mid-1970s, many Indian religious organizations had purchased physical structures (a temple, gurudwara, or church) where they could more formally and publicly practice their homeland religious rituals. But all these efforts focused on the US context and remained formally divorced from the Indian context (although some religious groups maintained relations with their parent bodies in India).

Indian Americans did not launch transnational organizations to make demands on the Indian government until the late 1970s. In my interview sample of 69 transnational organizations among Indians in the United States, only two were formed before the 1970s. An implicit claim in some studies on Indian Americans is that the absence of transnational organizations until the 1970s is simply a function of numbers and time; after all, transnational organizations take time to build, and the US Indian community was still small and very new during the 1970s (Kapur 2010). Other scholars have argued that Indian Americans' early inattention to India can be attributed to their middle-class, professional status. Their wealth at the time, while high, was newly earned (rather than inherited), and many were not ready to part with it. After all, they received more social recognition from material consumption than they did from philanthropic giving. As well, most members of the Indian diaspora were (and still are) suspicious of donor networks and often fear their money will not be spent as promised (Sheth 2010).

While I do not deny the validity of both these arguments, my interviews with elite Indian emigrants in the United States indicate an additional reason for their lack of collective organization during the Nationalist MDR, namely, resentment and remorse over the Indian government's actions. The Indian government's message under the Nationalist MDR that Indian identity was tied to India's geographic boundaries was welcomed by Muslims in India and by some Indian emigrants in Africa and the Caribbean, whose own loyalties were being questioned in their host countries. But scholars have noted that some Indians in these regions expressed remorse at feeling ignored by the Indian government and thus translated the official term "NRI" (which means "Non-Resident Indian") as "Non-Required Indian" (Rutten and Patel 2007: 180). Similarly, Indian Americans in my interviews (all of whom were highly educated) expressed remorse over and even feeling hurt by the Indian government's dismissive stance toward them during the Nationalist MDR. Many expressed guilt for leaving the nation after benefiting from state-sponsored education (which enabled them to emigrate to the United States), so the Indian government's critiques of a brain drain often touched a raw nerve among them. Many of my interviewees also expressed resentment that the Indian government did not recognize them or reach out to them during this period.

It was these deep feelings of abandonment, guilt, and resentment that an Indian movement designed to overthrow India's ruling party was able to tap with great effect by the end of the 1970s.

The Emergency and the Eventual Mobilization of Elite Emigrants

Despite their initial apathy, elite emigrants were eventually mobilized to help resist the Nationalist MDR, a mobilization that would help shape India's subsequent Neoliberal MDR.

Unlike poor emigrants' resistance, which was rooted in the material deprivations the Nationalist MDR imposed on them, middle-class emigrants' resistance was rooted in politics. Their mobilization took place in the context of the Emergency (1975–77), when Prime Minister Gandhi evoked her constitutional right to suspend India's democracy in the name of national security. The Emergency is often marked as the darkest hour of Indian democracy. Indeed, its authoritarian underpinning enabled an onslaught of harrowing state-induced violence, including slum clearances, forced sterilization campaigns, the imprisonment of over 100,000 people without due process, press censorship, and the suspension of basic civil liberties, such as freedom of speech. Gandhi felt particularly threatened by the growing strength of political opposition emanating from within India among the Communist left and the Hindu nationalist right. Some of these groups coalesced to form the Janata Party, while others took more radical, non-party forms. In an attempt at national solidarity, Gandhi depicted all such domestic opposition (party- and non-party-affiliated) as "antinational" and as foreign agents who wanted to penetrate India's borders and topple India's sovereignty.

In many ways, the Emergency signaled the last gasp of the postcolonial, Congress-led, Fabian-Socialist development paradigm, and with it the last breath of the Nationalist MDR.[23] Less often discussed is the role that the topic of emigration and Indian emigrants themselves played in the ending of the Emergency, and thus the demise of the Nationalist MDR. Hindu nationalist groups in India, for example, celebrated the diaspora in the anti-Emergency movement. As the Hindutva ideologue M. G. Chitkara wrote, "The world-wide protest, especially of the Indians living abroad, proved to be one of the decisive factors in upsetting the calculations of the dictatorial regime [in India]" (Chitkara 2004: 285, quoted in Anderson and Clibbens 2018: 1736). Similarly, left-wing organizations, such as the Indian Workers' Association and Socialist International; popular social movements, such known as the Jayaprakash Narayan movement; human rights organizers; and Quakers, tapped diaspora support against the Emergency. Across the political spectrum, the anti-Emergency movement targeted elite emigrants residing in the United Kingdom, United States, Canada, and East Africa.

Whether emigrants' role was factually decisive or merely symbolic is historically debatable, and the dearth of research on emigrants' involvement in the Emergency has left unresolved the question of who first sparked their involvement in the anti-Emergency movement. Among the Hindu right, scholars have shown that emigrants' involvement was spurred by leaders of the anti-Emergency

---

[23] Although Gandhi and the Congress Party were voted back into power a few years later, they returned with much weaker popular support and far more opposition parties with which to contend at the national and subnational levels.

movement in India rather than by members of the diaspora (Anderson and Clibbens 2018). This reading corroborates my own field research that suggests most Indians in the United States were reluctant to get involved in transnational activism before the Emergency. Therefore, unlike with poor emigrants who mobilized themselves and then attracted the attention of the Janata Party, middle-class emigrants were more likely *mobilized by* the groups composing the Janata Party.

Regardless of these details, it is clear that India's anti-Emergency movement reawakened the educated elite emigrant abroad as a figure who could and would exert their views and desires on the nation-state of India. For the first time since the anticolonial movement, an elite emigrant consciousness was forged. Moreover, elite emigrants' involvement in the anti-Emergency movement blasted open the closed borders of the postcolonial Indian state (and of the Nationalist MDR) to underscore the potentially positive impact that global forces could have on India—at least from the perspective of anti-Emergency supporters. Just as the Indian leaders of the anticolonial movement mobilized emigrants to gain global visibility as an antiracist movement, so too did Indian leaders of the anti-Emergency movement mobilize emigrants to gain global support as a pro-democracy movement. Exposing the often neglected role that educated elite Indian emigrants played in helping to end the Emergency thus helps us understand how and why the Nationalist MDR fell, as well as how and why India's subsequent Neoliberal MDR took the shape that it did.

Indian activists opposing Emergency rule tried to employ the "boomerang effect" by seeking support from abroad to pressure their own government at home (Keck and Sikkink 1998). Underlying this approach is a clear understanding of global power relations, requiring foreign pressure to come from a global superpower. Anti-Emergency activists mobilized Indian emigrants living in the United States and United Kingdom to form organizations, stage protests, lobby public figures, and expand media coverage in their host countries in order to influence their host governments to put pressure on Gandhi to end the Emergency. As well, anti-Emergency activists encouraged elite emigrants living in former British colonies, including East Africa, to provide information, funds, and moral support. In their study of emigrants' involvement during the Emergency, Anderson and Clibbens (2018) detail a wonderful example of an attempt to employ the boomerang effect when 200 people in the United Kingdom (including 65 members of Parliament, the famous economist E. F. Schumacher, the historian A. J. P. Taylor, and the Socialist Fenner Brockway) signed a petition alongside a prominent advertisement published in *The Times* on Indian Independence Day, August 15, 1975. The advertisement called for the release of social activist and anti-Emergency leader Jayprakash Narayan (who had been arrested in India) with a caption that read, "Don't let the light go out on India's democracy." A similar advertisement appeared in the *New York Times* on the same day. Drawing from this, the US Congress held hearings on civil liberties in India, relaying the negative press coverage and hearing statements by Indians for Democracy and other groups. Although the diaspora's assistance with attaining such negative international press did not result in concrete disruptions in bilateral relations between India, the United Kingdom, and the United States, an examination of India's Ministry of External Affairs reports, as well as Indian diplomatic mission reports, shows that it created substantial anxiety and anger within Gandhi's government (Anderson and Clibbens 2018).

As in the anticolonial movement, foreign locations provided elite Indian emigrants a safe space from which to work and mobilize while in exile. Given the pro-democracy tenet of the anti-Emergency movement, many activists emigrated to the wealthy countries of the West, such as the United Kingdom, the United States, and Canada. During the Emergency, the Indian government banned several organizations on the political left and the right, and many leaders were arrested on sedition charges. This spurred a new generation of young leaders to emigrate as students and activists. As readers familiar with contemporary India know, right-wing organizations involved in the anti-Emergency movement went on to gain substantial political power in India some decades later. What may be less familiar is that many of the contemporary leaders of India's Hindu right began their political career by emigrating and working with the diaspora during the Emergency. Subramanium Swamy, for example, studied at Harvard University, and Makarand Desai studied at the Massachusetts Institute of Technology during this period. But perhaps the most famous contemporary leaders of the Hindu right who were involved in interactions with the diaspora during the Emergency were Atul Bihari Vajpayee, who went on to become prime minister of India in the mid-1990s, and Narendra Modi, the current prime minister. In March 1977, Vajpayee was instrumental in organizing an international conference for the Friends of India Society International, which planted an initial seed for what would evolve into foreign outposts of the Hindu right's political party, the Bharatiya Janatha Party (BJP). Similarly, one of Modi's key roles during the anti-Emergency movement was to maintain contact with networks abroad and arrange for the transmission of information back to India (Anderson and Clibbens 2018).

In an interview with me, Dr. Subramanian Swamy, at the time the president of the Janata Party, a former cabinet minister of commerce, law, and justice, and a staunch supporter of right-wing Hindu politics, recalled his interactions with the US diaspora in the late 1970s, when he tried to get support for the new Janata Party. He explained, "During the emergency, when we were fighting Indira Gandhi, we received much support from UK and US. I went to the US to campaign. They were in a position to organize meetings because they had no censorship. We [in India] were under censorship. We broke the censorship in India by going abroad. And the West is such an important part of the world, that it helped to be there."[24]

To suppress the growing opposition movements gaining support from abroad, the Indian government under the Nationalist MDR eventually resorted to coercion—echoing the all-too-familiar state response experienced at the dawn of the Coolie MDR and the height of the anticolonial movement. The main weapons the Indian government had at its disposal to suppress Indian citizens abroad was the Passport Act, which enabled the government to impound the passports and/or stop the scholarships of student abroad whom the government deemed "undesirable," "antinational," or "unpatriotic." In addition to targeting individuals, India's diplomatic missions in the United States targeted emigrant organizations, such as Indians for Democracy. According to Anderson and Clibbens (2018), one of the emigrant students who lost his scholarship was Anand Kumar, a student in Chicago who became a sociologist in India and a founding member of a contemporary opposition party in India, Aam Aadmi Party.

The Final Shift: Suspending the 1922 Emigration Act and Acknowledging the Diaspora

The Emergency signaled the waning legitimacy of the Congress-led postcolonial state that relied on closed borders. Just as the Coolie MDR had resorted to emigration reforms in its final and desperate gasps for survival, so too did the Nationalist MDR.

First, at the height of the Emergency in 1976, the Indian government made an unprecedented shift in the Nationalist MDR and suspended the 1922 Act with little parliamentary discussion or debate. Between December 1976 and October 1977, the Ministry of Labor gave permission to 15,902 poor workers, whom the PGE identified as "semiskilled" and "unskilled," to emigrate.[25] By December 1977, the reported number of approved poor emigrants had jumped to 251,110.[26]

This quiet liberalization of emigration, however, was not enough to satiate the massive demand for low-wage labor in the Gulf countries. Therefore, hundreds of thousands more workers emigrated without government approval. During this period, countless new private recruiters emerged, and the small industry of

---

[24] Interview, March 14, 2011.

[25] Lok Sabha Sessions, Vol. 7, No. 4, November 17, 1977.

[26] This number includes emigrants to all countries, not just those going to the Gulf. Disaggregated data for this period is unavailable.

unregulated, exploitative migration mushroomed. Many interviewees recounted their pioneering approach during this era. "Ninety percent of Gulf emigrants are low income. They used to have no documents, no visa. They just went on big boats. Indian currency used to work there [in the Gulf], due to UK colonization. There were no visas required, so there was a lot of cheating by agents," recounted K. C. Joseph, minister of the Kerala government's Department for Overseas Keralites.[27]

It is this context of India's growing economic crisis, the 1970s oil boom in the Gulf countries, and rising pressure from within the state in which poor workers' demands for the freedom to emigrate finally became amplified enough to explode the legitimacy of the Nationalist MDR. In short, the liberalization of emigration in India was not the result of so-called neoliberal multilateral development agencies, which, in fact, emerged as a force decades later. *The liberalization of emigration in India was a result of poor workers' demands.*

As notable is that the demands by some Indian leaders to increase regulations on elite emigrants were never met. Elite Indian emigrants had no reason to support these demands, and other groups did not emerge to voice them. Instead, in the midst of the Emergency, while Gandhi was violently suppressing middle-class activists abroad, she also acknowledged their potential benefit to India. Anderson and Clibbens (2018: 1766) quote a 1975 memo by Gandhi: "India should use these people in its publicity drive in the same manner as Israel uses the Jews in [the] USA and elsewhere on their behalf. . . . The Israelis had a tremendous advantage. The Jews are the richest and most tenacious of the communities in [the] US. But we should make an effort. Thought should be given to organising Indian[s] abroad."[28]

In India's postcolonial history, this marked the first time the state officially acknowledged the diaspora as a potential boon. But as is clear from this quote, it was elite Indians abroad—those with "riches" and "tenacity"—whom the Indian state sought to tap. Gandhi's advisors were clear that she should invite Indians living in the United States, United Kingdom, and Canada to a convention in India because they could "contribute toward the mainstream of Indian life." In contrast, emigrants "who had settled in East Africa, Fiji, or the Caribbean" were thought to cause "misinterpretations" (Anderson and Clibbens 2018: 1766)[29] This marked an important shift in the Nationalist MDR, which had till then

---

[27] Interview, March 22, 2012.

[28] Summarized and quoted from Indira Gandhi in "A background note on attitude of publicity media in USA/UK/FRG/France to India and our efforts to project the correct picture in these countries" (n.d., probably December 1975), NAI, MEA, AMS Division, WII/102/31/75, Vol. 3.

[29] T. N. Kaul, Indian Ambassador to USA, letter to Indira Gandhi, March 23, 1976, NMML, T. N. Kaul Papers, S. No. 4, Part 1.

relied on ignoring its elite emigrants (at least officially) in order to bolster its claims of national pride and self-sufficiency.

By the late 1970s, it was clear that the Nationalist MDR was making way for a new MDR, which would once again try to use emigrants to fuel the nation's development agenda (rather than topple the nation's ruling state). Let us now turn to our analysis of India's contemporary MDR.

5

The CEO MDR (1977–Present)

Liberalizing Emigration and Tapping Emigrants' Financial Contributions

With the historical backdrop of the rise and fall of the colonial-era Coolie MDR (Chapter 3) and the rise and fall of the first postcolonial Nationalist MDR (Chapter 4), we are now ready to begin our analysis of India's contemporary MDR, which I call the CEO MDR. The CEO MDR promotes the liberalization of poor and wealthy workers' emigration to fuel a new development model in India that valorizes global markets (for people and capital), the private accumulation of wealth, self-sufficiency, and entrepreneurship (among elite *and* poor emigrants). As argued in previous chapters, understanding the contemporary MDR's ancestral lineage enables us to decipher how it is (and is not) unique relative to earlier MDRs and why it is so strikingly solid. While this chapter unpacks how the CEO MDR echoes past MDRs, the next chapter highlights what is unique about the CEO MDR. As we saw in Chapter 3, exporting poor and elite emigrants to fuel domestic development is not a historically unique strategy for India; in fact, it is reminiscent of the colonial-era Coolie MDR.

How, then, did India's postcolonial government attain domestic consent for a colonial-era-like MDR? To answer this question, this chapter and the next trace the start of the CEO MDR to 1977. Doing so exposes the exploratory phase of the 1970s and 1980s, when poor and elite emigrants played a vital, but understudied, role in fomenting consent for India's new CEO MDR. In turn, the CEO MDR (and emigrants' role therein) helped build consent within India for a new development model of neoliberal globalization, which was officially launched decades later. In other words, *the global movement of people presaged Indians' consent to the global movement of goods and services, not the other way around.* This chapter details how emigrants' financial contributions from abroad (in the form of remittances, savings accounts, investments, and bonds) helped

The Migration-Development Regime. Rina Agarwala, Oxford University Press. © Oxford University Press 2022.
DOI: 10.1093/oso/9780197586396.003.0005

the state reframe emigrants as a resource for India (rather than an embarrassment, as in the Nationalist MDR) and build consent for foreign capital inflows. The next chapter examines the role of elite emigrants' social and ideological contributions.

But as with previous MDRs, the CEO MDR balances on several class-based contradictions. To cement its legitimacy in relying on poor workers' foreign wages, the state still remains tethered to the electoral expectations of state protections for poor workers that defined the Nationalist MDR. This constraint has forced the state to retain some restrictions over poor workers' emigration, provide some welfare, and reincorporate them into India's economy upon return (since so many are temporary migrants).

To cement its legitimacy in relying on elite emigrants' financial contributions from abroad, the state returned to a practice first launched by independence leaders during the early 1900s and reincarnated during the anti-Emergency movement of the 1970s: appealing to the shared racial and ethnic bonds between domestic Indians and those residing abroad. While this helped build some domestic consent for the use of foreign resources (from less foreign Indians abroad), it did not draw massive contributions from elite emigrants. Therefore, unlike with poor emigrants, the government has also offered additional incentives to elite emigrants, making their financial contributions costly, volatile, and still less than poor workers' contributions (which is striking given elite emigrants' higher salary base). This raises a question I address in Chapter 6: Why does the CEO MDR continue to woo elite emigrants?

Launching the CEO MDR: The 1970s and 1980s

The CEO MDR, and its new approach to liberalized emigration, began in the late 1970s. Although it arrived alongside a worldwide turn toward neoliberal development strategies that aimed to strengthen private enterprise and to free markets from government control, it came decades *before* India officially began liberalizing its markets for goods and services in 1991. Some scholars have traced the roots of India's liberalization to the 1980s, when the government began its privatization efforts (Kohli 2012). Others have traced it to the late 2000s, when India began pairing liberalization with globalization, opening its borders to the international trade of goods and services for the first time since Independence. Interestingly, none of these studies accounts for India's approach to the international movement of people. Those who examine contemporary emigration from India, therefore, usually follow these studies and begin their accounts in the late 1990s and 2000s.

As detailed in the previous chapter, the Janata Party (a coalition of political parties from the right and left who were united in their opposition to the hegemonic Congress Party) was instrumental in undoing the Nationalist MDR and thus setting the ground for the CEO MDR. During the early 1970s, India's *poor workers* (not just northern powers promoting neoliberalism) demanded the liberalization of emigration because they had suffered under the failed promises of the Nationalist MDR and thus sought the right to seek employment abroad. And the Janata Party supported these demands. The Janata Party also mobilized the previously unorganized population of educated emigrants to fight a global pro-democracy movement that ultimately overthrew Indira Gandhi's Emergency rule. The anti-Emergency movement thus helped legitimize elite emigrants' right to shape and participate in India's economic and political development from afar.

Upon winning the national elections in 1977 (which Gandhi had called for), the Janata Party sought to transition the nation into a new MDR that could redefine the nation's development agenda. The Janata Party was the first non-Congress party to rule India's national government, and its electoral victory is widely accepted as signaling the end of the Fabian-Socialist development model defined by national borders, state ownership of public assets, state planning and control over the economy, and state protection within closed borders (for goods, services, and poor workers).

What is less highlighted is how the Janata Party used emigration policies for the poor and elite to explore and attain domestic consent for a new development agenda. This new agenda no longer associated globalization with imperialism. Rather, it evoked India's sovereignty and pride *through the celebration of global markets and open borders*—first for people and eventually for goods and services. As well, this new agenda no longer celebrated state ownership and protection. Rather, it celebrated *privatization in the economy and in the social sector,* an ideal that emigrants had long practiced abroad.

Although the Janata Party's rule was brief (only three years), its impact on the nation's migration practices was lasting. Upon her return as prime minister under the Congress Party in 1980, Indira Gandhi continued to pursue the transition toward the new MDR that the Janata Party had started. And in 1985, Rajiv Gandhi of the Congress Party cemented further consent for the CEO MDR. Let us now examine exactly how the government implemented this new agenda among poor and elite emigrants.

Understanding the Liberalization of Poor Workers

A key feature of the CEO MDR is that it has progressively liberalized the emigration of poor workers. But recognizing the historical roots of this liberalization offers three important corrections to the common understanding of India's contemporary emigration practices as a simple reflection of neoliberalism.

A Demand from Poor Workers

First, poor workers demanded the liberalization of their emigration. In fact, it was poor workers' resistance to the Nationalist MDR that gave the Janata Party the ammunition it needed to launch a new MDR. Moreover, the Janata Party included left-wing parties that represented a pro-worker bloc. Therefore, in its election campaign, the party vehemently opposed the Nationalist MDR's protective restrictions against emigration, explicitly pointing to poor workers as a reason for this opposition. Upon entering office, the Janata government delegitimized the previous Congress rule by claiming the Nationalist MDR *abused* poor workers by restricting their emigration. Once at the helm of Parliament, the Janata Party enabled those who had long opposed the Nationalist MDR to repeatedly air their views. Members of Parliament from different ideological orientations joined in reframing the 1922 Emigration Act as "an instrument no longer of exploitation by the colonial powers, but an instrument of corruption and bribery in the hands of a large number of officers who collectively call themselves the Protector of Emigrants . . . [who] are out to destroy and exploit [poor emigrants] for their own profit."[1]

The pro-worker government of the state of Kerala was another leading voice in bringing down the Nationalist MDR and launching a new MDR. In a passionate speech, Vayalar Ravi, member of Parliament from Kerala (who later served as the minister of overseas Indian affairs), reiterated the need to wrest control over emigration decisions from the government, because government officials were prone to abusing their powers while simultaneously increasing the number of administrative personnel responsible for controlling emigration.[2] The liberalization of poor emigrants was thus viewed as a welcome release from the slow and corrupt state clearance process.

To this day, those on the political right *and* left, as well as those representing poor workers, support the liberalization of poor workers' emigration. As a joint secretary in the MEA's Office of Overseas Indian Affairs explained to me, "We are not in the business of restricting freedom of movement."[3] K. C. Joseph, minister for rural development, overseas Keralites, and planning and culture in the government of Kerala, went so far as to promote liberalization even in the face of exploitation. Without pause, he explained to me that regulations are viewed by many poor emigrants as anathema to liberty: "The government is trying to limit illegal [i.e., exploitative] migration, but we can't restrict it too much, because people will be upset. We already have so many restrictions."[4]

---

[1] Lok Sabha Debates, Vol. 8, Nos. 31–40, April 18, 1978, 359.
[2] Lok Sabha Debates, Vol. 16, No. 9, July 27, 1978.
[3] Interview, January 4, 2019.
[4] Interview, March 22, 2012.

Recognizing poor workers' role in liberalizing Indian emigration is important not only to nuance our understanding of history and deepen our understanding of the CEO MDR's foundation but also to strengthen the target of our future trajectories. Liberalized emigration may not be the primary problem facing poor workers today. Indeed, in the context of failed domestic employment generation, emigration is one of the only options available to the world's poor workers.

Retaining State Protection

This raises a second correction to our understanding of the liberalization of poor workers' emigration: it remains tethered to the protective promises of the Nationalist MDR.

Poor workers have consistently demanded that liberalized emigration must take place alongside *rights-based protection* rather than the paternalist protection that began under the Nationalist MDR and still persists today. These demands were especially pronounced under the Janata Party. In a damning critique of Janata's Ministry of Labor, for example, worker representatives on the Inter-ministerial Committee on Emigration wrote, "The lure of jobs is understandable; the recruiting agents' greed to make quick money, though reprehensible, is also understandable; what is not understandable is the failure of the licensing system of the Labour Ministry during 1976–79 [i.e., under Janata]."[5]

India's poor workers also tried to cement the protective state as something to valorize on the global stage. In the early 1980s, Chitta Basu of the left-wing Forward Bloc in West Bengal noted the Indian government's own public-sector undertakings abroad had abused Indian workers, exclaiming, "Such reports project a very bad image of public sector abroad and surely bring a bad name to the country. The Committee feel that public sector undertakings are expected to be model employers and this expectation is not only with reference to the workers at home but also abroad."[6]

To retain its legitimacy among the mass electorate, the Janata Party was thus forced to follow the Nationalist MDR's claims to protect vulnerable Indian workers while still legally liberalizing their ability to emigrate.[7] To address this challenge, the Janata government launched a series of exploratory parliamentary discussions on the topic. My review of parliamentary debates reveals that for the first time since Independence, the emigration of poor workers became a repeated topic across parliamentary sessions in this period. Significantly, and in contrast

[5] Ministry of External Affairs, Estimates Committee Report, 1980–81, 16th Report, "Overseas Indians in West Asia, Sri Lanka, Malaysia, Burma, Indonesia, and Singapore," Part 1, West Asia, 25.

[6] Lok Sabha Debates, Vol. 40, No. 15, August 12, 1983, 285.

[7] Lok Sabha Sessions, Vol. 7, No. 4, November 17, 1977.

to the contemporary era, the challenge facing emigrant workers was framed and understood as a "labor" challenge. The Janata government initiated a fact-finding mission by Minister of Labor Ravindra Varma to visit poor Indian emigrants in the Gulf, and it immediately announced that it was considering amending the 1922 Emigration Act.[8] In 1978, the government set up a larger Inter-ministerial Committee—comprising of the Ministry of External Affairs (MEA), Ministry of Industry and Home Affairs, and Ministry of Labor—to study the situation of overseas Indian workers.[9] In its explorations, the government drew on the same rhetoric of "national dignity" and "fairness" that the previous Nationalist MDR had used to forbid poor workers' emigration. For example, in 1978, Minister Varma announced, "It is the responsibility of the Government to ensure that consistent with fair conditions of work, and fair wages for work, and national dignity, every effort is made to see that such offers [i.e., employment abroad] are availed of."[10]

Several members of Parliament also tried to enact material forms of government protection for emigrant workers by demanding the creation of a centralized government-run Manpower Corporation that could recruit, register, and train poor emigrant workers and study global labor market demands to help workers find suitable employment. They demanded the government enforce fair wages and work conditions for poor emigrants by accrediting foreign employers and making labor-supply agreements with receiving-country governments. These demands reflected the still firm faith in the state to protect vulnerable citizens. In the late 1970s, Atal Bihari Vajpayee, a member of the Hindu-right party, Bharatiya Janata Party (BJP), served as the minister of external affairs (or foreign minister), and for decades he raised the issue of emigration in parliamentary debates. When Vajpayee became prime minister in the late 1990s, he reinserted emigration into a more central stage in parliamentary discussions (Khadria 2007: 131). As prime minister, he was facing substantial domestic resistance to increased globalization, and in response he reengaged poor emigrants' demands for government labor market protections, calling for what was renamed the Manpower Export-Promotion Corporation. In addition to protecting workers, the corporation promised to market Indian workers abroad by partnering with other export promotion agencies.

The demands and debates that took place around state protection *alongside* the liberalization of emigration are usually omitted from studies on contemporary Indian emigration. But they are key to exposing the vulnerabilities in the

---

[8] Lok Sabha Debates, Vol. 2, Nos. 1–10, June 16, 1977.

[9] Ministry of External Affairs, Estimates Committee Report, 1980–81, 16th Report, "Overseas Indians in West Asia, Sri Lanka, Malaysia, Burma, Indonesia, and Singapore," Part 1, West Asia, 21.

[10] Lok Sabha Debates, 6th series, No. 9, March 1, 1979, 10, emphasis added by author.

CEO MDR that have emerged as a result (which I detail later in this chapter and the next) and potential avenues for the future (which I explore in the final chapter).

From Protected Emigrants to Liberalized Men

An important consequence of the CEO MDR's liberalization of poor emigrants is that it has been entirely male. Regulations and restrictions on the emigration of poor *female* workers have, in fact, increased under the CEO MDR. This stands in sharp contrast to other contemporary sending countries, such as the Philippines, that specifically target and market their female emigrants (Parrenas 2004; Rodriguez 2010).

In India, the gendered discrepancy in the liberalization of poor workers' emigration was justified as a response to emigrant organizations. Indeed, government representatives from Kerala had long demanded increased restrictions on the emigration of poor women, citing cases of severe exploitation among female Indian domestic workers in the Gulf. Although these demands to protect poor female emigrants were ignored by the national government for decades, under the CEO MDR restrictions preventing poor women's emigration suddenly passed through the Parliament with relatively little discussion or debate. An additional reason given to retain emigration clearances over female emigrants has been the foreign exchange earned through the attestation of the documents required as part of the clearance procedure.[11]

During the 1980s, all uneducated female emigrants to the Gulf countries who were less than 40 years old required an additional attestation and certification from the Indian mission in the host country (whether or not they were going for employment).[12] This was later reduced to 30 years old, which still exceeded the restriction on male emigrants. In 2015, nurses (who are predominantly female) were also included in the restricted category (despite their education and skill level).[13] In addition to requiring these women to get government clearance, the restrictions also forbade women to use private recruiters. Women were allowed to migrate only through state-run recruitment agencies.

Although all the recruiters I interviewed vehemently denied working with female emigrants, almost all had piles of applications from women "in process" on their desks. In short, poor women have been pushed into the extralegal sphere of illicit emigration under the CEO MDR. As I show in Chapter 7, this gendered

[11] Ministry of External Affairs, Estimates Committee 1993–94, April 22, 1994.

[12] Parliament Debate, 12th series, Vol. 6, No. 3, December 2, 1998.

[13] Government of India, Overseas Indian Affairs, Question No. 415, July 22, 2015, Gen. V. K. Singh, Minister of State for Overseas Indian Affairs.

dynamic of poor workers' emigration has shaped the male-dominated character of poor migrants' organizations from below.

The 1983 Emigration Act

In 1983, after seven years in the making, the Indian government passed a new Emigration Act, thereby institutionalizing the CEO MDR's liberalization of poor, male emigrants. Unfortunately, however, the 1983 Act failed to uphold workers' demands for rights-based protections. Although the Janata Party initiated the new act, the Congress Party under Indira Gandhi passed it.

The 1983 Emigration Act retained the regulatory practice (started under the 1922 Emigration Act) of dividing Indian emigrants into two groups: (1) those who require government oversight/protection and must attain government clearance (in the form of a stamp in their passport) to emigrate because they are not educated and are thus deemed poor and "vulnerable" and (2) those who do not require any government clearance to emigrate because they meet the minimum education level to be considered "nonvulnerable."[14] The 1983 Act also retained the statutory authority first launched under colonialism, the Protector General of Emigrants (PGE) under the Ministry of Labor, to be responsible for the welfare and protection of emigrants in category 1. Under the PGE, 10 regional Protector of Emigrants (PoEs) provide clearance stamps in the passports of emigrants in category 1. Without the coveted stamp, uneducated emigrants cannot clear customs at the Indian border.

However, unlike in the Nationalist MDR, when PoEs were encouraged to deny clearances, PoEs under the CEO MDR were now *encouraged to provide them*. Until recently, the PoE offered an ever-increasing number of clearances each year. Between 2000 to 2014, the number of clearances more than tripled, from 243,182 to 804,000 (Ministry of Overseas Indian Affairs 2015)—a trend

---

[14] Under the 1983 Emigration Act, clearance requirements also depend on country of destination and purpose of travel, thereby creating a dizzying and ever-changing set of rules. At the time of writing, uneducated emigrants traveling for Haj and Umrah to Saudi Arabia or to perform Ziarat in Saudi Arabia, Syria, Iran, Iraq, Jordan, Egypt, and Yemen do not require clearance. However, uneducated emigrants traveling to one of 18 specified countries for employment do require clearance. These countries are United Arab Emirates, Saudi Arabia, Qatar, Oman, Kuwait, Bahrain, Libya, Jordan, Yemen, Sudan, Syria, Lebanon, Afghanistan, Malaysia, Thailand, Indonesia, Iraq, and Brunei. Uneducated emigrants traveling to these countries for reasons other than employment (such as tourism, business, or family visit) do not require emigration clearance but must carry specified documents (such as a two-way return ticket and a sponsor letter). Since most of the countries exempted from clearance requirements (such as Japan, New Zealand, Australia, Canada, United States, Singapore, South Korea, South Africa, Thailand, and countries in Europe) do not accept uneducated Indian immigrants, the clearance requirements clearly target poor workers seeking to emigrate for employment in the Gulf.

that India's foremost scholars of emigration said "suggested a new dynamism" in the government's approach (Kumar and Rajan 2014: 18).

In addition, since the 1983 Act was passed, the national government (across political parties) has progressively diluted the requirements for clearances, thereby folding more poor workers into the second category of liberalized "emigration clearance not required" emigrants. In 1991, the Congress-led MEA recommended amendments to the 1983 Act that would abolish the Ministry of Labor's obligation to review and approve employment contracts for emigrants in category 1.[15] Although the recommendation did not pass Parliament, the subsequent BJP government led by Vajpayee did simplify the emigration procedures by lowering the number of destination countries requiring clearance, facilitating cyclical migration, and eliminating the requirement for a return airline ticket deposit. Six additional categories of emigrants were also exempted from emigration clearance requirements and were thus free to emigrate without any government approval of their contract terms.[16] In December 2004, the government announced the education requirement to emigrate without government clearance would be lowered from graduation (12th grade equivalent) to 10th grade, thereby redefining the category of "vulnerable worker" and increasing the number of "nonvulnerable" workers free to emigrate without government clearance.

State Protection under the 1983 Act

Unfortunately for India's poor emigrants, the 1983 Act *ignored poor workers' demands for liberalization with rights-based protections from exploitative employers abroad.*

Although there was a broad consensus (from left to right) around the liberalization of poor workers' emigration when launching the CEO MDR, there was much less consensus around the types of protections the government should offer poor emigrants. Pro-worker parties pushed the government to uphold workers' original demands for rights-based and material protections, and complaints were periodically raised in Parliament about the lack of enforcement over the regulation of recruiting agents, too few personnel assigned to approve emigration applications (thereby slowing the outflow), the need for additional

---

[15] Ministry of External Affairs, Estimates Committee, 1991–92, 10th Lok Sabha, Delhi, 5th Report, February 14, 1992.

[16] These include supervisors, professional workers, and semiprofessional workers; light/medium/heavy vehicle drivers; clerical workers (including stenographers, storekeepers, timekeepers, typists); and cooks (excluding those who seek employment in households). Recruiting agents must attest to the emigrant's trade.

data on emigrants, complaints of government corruption, and demands for in-surance and welfare funds for workers similar to those offered by other sending countries, such as Thailand and South Korea.

However, rather than meeting workers' demands for rights-based protection with liberalized emigration, the 1983 Act emphasized liberalization itself as a form of state protection. As the Estimates Committee declared in 1980, the pur-pose of the 1983 Act would be to "avoid over-regulation which may result in creating difficulties for genuine workers seeking employment abroad."[17] In 1983, Minister of Labor Veerendra Patil emphasized, "I repeat that the main purpose of this Bill is to promote the export of labour."[18] Although a decade earlier, Gandhi had vehemently upheld the emigration restrictions of the Nationalist MDR, in a 1982 parliamentary session she plainly stated, "I fully agree that the interests of our workers should be safeguarded. However, what has actually happened is that such employment markets are being closed to us. And these people there are looking toward the Philippines and other countries for their labour. That also is harmful to our people because they could make good money there."[19] Minister Patil reiterated, "The main approach has been to protect the emigrant workers from exploitation . . . but at the same time not to have the cumbersome procedures which will reduce the competitiveness of Indian labour in the over-seas labour market."[20] This was a stark shift from an earlier era that promised protection at the expense of economic accumulation.

In 2004, the BJP government claimed, "Indian workers seeking employment abroad, particularly in Gulf countries, are expected to be *better protected* by the liberalisation of emigration procedures."[21] The BJP government also claimed that further liberalization would protect workers from having to pay rents to government officials and recruiting agents in return for bureaucratic clearances to emigrate. As in the Coolie MDR (see Chapter 3), government officials also framed poor workers' emigration as an opportunity to overcome one's low caste status. One emigrant official in the Kerala government, K. Satish Nambudiripad, extolled the riches of emigration: "More money came in. Everyone from low to high strata could go to the Gulf. Initially it was only the lowest strata. Leaving home was considered a failure. It meant you can't make it. When you cross the seas, you lose your *varna, jati* [caste]. . . . [B]ut then you started to see in the

---

[17] Ministry of External Affairs, Estimates Committee Report, 1980–81, 16th Report, "Overseas Indians in West Asia, Sri Lanka, Malaysia, Burma, Indonesia, and Singapore," Part 1, West Asia, 25.

[18] Lok Sabha Debates, Vol. 40, No. 15, August 12, 1983, 290.

[19] Lok Sabha Debates, Vol. 30, No. 4, July 14, 1982, 12.

[20] Lok Sabha Debates, Vol. 40, No. 13, August 10, 1983, 469.

[21] Government of India, Labour and Employment, Question and Answer, December 6, 2004, 1, emphasis added by author.

Muslim [i.e., early emigrant] pockets *very* big houses. A lot of wealth. A lot of gold. Big huge properties. It was very visible."[22]

Some government officials I spoke with even extolled the government's "protection" of poor emigrants as a *new* government priority in emigration under the CEO MDR. Basant Kumar Potnuru, a research officer in the government think-tank for emigrants (then called the Indian Council of Overseas Employment, now called the India Centre for Migration) said, "It is only recently that the Indian government mechanisms have emerged as a source of protection. The awareness part is still lacking."[23]

In addition to redefining state protection as liberalization itself, the 1983 Act effectively silenced further debates around rights-based protections for poor emigrants. In my review of parliamentary discussions, successive prime minsters, as well as ministers of labor and external affairs, from the late 1970s through the 1990s constantly dismissed complaints raised during parliamentary sessions, never let the discussions go too far, often denied that any complaints of exploitation had come to their attention, and sometimes offered vague claims that steps were being taken by the government to offer training of emigrants and research on labor demand needs. Chitta Basu of the Forward Bloc in West Bengal tried to expose the government's tactics, noting early on that the 1983 Act was simply helping the government hide the exploitation that recruiters facilitated. He proclaimed that "[m]alpractices are being institutionalized" through this Act, since the Act does not stipulate strong penalties for malpractice and exploitation.[24] In 1991, the Gulf War exposed the emptiness of the government's promises to protect poor workers. Shortly after the war began, the government was forced to repatriate hundreds of thousands of poor emigrants working in the Gulf, and the government's inability and/or unwillingness to provide for poor migrant returnees became painfully clear.

But our historical analysis of MDRs shows the government's claim of protecting poor emigrants by liberalizing their emigration is clearly not new. In fact, it echoes similar claims made under the Coolie MDR. And similar to the Coolie MDR, the claim has created several contradictions for the CEO MDR. First, despite government officials' feverish support for liberalized emigration as a form of state protection, persistent demands for greater state protection have prevented the CEO MDR from fully liberalizing all emigration. In the name of state protection, therefore, the CEO MDR still restricts and controls the emigration of thousands of poor workers. As secretary of the Ministry of

---

[22] Interview, January 11, 2017. Nambudiripad is the former CEO of NORKWA-Roots, an office responsible for emigrants in the Kerala government.

[23] Interview, March 20, 2012.

[24] Lok Sabha Debates, Vol. 40, No. 15, August 12, 1983, 284.

Overseas Indian Affairs Alwin Didar Singh explained to me, government clearance is required only for the "eighteen countries that have less strong labor regimes. It ... attempts to protect [poor emigrants]. We create [memorandums of understanding] with [receiving] countries, through the labor wings in our embassies. We take care of working conditions, health insurance, domestic labor."[25] These poor workers must still fill out complicated paperwork and pay fees to the government—burdens not required of educated emigrants going to the same countries. Clearances are provided only in certain circumstances and are subjected to a series of requirements, which the PGE is responsible for enforcing. Although PoEs are responsible for reviewing poor migrants' employment contracts to ensure proper wages, working hours, travel expenses, and medical care, they remain notorious for denying clearances to those unwilling to pay a bribe.

Second (as I detail in the next chapter), because the CEO MDR's liberalization of poor workers' emigration has relied on temporary migration to the Gulf, the state's continuing claim to protect workers has forced it to help reincorporate poor emigrants into the Indian economy upon their return and to provide them with some welfare.

Reframing Poor Emigrants as a Financial Resource

To justify its initial liberalization of poor male emigrants, the national government in the late 1970s had to replace the Nationalist MDR's framing of India's global image as a "non-coolie nation" that forbade poor workers' emigration. Instead, the government reframed India as a "development donor" that sends workers to developing countries, such as those in the Middle East. This new frame was significant in that it articulated poor Indian emigrants as a form of national currency that could boost India's global image as a facilitator of third world solidarity, and South-South migration as a form of multilateral cooperation. In contrast to earlier decades, when government officials repeatedly framed the emigration of poor workers as an "embarrassment" for India's image on the global stage, Prime Minister Morarji Desai of the Janata Party reframed emigration as a way for India to "assist friendly developing countries in the task of development of [their] economies."[26]

But soon the government moved beyond the symbolic benefits India could attain by exporting laborers and highlighted the financial benefits of remittances, or wages earned abroad, that India could gain.[27] Thus, poor emigrants were once

---

[25] Interview, January 19, 2011.

[26] Lok Sabha Debates, Vol. 4, July 14, 1977, 132.

[27] Lok Sabha Debates, Vol. 19, No. 5, November 24, 1978.

again framed as a resource for Indian development (as they had been during the Coolie MDR). When trying to explain the long delay in writing and enacting the 1983 Act that liberalized poor workers' emigration, Minister of Labor Patil pointed to the "sensitive" nature of emigration that affects "not only workers, but also the finances and the foreign exchange and the balance' of payments of our country."[28] In other words, by legalizing poor workers' emigration, the Indian government legitimized remittances, indicating a new willingness to rely on foreign capital for domestic needs.

To retain their legitimacy as protectors of vulnerable workers, national government officials supported a 1970 effort to create new bank accounts designed for the foreign exchange deposits of remittances.[29] Members of Parliament also discussed a proposal submitted by the Kerala government to the Reserve Bank of India to use remittances to help individual emigrants purchase land and construct houses, as well as to fund rural development programs for dairy, poultry, and fish farming; village industries; irrigation; and electricity transmission and distribution.[30] Some also called on the government to regulate remittances to maintain the "dignity and self-respect of every citizen" by requiring the funds to be channeled toward employment projects rather than toward individual spending on construction and land.[31]

In an unprecedented and overt declaration of appreciation to poor emigrant workers, Minister Patil declared in 1983:

> I will also like to add Government's appreciation and also admiration for the Indian emigrant workers, who leave their homes and hearth to go to foreign lands. These workers do need help in safeguarding their interests here and also to protect them from exploitation by unscrupulous persons. They are not only earning a good name for the quality of Indian labour; but they are also helping the economy of their mother country by sending a huge amount of foreign exchange, which is badly needed for the development of the country. The present Emigration Bill is a token of our gratitude to them and should be passed urgently.[32]

---

[28] Lok Sabha Debates, Vol. 40, No. 15, August 12, 1983, 292.

[29] These are known as the Non-Resident (External) Rupee Account and the Non-Resident (External) Ordinary Rupee Account.

[30] Lok Sabha Debates, Vol. 19, No. 10, December 1, 1978.

[31] Lok Sabha Debates, August 11, 1983, Eduardo Faleiro, 331.

[32] Lok Sabha Debates, Vol. 40, No. 13, August 10, 1983, 471.

Such recognition of poor emigrants' remittances, however, represented a rare and fleeting moment in Indian parliamentary debates. Although remittances flooded India's coffers thereafter, the government's recognition of the emigrants behind the remittances quickly faded.

The Extraordinary "Success" of Remittances

The sheer volume of remittance flows, their ability to directly meet poor families' consumption needs, and their success in stabilizing India's economy during repeated economic crises helped build widespread acceptance within India for the domestic use of wages earned abroad. In my review of parliamentary debates, which are littered with critiques against globalization and foreign direct investment (FDI), not once did anyone criticize the use of emigrant remittances after the late 1970s. In short, by tapping poor workers' financial contributions, the Indian government had successfully legitimized at least one opening for foreign capital flows.

The volume of remittances that India received (then and still today) has been nothing short of extraordinary. As part of the government's new approach to tapping its emigrants for their financial contributions, politicians demanded and got data on remittances for the first time. In 1977 India earned US$934 million in remittances, and by 1980 total remittance earnings had increased to US$2.76 billion (World Bank n.d.). Today, India is the top remittance-receiving country in the world, with US$76 billion.[33] These remittances account for nearly 3% of the national GDP, 25% of income in some states, and 45% of income in some districts (World Bank n.d.). They regularly exceed the combined annual amount received from FDI, FPI, overseas development aid, and bank deposits from Indian emigrants (Reserve Bank of India 2018).[34] And they are only slightly less than the net earnings India receives from its widely acknowledged export of software services (Reserve Bank of India 2018).[35]

As noted in Chapter 1, debates abound on the impact of remittances on sending-country development. Remittances have been found to exacerbate inequalities between emigrant and nonemigrant households as well as intrahousehold gender dynamics. And evidence of their long-term impact has

[33] For the most current figure, I have cited 2019 given the extraordinary circumstances of 2020 due to the COVID-19 pandemic (World Bank n.d.)

[34] In 2019–20, FDI was US$43 billion; foreign portfolio investment was US$ 1.4 billion; overseas development aid was US$3.8 billion; and NRI deposits were US$8.6 billion (Reserve Bank of India 2018).

[35] Remittances combined with emigrants' bank deposits (which stem mainly from elite emigrants) exceed net earnings from software services.

been mixed. But India's remittances have offered the nation repeated short-term fixes. First, they are widely acknowledged as meeting the daily consumption needs of the poor, since they are transmitted directly to emigrants' families. In India, they are estimated to cover 30% to 40% of the annual household consumption expenditure for remittance-receiving households in urban and rural areas (World Bank n.d.).

Second, remittances have helped India weather multiple financial crises. The foreign exchange through remittances has been credited for offsetting India's merchandise trade deficit and keeping its current account deficits modest during the 1970s global crisis. Scholars at the time celebrated remittances for enabling India to manage the rising price of oil imports (Weiner 1982). In the 1990s, when India was recovering from the brink of financial collapse, remittances once again offered a countercyclical respite (Reserve Bank of India 2006). In 2009, when the world was reeling from the global financial crisis, India's remittances financed nearly 45% of its total trade deficit (Overseas Indian Facilitation Centre 2009).

Remittances' anticyclical power is usually attributed to the fact that India's human supply chain for low-wage labor has not been channeled toward advanced economies (the source of most global economic cycles) but by the pull of a commodity: oil. In the 1970s, Gulf countries increased their labor demand just as most of the world was suffering from economic decline. Even in the 1980s, when oil prices fell by 50% and the Gulf's demand for construction workers declined, the need for (often female-dominated) service workers (such as domestic workers, nurses, and sales staff) rose. After the 1991 Gulf War threatened to expose the vulnerability of relying on foreign funds, spiking oil prices revived the demand for reconstruction work in the Gulf. Combined with the dearth of local labor in the Gulf, Indian emigrants were soon pulled once again to the region.[36] And despite a short dip in labor demand after the 2008 financial crisis, the housing boom in Dubai further increased demand for Indian workers through the new millennium (Buckley 2012).

What makes the size and impact of India's remittance flow so extraordinary is that most of it stems from the relatively low wages that India's poorest emigrants earn. Although data on the class of remittance-sending emigrants is not available, scholars and policymakers (globally) have shown that poor emigrants tend to send remittances directly to family and loved ones at home to cover daily consumption needs. Elite Indian emigrants, on the other hand, tend to send fewer remittances since their family members' daily consumption needs are already met or their family members have emigrated

[36] For a summary of the political underpinnings of the dearth in local labor supply in the Gulf, see Castles and Delgado Wise (2007).

with them. Although elite Indian emigrants send some remittances, they are better known for sending direct investments, portfolio investments, or bank deposits (see next section). The Gulf countries (which host nearly 90% of India's poor emigrants) therefore account for more than the majority of India's total remittances (Reserve Bank of India 2018). Meanwhile, countries where the wealthiest Indian emigrants reside account for a lower share of total remittances, the United States accounting for 23% and the combined total of the United Kingdom, Canada, Australia, Germany, and Italy accounting for only 5% (Reserve Bank of India 2018).

As noteworthy is the fact that India does not give a premium exchange rate for remittances. This is in contrast to other Asian countries, as well as to the multitude of incentives the Indian government provides elite emigrants to attract their savings and investments (see next section). Also unlike other Asian countries, the Indian government does not require emigrants to send remittances. According to foreign exchange control regulations, India's only requirement is that remittances be sent through the official banking system, and balances held abroad should be repatriated when a migrant returns to India.

Paying for Racial Solidarity among Elite Emigrants

In addition to reframing India's approach to poor emigrants, the CEO MDR has altered India's approach to educated elite emigrants. As shown at the end of the previous chapter, educated emigrants had displayed their ability to affect change in India during the anti-Emergency movement by providing ideas, information, safe havens, global media campaigns, and financial support. These efforts helped restore India's democracy and made way for the new Janata government that was eager to change India's developmental strategy.

Rather than ignoring its elites abroad and claiming its self-sufficiency from the West (as in the Nationalist MDR), the post-Emergency Indian state of the late 1970s explored the option of *using* its elite emigrants, especially those residing in the wealthy receiving countries of the United States and United Kingdom, to help change India's domestic development agenda. To this end, the new government tried to tap elite emigrants' foreign investments and savings in what scholars have called "ethnic direct investment," or EDI (Ye 2014). EDI offered a first step toward gaining consensus in India for FDI. EDI was viewed within India as less threatening to India's pride and sovereignty because emigrants' "Indian" blood and affection tempered the foreignness of their financial contributions from abroad.

To attract elite emigrants' financial contributions to India, the government, especially during the transition period of the 1970s and 1980s, highlighted the racial or ethnic solidarity bonds between Indians in India and those abroad. Specifically, the government appealed to the cultural and emotional bonds domestic Indians share with its elite emigrants. As one government official noted, "Traditionally investment in the bond market is done after looking at security, liquidity, safety and returns. We will add Emotional Property to tap funds from NRIs [i.e., Non-Resident Indians]. We would appeal to their emotions and ask them to lend for development in the motherland" (Raghuram 2008). References to the "mother country" and "India's children abroad" are rampant in the parliamentary discussions on emigration during this period. Some scholars of Indian emigration still argue that "emotional ties with India" ranked as the single highest motivating factor spurring diasporic capital flows (Krishnamurty 1994: 11).

However, while appeals to racial solidarity helped attain some domestic consent for foreign investment and savings, they were not sufficient to attract emigrants' financial contributions. Therefore, the government also offered additional financial incentives, thereby effectively paying a state subsidy to elite emigrants. These incentives are often dismissed in scholarly studies on elite emigrants' savings and investments in India. But a comparison with poor workers' financial contributions through remittances (which receive no incentives) makes them impossible to ignore.

Indian Americans: Elite, Recent, and a Third Wave

The elite, recent, and steadily growing population of Indian emigrants in the United States provided an ideal test group for the Indian government's new attempts to recognize and tap elite emigrants as a financial resource. In particular, Indian Americans' elite status was expected to bring major financial contributions, while their recent and growing, status was assumed to ensure their fresh emotional, cultural, and personal connections to India.

Indian Americans today occupy strikingly elite socioeconomic class positions, earning them the appropriate title of "the other one percent" (Chakravorty, Kapur, and Singh 2017).[37] In fact, among receiving countries, the United States represents the most homogeneous concentration of Indian

---

[37] Since 1965, US immigration laws have restricted Indian immigration to an educated and professional minority (and sometimes their families). Further research should examine why (unlike other immigrant groups) poor Indians have not entered the United States through extralegal means. One reason might be that India's MDRs have never channeled the human supply chain for low-wage labor toward North America. Under the Nationalist MDR, the government tried to forbid any such supply chain. Under the CEO MDR, the government focused India's human supply chain toward the Gulf countries, and since then it has become self-reproducing. In other words, sending-country MDRs are at least as influential as receiving-country laws in shaping global migration patterns.

elites. Over 95% of Indian Americans enjoy secure legal status in the United States, and nearly 82% report being able to speak English "very well." As a result, they are well-integrated into the high-wage segment of the US labor market and represent the wealthiest and most educated ethnic group in the United States. Today, 85% of Indians in the United States over the age of 25 have more than a high school education, and 43% have a graduate degree. Their median household income is US$119,000, and their poverty rate is only 6%. On average, therefore, Indian Americans enjoy a higher socioeconomic status than Americans overall as well as Indians in India (American Community Survey 2019; Ministry of External Affairs, Non Resident Indians and Persons of Indian Origin Division 2000).[38]

As illustrated in previous chapters, the numbers of elite Indian Americans have grown. After the small "first wave" of Indian farmers, ex-soldiers, and intellectuals who migrated there in the early 1900s (see Chapter 3), Indians were barred from entering the United States between 1917 and 1965. The larger "second wave" of Indians, who arrived during the mid-1960s and 1970s, entered under the 1965 Immigration and Nationality Act (Hart-Celler), which allowed entry only to educated, tertiary-level students and professionals (and their families) (see Chapter 4). Although accompanying family members were often less educated, they still occupied middle- and upper- caste and -class status, working as business owners of gas stations, motels, and convenience stores. Second-wave Indians therefore were clearly elite relative to poor Indian emigrants in the Gulf, but they were not necessarily connected to India's domestic elite. In fact, under the Nationalist MDR, they were often shunned by India's domestic elite.

The 1990s began what is commonly known as a "third wave" of Indian immigration to the United States, which further cemented Indian Americans' elite status, as well as their particular image under the CEO MDR. In the 1990s, US employers recruited skilled Indians to staff the expanding IT sector. This recruitment catalyzed the largest wave of educated Indian immigrants to the United States in absolute terms (although its annual growth rate of nearly 10% was lower than the 20% experienced by the second wave). By 1990, the number of Indian immigrants in the United States had more than doubled since 1980, reaching 450,406; by 2000 it doubled again, reaching 1,022,552, and by 2019 it doubled yet again, reaching a new high of 2,688,000.[39] Today, Indians represent the third-largest immigrant group in

---

[38] These figures include foreign-born and US-born Indians, since the difference in socioeconomic characteristics between these two groups is minimal (with foreign-born Indians earning slightly more than US-born). Note: 67% of Indians in the United States are employed, while 30% are not in the labor force, representing a large share of dependent family members.

[39] American Community Survey (2019); Gibson and Jung (2006).

the United States (after Mexicans and Chinese), and the United States represents the second-largest receiving country of Indian emigrants (American Community Survey 2019; Ministry of External Affairs 2020).[40]

In addition to Indian Americans' elite and growing status, Indian government officials highlighted to me Indian Americans' recent temporary status in the United States. This was assumed to reflect Indian Americans' strong emotional bonds to India, which could facilitate the government's ability to tap their financial contributions. Most Indian Americans today are still first-generation immigrants. In addition, a large share of third-wave Indian immigrants arrive on temporary visas and thus must return to India after a certain period—a phenomenon known as "circular migration." This trend contrasts with earlier waves of Indian immigrants, who arrived with permanent visas and often with family members. In 2019, educated Indians accounted for an astounding 75% of US H-1B visa petitions (a coveted visa that allows skilled foreign citizens to temporarily work in the United States).[41] Nearly 80% of these were from Indian males (US Citizenship and Immigration Services 2019). (I will return to the gender implications of this trend within Indian Americans' transnational organizations in Chapter 8). Although circular migration has long been the norm among India's poor emigrants in the Gulf, it did not shape elite emigrants until the late 1990s, when new US immigration laws favored temporary work visas for educated and professional workers. Circular migration also represented the increasingly globalized nature of Indian capital in the late 1990s and 2000s.

Rather than critiquing circular migration as unfair (as many immigrant-rights activists do), Indian government officials celebrated it as a solution to the age-old problem of the country's brain drain. One government official told me

---

[40] In 2019, the population of Mexican immigrants in the United States was 11.2 million and Chinese immigrants was 2.9 million. In 2020, the United Arab Emirates hosted 3.4 million Indian immigrants, and Saudi Arabia hosted 2.4 million.

[41] In 2019, Indians accounted for 313,944 of H-1B visa petitions. Between 2007 and 2017, the annual approval rate was approximately 75%. H-1B visas are generally given for three years, with a possibility of an extension of another three. Despite periodic dips in the total number of H-1B visas granted (for example, just after the 2008 US financial crisis and in 2018 under Donald Trump's more aggressive nativist policies), the number issued today far exceeds the pre-2008 numbers. Throughout, Indians have consistently remained the single largest immigrant group to receive this visa (US Citizenship and Immigration Services 2007–17, 2018. A smaller share of educated Indian immigrants arrive in the United States on L-1 visas, which are given to managers and executives or specialized knowledge workers who are employees of an Indian firm for a period of seven years for managers and executives (L-1A visa) or five years for knowledge workers (L-1B visa). India is also the top receiving country of L-1B visas. In 2019, 18,354 L1-B visas were received by Indians (US Department of State, Bureau of Consular Affairs n.d.).

that circular migration "is the key point": "We won't have strong diasporas for long. We will just have global citizens."[42] As I show in the next chapter, the celebration of circular migration is stunted as it does not address sending states' responsibility to reincorporate emigrants upon their return. For India's poor emigrants, this has been a major strain. But for elite emigrants, government officials defended US immigration laws, reflecting the CEO MDR's new narrative around elite emigration—not as something to ignore or be ashamed of but as something India could gain from.

Reframing Elite Emigrants as a Financial Resource

As it had with poor emigrants, the Janata government reframed educated, elite emigrants as a potential solution to the economic crisis besieging the Indian economy in the 1970s. At the time, China and the Philippines were beginning to show that, in addition to yielding short-term finances in the form of remittances, elite emigrants could also be an ideal source of long-term financing through their investments and savings (Guha and Ray 2000; Ye 2016). Emigrant investments are widely understood as distinct from remittances; a 2018 report found that only 8% of remittances are invested in real property or equity (while 20% are placed in bank accounts and 60% are for family maintenance and consumption) (Reserve Bank of India 2018). Diaspora savings are also considered distinct from remittances, as the former are drawn from accumulated wealth and can be held long term, while the latter are drawn from income and are often consumed in the short term. Therefore, the Indian government heralded elite emigrants abroad as potential investors and long-term savers who could stop the bleeding of the Indian economy (Seshadri 1993). In doing so, the government offered India a second pilot experiment for foreign capital flows. But the experiment did not come for free.

Using EDI to Build Consent for FDI: 1970s and 1980s

The introduction of Indian emigrants as potential investors in India began with the Janata Party's willingness to use FDI as a solution to the economic crisis. In the face of massive trade deficits, the Indian rupee had already been devalued by 20% in 1967, and it was headed in an inexorably downward spiral through the 1970s. To save the economy from collapse, the Janata Party prioritized FDI as

---

[42] Interview, January 25, 2011. Indian government officials did acknowledge to me the unjust taxation that elite circular emigrants in the United States and United Kingdom endure because these countries refuse to exempt Indian emigrants from paying social security taxes (which they will likely never receive back due to their forced return to India). India has secured such exemptions (known as Totalizing Agreements) with 19 other receiving countries.

the centerpiece of a new industrialization drive. At the time, however, most government officials, the public, and the domestic private sector viewed FDI with great suspicion. There were few precedents for FDI-driven development; even the developmental state model of Japan, which had embraced foreign trade and international loans, had remained restrictive toward FDI.

In the face of such domestic opposition to FDI, Indian emigrant investors became an ideal compromise solution—more familiar and trustworthy in skin and blood and more likely to have a native Indian's tolerance of Indian society, but still foreign in access to resources. The government-owned State Bank of India has even been said to think Indian emigrants would be more understanding if India had a financial crisis and would agree to accept their returns in rupees if necessary (Ketkar and Dilip 2007). As early as 1975, the government's Indian Investment Center held seminars for elite Indians abroad to invite their EDI into new Indian industries (Fisher 1980). India also became one of a handful of countries that tracked EDI. Because the government sought investments in Western currencies, it appealed especially to elite emigrants in North America and Europe. As reported in *India Abroad*, a popular Indian emigrant newspaper in the United States, "The employment histories of Indian immigrants in the United States have given them money to spare, technical and management expertise . . . entrepreneurial zeal . . . and important networks within scientific, industrial and financial institutions . . . which might be of great benefit to India" (India Abroad, March 1, 1991 B:15).

The Janata Party's acknowledgment of EDI as a less threatening "foreign" vector into the global economy continued under Indira Gandhi and the resurgent Congress Party's subsequent government in 1980. Upon losing power in 1977, Gandhi herself had sought support from elite emigrants. Despite the travel restrictions the ruling Janata Party had placed on her, she received an exceptional invitation from the British government to travel to the United Kingdom, where she was lavishly hosted by the Indian emigrant and business tycoon Swaraj Paul. Paul raised funds and organized rallies and meetings for her to meet other wealthy emigrants in the United Kingdom as part of what came to be known as her "come-back tour" in London (Ye 2016). These experiences, along with the influence of her son, Sanjay Gandhi, forced her to show greater openness to global partnerships and private business than ever before.[43] Upon returning as prime minister in 1980, Gandhi appointed P. C. Alexander, an emigrant who had worked at the United Nations, International Monetary Fund, and the World Bank in the United States, as her commerce minister, which scholars have argued symbolized a major turning point in India's global leanings (Ye 2016).

---

[43] This is famously illustrated by Indira Gandhi's support of Sanjay Gandhi's involvement in the private Indian automobile company Maruthi.

In 1985, Rajiv Gandhi was unexpectedly thrust into the prime minister's seat (and leadership of the Congress Party) upon the assassination of his mother. Rajiv, who had been educated in the United Kingdom and married an Italian woman, became famous for further expanding upon the globalization trajectory begun by the Janata Party and continued by his mother. He was elected to power under a promise to bring India into the 21st century through relaxed controls on foreign capital. But soon after he took office, planners and economists resisted his initial visions, worrying that floods of foreign investors would enter Indian industry as they had in Taiwan, South Korea, Singapore, and Hong Kong (Ye 2016). Although Rajiv was thus forced to reverse his earlier efforts to open India's borders to FDI, he continued to reach out to Indian emigrants in the hopes of attracting EDI. In 1988, during his first visit to North America, he hosted the first reception for Indian emigrants living in the United States, personally encouraging them to reconnect with India.[44] He invited the leaders of all transnational organizations to the embassy for the first time. He also hosted the first Indian cultural festivals in Washington, DC, and Paris.

But the government's attempts to attract EDI could not rely on appeals to racial solidarity alone. They required material sweeteners. In sharp contrast to poor emigrants, who were demanding greater assistance in making (albeit much smaller) industrial investments at the time, elite emigrants were given government assistance (at the national and state levels) in planning and setting up new industries, acquiring raw materials and credit, becoming partners in local Indian firms, and finding Indian co-investors (since emigrants who planned to repatriate profits could not be the sole shareholders in a venture). In some cases, subnational state governments became partners in EDI ventures, offering tax concessions along with special rights to import equipment, move currency in and out of the country, and repatriate profits.

Another avenue the national government (first under the Janata Party and then under the Congress Party) used to offer material incentives in return for elite emigrants' financial contributions was adding new life into an existing, but dormant, tax category called "Non-Resident Indians," or NRIs. By the early 1980s, the term had entered the official lexicon within India and could be seen throughout the parliamentary debates. By that time, it had become a "catch-all category for Indian middle classes in the diaspora" (Shukla 1999: 26). Over the course of the decade, the definition of NRIs was extended to include family members of elite emigrants. On March 1, 1991, for example, a Citibank advertisement in India Abroad soliciting NRI deposits included all "Indian nationals and foreign passport holders of Indian origin . . . even wives of Indian citizens and those whose

---

[44] Indira Gandhi had also visited the United States in 1983 to improve relations between the US government and Indian Americans; however, the visit was not as successful.

parents or grandparents were resident in undivided India." Despite this expanded definition, the NRI term remained associated with elite emigrants.

The Indian government explicitly expressed its motivation for creating this ethnic category to tap elite emigrants' long-term financial resources for the Indian economy. To do so, the government launched new programs that constructed NRIs as a unique category that enjoyed investment privileges unavailable to local Indians or to non-Indian foreigners. Even the 1973 Foreign Exchange Regulation Act, which was designed to keep out foreign money and influence, made an exception for "Indian persons not residing in India" (i.e., NRIs), explicitly distinguishing Indians abroad from foreigners. Until 1991, Indian emigrant investors also received exemptions from the tight restrictions applied to non-Indian foreign investors. To retain its legitimacy with the majority of Indian government officials who were wary of foreign investment, the government emphasized that it would still regulate and control NRI investment in accordance with its development agenda. Nevertheless, the unique privileges offered elite emigrants material incentives and proof of the Indian government's recognition of their status at long last.

In addition to special investment privileges, the government in the 1970s offered new savings deposit schemes, again with attractive incentives and subsidized risk, to entice Indian emigrants to deposit foreign currency accounts in India for the first time. These accounts not only drew remittances; they also sought to attract capital from the accumulated savings and wealth of elite emigrants. To this end, the state-controlled Reserve Bank of India initiated two programs. The first was to create the Foreign Currency Non-Resident (External) Ordinary Account, which insured the depositor against exchange rate fluctuations by providing a fixed rate. The second was the Non-Resident (External) Rupee Account, which offered a higher interest rate without the guarantee of a fixed exchange rate. By 1982 these initiatives were expanded further, offering even higher interest rates, tax exemptions on capital gains, and even a guaranteed option of repatriating funds in the hopes of attracting more NRI deposits in Indian banks, investments in India, and buying real estate in India (Nayyar 1994; India Abroad, November 10, 1989:19). Throughout the 1980s, much like remittances, elite emigrants' savings deposits were celebrated for helping to balance India's trade deficits, maintain India's ever-precarious foreign currency reserves, and finance India's imports of industrial machinery and raw materials. By 1990, they were worth a cumulative total of US$10.412 billion (although their annual inflow was much lower than that of remittances [Reserve Bank of India 1991]).

Expanding Initiatives after the 1990s

Despite some concerns, the initial performance of emigrants' savings and investments laid the groundwork for the post-1991 government to expand India's openness to global resources from all foreigners, not just those with Indian heritage. In July 1991, Prime Minister P. V. Narasimha Rao of the Congress Party relaxed FDI regulations for the first time since the mid-1970s to allow foreign firms to hold a controlling 51% interest in companies in India. Rather than allowing only Indian emigrants to send foreign investments, the government now provided access to *all* foreign investors to engage in Indian real estate, stock markets, and even certain "strategic" industries. Although emigrants were instrumental in laying this groundwork, their success ironically lost them many of the unique investment privileges they had enjoyed during the early years of the CEO MDR.

However, even in the post-liberalization era, resistance against FDI and the global trade of goods and services remained alive in India. EDI and emigrants' savings programs continued to serve a useful and more acceptable vector through which to tap foreign funds through the 1990s and 2000s. The government thus expanded its programs to attract EDI and diaspora savings and launched new programs to attract a new financial flow from elite emigrants—that is, diaspora bonds. Once again, the government instituted a plethora of incentive packages to attract these financial flows.

First, the government built new institutions designed to facilitate elite emigrants' investments. However, these institutions did not succeed (and were, in fact, shut down by 2015), and they were costly to build in terms of government finances, time, and personnel. In 2011, the government funded a new subunit under the new Ministry of Overseas Indian Affairs, called the Overseas Indian Facilitation Centre (OIFC), that created an online business networking portal designed to answer questions for potential diaspora investors; published articles on how to invest in the Indian stock market, buy land, and handle Indian FDI regulations; sent e-letters to overseas subscribers and embassies to explain opportunities in India; and held roadshows abroad with the ministry's secretary, Indian business owners, and potential investors in the United Kingdom and United States. Although OIFC's CEO, Shefali Chaturvedi, underlined that it does not focus solely on investments, their work was geared almost entirely toward investment attraction.[45] OIFC viewed remittances as an already steady stream of income for India, and thus did not aim to attract remittances but rather worked to divert them from bank deposits into investments.[46] Echoing almost the same sentiments expressed by the Janata Party and the Congress Party of

---

[45] Interview, January 20, 2011.
[46] Interview, January 20, 2011.

the 1970s and 1980s, OIFC staff articulated to me more than two decades later that they target elite emigrants as financial resources. As one executive at OIFC explained, "We are geared toward diasporas in developed countries, since the diaspora in the Caribbean have very different needs than economic engagement... [W]e care about business-related queries."[47]

Some subnational governments also offered incentive packages to attract investments from Indian emigrants in the 1990s and 2000s. India's federalist structure allows investments to come directly to state governments (unlike remittances, which are handled by the national government). For example, the government of Andhra Pradesh, the home state of a large proportion of elite third-wave emigrants working in the US IT sector, created a state-level investment board and offered customized services from the state government's Department of Industries and Commerce for large-scale investments in food processing and textiles. Although these are not exclusively designed for NRIs, T. S. Appa Rao, secretary of industries and commerce, explained to me that NRIs often benefit the most from them, since NRI investments are often above the required cap placed on foreign investments.[48] Officials in the state governments of Andhra Pradesh and Gujarat also told me of intentions to draw NRI investments to state-based research-and-development facilities, education centers, and software technology parks.

Second, the government offered additional incentives to attract more diaspora savings. In January 2000, it agreed to relax currency controls and replaced the Foreign Exchange Regulation Act with the Foreign Exchange Management Act, enabling Indian emigrants who did not hold Indian citizenship to deposit savings in India. In July 2002, the Reserve Bank of India liberalized capital accounts, allowing NRIs to repatriate up to US$230,000 from Non-Resident (External) Ordinary Accounts to cover medical and educational expenses, including an annual amount of US$100,000 accrued from the sale of property held for at least 10 years. Scholars have celebrated Indian emigrants' savings deposits. For example, some have noted with a slightly misleading flair (because they draw on figures of the cumulative total rather than annual flows), "Although Indian immigrants account for 0.1% of the US population, they provide 10% of India's national income" (Koshy and Radhakrishnan 2008: 305).

Finally, the Indian government in the 1990s introduced NRI bonds (with a five-year maturity) to attract elite emigrants' long-term financial contributions. Bonds differ from saving deposits in that they cannot be withdrawn at any time, so they can be used by the government to finance investment. Bonds are considered less degrading for a country than asking for foreign aid, and bonds boost a country's sovereign credit ratings. Moreover, they have been used to

---

[47] Interview, Ankit Gupta, January 20, 2011.
[48] Interview, May 24, 2011.

assist India during moments of economic crisis. In 1992, following the balance-of-payments crisis that spurred India's official 1991 liberalization efforts, the government (with Manmohan Singh of the Congress Party as finance minister) issued India Development Bonds, which offered emigrants attractive yields and raised approximately US$1.6 billion (Ketkar and Dilip 2007). To market the bonds, the government promised NRIs they could "own [their] dream house in India," "secure old age retirement," and "provide income for [their] family in India" (India Abroad, January 25, 1991a:7). In 1998, the government launched Resurgent India Bonds to appeal for emigrants' financial contributions following global sanctions on India due to the government's testing of nuclear weapons. These bonds raised approximately US$4.5 billion. In 2000, the government launched the India Millennium Development Bonds, which raised US$5.5 billion. In 2013, the government issued a swap facility that raised US$30 billion (Reserve Bank of India 2013).[49]

As with NRI savings, NRI bonds resulted in substantial fanfare and have been framed as an ideal win-win solution for India's economic needs. Emigrants received above-market returns, and India could pay a below-market country risk premium. On February 29, 2000, a *New York Times* article entitled "Web Moghuls' Return Passage to India" became a major source of pride for the Indian American community (Dugger 2000). As Priya Viswanath (2000: 12) writes, "The Silicon boys had responded to an [Indian] government that had challenged them to raise a billion dollars for the institutes that educated them."

The Less Extraordinary Flow of Diaspora Investments and Savings

While the celebrations of elite emigrants' financial contributions are not without merit, they miss important inequalities built into them, which can be exposed only when we compare them to poor emigrants' financial contributions. In comparison, elite Indian emigrants' financial contributions have been less than extraordinary.

First, elite emigrants' savings and investments have cost the government more to attract (in the form of incentives) than have remittances. Efforts to draw elite emigrants' investments and savings have included several incentives from the Indian government, effectively providing elite emigrants with a subsidy that was never offered to poor emigrants. While markets will suggest that such incentives

---

[49] This effort was not limited to NRIs. Although these bonds targeted infrastructure financing in India, less than one-third of the funds were used for such financing, with the remainder entering general revenues.

are part of the price, a moral compass might suggest similar incentives/subsidies be paid to poor workers who must send financial remittances to India for the sake of their families' survival.

Second, elite emigrants' investments and savings have been more volatile than remittances. According to one estimate, from 1975 to 2018 the variation of annual flows of remittances was 49.1, whereas the annual flow variation of net NRI deposits was 62.8 and net FDI inflows was 57.6 (Kapur 2018). To make the programs attractive, the government allowed depositors to withdraw their funds from India at any time. Moreover, elite emigrants' location in wealthy receiving countries ensures their financial contributions will likely reflect global market booms and busts rather than offering a countercyclical financial flow, as poor workers in the Gulf often have.

The volatility of NRI deposits was painfully experienced during the 1991 Gulf War. In addition to spiking oil prices, the Indian economy was facing inflationary pressures, overvalued exchange rates, and rising fiscal deficits. Commercial lenders were shying away, and India's credit rating in the international loan market plummeted as a result. In this context, elite emigrants abruptly pulled their savings, causing nearly US$1 billion in NRI deposits to exit India. This loss offset the earlier gains made from emigrant capital during the late 1970s and 1980s. Most elite emigrants cited unease about the Indian economy, while some also expressed frustration with the severe exchange restrictions in India. The Gulf War thus showed that elite emigrants' savings deposits during the 1980s did more to delay rather than avert the crisis. As V. Krishnamurty (1994: 7) eloquently argues, there are two different trajectories and class implications for the varying types of emigrant assistance: "Remittances bring down the measured deficit, while deposits help to finance it." Indeed, the sudden loss of foreign exchange from elite emigrants' savings deposits (combined with a concurrent drop in remittances due to the forced repatriation of poor emigrants) during the Gulf War caused foreign exchange reserves to fall so low that the Indian government could not afford essential imports. The resulting balance-of-payments crisis eventually forced India to accept a series of economic reforms as part of a loan package from the International Monetary Fund and the World Bank in 1991—thereby launching the official start of India's version of neoliberalism (Nayyar 1994).

Third, the volume of elite emigrants' financial contributions is less than poor workers' remittances, which is especially surprising given the enormous disparities in poor versus elite emigrants' salaries. If we take into account India's public expenditure on elite emigrants' education, as well as the tuition money paid from India to foreign universities for elite emigrants' foreign education, elite emigrants' financial contributions dim even further. While celebrations of diaspora savings usually focus on cumulative totals, a more accurate measure is the annual flow, which has been consistently one-tenth (or less) than the annual remittance flows; in some years, it has been negative, representing an outflow from India's reserves.

Diaspora investments have been particularly low, especially relative to other countries, such as China. In 1989, India's former minister of finance announced at a seminar for Indian business owners that 957 NRI project proposals, totaling a mere US$240 million, had been sanctioned between 1983 and 1988 (The Hindu, July 13,1989:9). From 1991 to 2003, only 4.2% of Indian FDI came from NRIs.[50] The remaining 96% came from multinational corporations. Although many of these corporations are headed by or heavily staffed by Indian emigrants, the true impact that emigrants have had on corporations' FDI is difficult to measure. By 2001, NRI investment totaled only $US0.2 billion, while Chinese diaspora investment totaled US$32 billion.

Even at the subnational levels, where ethnic, linguistic, and cultural ties are particularly tight, the results have been thin. As noted by the Gujarat government, "The Indian figures [of diaspora investments] look dramatically puny in comparison to China. . . . [I]nfrastructure aid by the Gujarati diaspora . . . has not been experienced so far . . . and large-scale business investment by Non-Resident Gujaratis has not happened in a very major way" (Singh 2011: 2). In Andhra Pradesh, government officials expressed a similar sentiment. T. S. Appa Rao, secretary of industries and commerce in the state government, complained, "Our NRIs are mainly professional, so the investment is not so deliberate. They are not entrepreneurs. So they are investing in real estate. But this is totally private."[51] OIFC's CEO Chaturvedi said her partnerships with state governments had not yielded much in terms of investment, and some state governments were even turning away diaspora investments. By 2015, the low levels of emigrants' EDI forced OIFC to shut down. Shortly after its closure, Chaturvedi explained, "Originally the vision was to make OIFC for profit and self-sustainable. But after three years of experience, we realized it's going to mainly be about promotion. We can't change the client. We try to connect them to profitable service providers, but after getting questions answered, when it's time to make a deal, they retreat to 'think about it.' So we saw we will always have to be funded by the government."[52]

Scholars have attributed India's relative failure to attract EDI to elite Indian emigrants' occupational status as professionals in education, health services, and engineering. Unlike wealthy Chinese emigrants, most of whom are entrepreneurs, scholars argue that Indian professional emigrants are less likely

[50] Interview, OIFC CEO Shefali Chaturvedi, January 20, 2011.
[51] Interview, May 24, 2011.
[52] Interview, January 20, 2011.

to engage in direct business investments and are less likely to have the necessary personal connections with Indian businesses and local officials (Ye 2014).
Scholars comparing China and India have also shown that there is no "India
Circle" of manufacturing production chains fueled by ethnic business networks
(as there is among the Chinese diaspora) (Tsai 2010; Wei 2005). Indian government officials expressed similar theories about the impact of Indian Americans'
occupational status. Chaturvedi explained, "We don't only focus on high net
worth individuals. We want to make [everyone] feel welcome and invited. So
we need to understand the profile of the diaspora. If they were all entrepreneurs,
then I would talk business. But the diaspora is largely professional in the US ... so
we also care about little investments. Not just the huge FDIs."[53]

* * *

As I have shown in this chapter, despite the clear vulnerabilities in its new emigration approach, as well as the devastating economic crisis that it failed to avert
through global resources, the CEO MDR from the late 1970s onward attained
domestic consent to liberalize the emigration of workers and tap both poor and
elite emigrants as a legitimate vector through which to channel foreign financial flows into India. Poor emigrants under the CEO MDR have yielded massive financial contributions, which have been relatively cost-free for the Indian
government. The CEO MDR has successfully reframed state protection of poor
emigrants as increased liberalization for most and continued restrictions for
some. And the state has not provided poor emigrants with financial incentives for
their remittances or rights-based protections. In contrast, elite emigrants' financial contributions have paled beside their massive salaries. Moreover, they have
been volatile and costly for the government to attract. An important question,
therefore, remains: Given the uneven impact and vulnerabilities of emigrants'
financial contributions, how has the CEO MDR managed to survive? Let us now
turn to answering this question.

[53] Interview, January 20, 2011.

6

The CEO MDR's Elite Class Pact of "Global Indians"

Chapter 5 explained exactly how and through whom the CEO MDR was able to attain domestic consent for a colonial-era-like MDR that is utilizing poor and elite emigrants' labor as an economic resource to fuel India's development. Specifically, it showed the vital role that both poor and elite emigrants played, starting in the late 1970s, in the CEO MDR's ability to liberalize emigration and valorize the global movement of people and capital. Doing so deepens our understanding of neoliberalism by exposing its strikingly solid foundation. But Chapter 5 also exposed the deep class distinctions the CEO MDR has instituted between poor and elite emigrants' financial contributions and the weaknesses underlying this strategy. Poor emigrants' financial returns have been massive. But to retain legitimacy, the CEO MDR remains tethered to an electoral expectation of state protection for "the vulnerable" that it has yet to meet. And to attract elite emigrants' financial contributions, the CEO MDR extended costly incentives in return for lukewarm and volatile returns. Chapter 5 thus ended with a puzzle: How and why has the CEO MDR survived despite the vulnerabilities experienced by relying on emigrants' foreign financial resources?

This chapter answers this question by detailing an aspect of the CEO MDR that makes it historically unique: since the late 1970s, the Indian government has tapped elite emigrants' social and ideological contributions in the form of their ideas, ideals, tastes, networks, and technical expertise. Unlike the government's efforts to tap elite and poor emigrants' financial resources, the government's attempt to tap emigrants' social and ideological contributions have only targeted elites in the wealthy capitalist countries of the West, particularly the United States. Doing so has necessarily shaped the content of the social contributions received.

To draw elite emigrants' social contributions, the Indian government first reframed elite emigrants in the West as successful role models for a new India.

The Migration-Development Regime. Rina Agarwala, Oxford University Press. © Oxford University Press 2022.
DOI: 10.1093/oso/9780197586396.003.0006

Government officials met with these emigrants abroad, granted them new awards that publicly recognized their achievements and experiences with capitalist market economies, and used them as transmitters to improve India's bilateral relations with their host countries. These status markers encouraged elite emigrants in the West to reverse their earlier resentment toward the Indian government and join it in shaping a new development agenda. To this end, elite emigrants were invited back to India to serve in powerful policy positions in the national government, forge partnerships with and even start businesses and social organizations, and interact (much more than before) with domestic elites as policy advisors, business partners, and philanthropists. Similarly, the government encouraged educated and professional Indians to emigrate to work in Western private companies or in foreign branches of Indian social organizations, framing them as what Ajantha Subramanian (2015: 291) has eloquently exposed as "India's greatest export, widely understood to exemplify the country's comparative advantage in the global marketplace."

These global exchanges facilitated new partnerships between Indian and foreign-based firms and social organizations, increased foreign trade, and facilitated the exchange of ideas in three new areas—in all of which elite Indian emigrants were framed as experts. First, they helped launch export-oriented private businesses within India in sectors such as healthcare, telecommunications, and software—the very same industries in which elite emigrants were employed. Second, they helped launch a private, voluntary sector for social welfare in India that drew from the US model and helped legitimize emigrants' involvement in India's economic development and poverty alleviation. Third, during the 1990s they were used to expand India's real estate sector in investment and architectural styles that mimicked those in the United States. The impressive performance of the new private corporations, the growth of voluntary organizations, and the soaring real estate prices during this period, combined with the new personal and professional networks forged between domestic and emigrant elites, helped convince domestic elites (in government and in business) to eventually welcome, value, and even celebrate Western/American tastes and their underlying ideals of globalization, privatization, and self-sufficiency.

It is this aspect of the CEO MDR, I argue, that has exacerbated unique class inequities and ensured its reproduction. Most important, elite emigrants' social and ideological contributions and exchanges with Indian elites in government and business have forged *a powerful new class pact* among "global Indians" who dominate India's development agenda and attain material wealth and status in the process. For the first time in India's history, the state has deliberately folded its elite emigrants into its domestic elite pact. The CEO MDR, therefore, is much more than a simple turn to "free" global markets. It has ensured the Indian state orchestrates and benefits from the newfound privatization and globalization of business, social welfare, and real estate, as well as a celebration of individual (rather than national) self-sufficiency.

But elite class pacts in a democracy require consent from below. Poor emigrants, despite their massive financial remittances, do not enjoy any power to collaborate with or shape India's development agenda through their social contributions under the CEO MDR. As I detail in this chapter, while the elite class pact cemented consent for a new development ideology among domestic elites in the 1970s and 1980s, during the 1990s and 2000s the government tried to secure poor emigrants' consent to elite ideals of high-tech modernity, private-sector development, self-sufficiency, and hard work. To do so, the CEO MDR has combined poor and wealthy emigrants into a single, cross-class identity of "the Indian migrant," thereby occluding the class differences in emigrants' needs and interests and deflecting attention away from wage labor. To construct this identity, the government (1) built new single-point institutions that offer services to both poor and elite emigrants and transmit elite ideals for all migrants and (2) reframed poor emigrant workers as "entrepreneurs" and CEOs. Given India's long history of legally distinguishing emigrants by class, this attempt to combine emigrant classes into a single category is significant. But given the minimal impact these efforts have had on improving poor emigrants' material needs, the CEO MDR has also been forced to launch paternalist welfare programs, thereby ironically resuscitating the image of the "vulnerable migrant" it had worked so hard to obliterate. Chapters 7 and 8 will unpack how poor and elite emigrants have experienced and responded to the CEO MDR.

Employing a Currency of Status Recognition with Elite Emigrants

To attract elite emigrants' social contributions, the national government since the late 1970s has employed a currency of status recognition, reframing elite emigrants' successes and their host country's ideals as role models for a new India to emulate. This marked a stark shift from earlier MDRs, where the state controlled (under the Coolie MDR) or dismissed (under the Nationalist MDR) its elite emigrants.

Central to this approach was building relations with elite Indian emigrants in wealthy capitalist countries, particularly the United States. Upon entering office in 1977, the Janata Party "pledged to strengthen ties with the U.S.A. . . . to help correct the grave imbalances in the world economic order" (Kumar 1978: 590). Rebalancing India's already strong relationship with the USSR with a strengthened relationship with the United States was considered a way "to establish a new and equitable international economic order," which would ensure "peace as the only effective means of salvation for all human beings . . . and for the safety of the planet itself" (Kumar 1978: 589). The CEO MDR's focus on the United States continues to this day. As G. Gurucharan, then CEO of the Indian Council of Overseas Employment,[1] told me, "When we say 'diaspora,' we really mean Indo-US people. . . . To me, Indian Americans are the *ideal* diaspora."[2] Even the Annual Report of the Ministry of Overseas Indian Affairs (MOIA 2015: 8) listed one of its four key policy imperatives as "Anchor diasporas' initiatives in the [United] States."[3]

From the start, the CEO MDR has used Indian Americans to help build new ideals within India—ideals the United States represented. Janata Party leaders therefore traveled to the United States to build upon the diaspora connections they had earlier formed during the anti-Emergency movements. During these trips, Janata officials appealed to American ideals of democracy, capitalism, anti-Islamism, and anti-Communism, claiming they shared these ideals with Indian Americans. As Subramanian Swamy, then president of the Janata Party, former cabinet minister of commerce, law, and justice, and staunch supporter of right-wing Hindu politics, explained to me, "My work with Janata abroad is ideological. . . . We join on ideology. We preach about free market, against Islamic rule, for democracy. All this helps us gel with America. We are pro-US." He went on to extol Indian Americans as an asset to India: "The Indians in the US give us [the Indian government] names and access to a network."[4]

At the micro level, Indian Americans were celebrated for their work in the private sector, requiring less government involvement in the corporate sector as well as in the voluntary sector of philanthropy. Indian Americans' success in the world's most profitable private market became an ideal vector through which the CEO MDR could promote the American values of individual "success" through "hard work," education, and privatization within India. As India's former finance minister P. Chidambaram said, "The phenomenal success achieved by Indians abroad by practicing free enterprise meant that if Indians were allowed

---

[1] The Indian Council of Overseas Employment was a think-tank based in the Ministry of Overseas Indian Affairs that examined how India should address issues of migration.

[2] Interview, January 25, 2011, emphasis in original. Although this book focuses on elite emigrants in the United States, those in the United Kingdom, and to a lesser extent in the Middle East, were also pursued during this period and deserve further study. For example, Dhirubhai Ambani worked in Yemen before returning to India to launch Reliance Industries, now a Fortune 500 company, and Indians in the United Kingdom began Hinduja Brothers.

[3] The other three imperatives are listed as (1) offer customized solutions to meet the varied expectations of the overseas Indian community; (2) bring a strategic dimension to India's engagement with its diaspora; and (3) tap the investible diasporic community for knowledge and resources in diversified economic, social, and cultural areas.

[4] Interview, March 14, 2011.

to function in an open market, they could replicate some of that success here [in India]" (Chidambaram 2002, quoted in Chakravorty, Kapur, and Singh 2017: 273).

The Indian government under the CEO MDR thus sought to tap Indian Americans' knowledge of American business practices, management techniques, and entrepreneurial experience, as well as their "world-class" professional skills, especially in medicine and IT. Within India, elite emigrants became known as the "knowledge diaspora." Government officials I interviewed repeatedly pointed out Indian Americans' high socioeconomic status in the United States as a sign of their success, their power, and thus their "worth" to India. One official commented, "Indian Americans have become significant in the knowledge sector—academia, IT, science, and some business. So, they are very influential."[5]

Through the 1970s and 1980s, the Janata Party and subsequently the Congress Party encouraged elite emigrants' emotional bonds to India, offering them as role models within India and inviting their involvement in shaping India's development trajectory. This approach echoes that used in other countries, such as China (Zhou, Wang, and Lee 2010). Elite emigrants were permitted to share and promote their ideals while living permanently abroad or upon their return to India (a phenomenon that grew in the 1990s due to new visa restrictions in receiving countries). In return, the national government promised to change Indian entry laws to allow these emigrants (even those with foreign citizenship) easier return access to the "motherland." The government also sponsored seminars for overseas Indians to meet with government officials and appointed the Indian Council for Cultural Relations to directly handle issues concerning overseas Indians.

At first, suspicions against American-style capitalism that valorized entrepreneurship, free markets, and the private sector remained strong within the Indian government. To ease into the shift, the government first showcased elites moving to developing countries. Prime Minister Morarji Desai of the Janata Party heroicized them as an "export of our technical know-how," while vilifying those who go "merely to earn more money by better employment." Echoing the defensive stance of the Nationalist MDR, Desai reiterated that India cannot compete with developed country wages and will "not suffer [when the elites leave]. . . . We have enough . . . technical people [in India]."[6] Following this, the Janata Party lifted a short-term ban that had been placed on some nurses and doctors, shifting the understanding of their emigration as a drain on India to an opportunity for geopolitical gain. Minister of Health and Family Welfare Jagdambi Prasad Yadav

[5] Interview, January 25, 2011.
[6] Lok Sabha debates, Vol. 18, No. 23, August 16, 1978, 6.

announced, "The deputation of nurses abroad is being allowed where such deputation is considered by the Ministry of External Affairs to be in the interest of our political and economic relations with the country concerned."[7]

These initial actions paved the way for the Indian government to eventually use the success of elite Indians abroad as a reflection of a more globalized, developed India. As Alwin Didar Singh, secretary of MOIA, explained to me, "As the Indian diaspora's brand increases, it helps India's brand increase. . . . If the diaspora assists us in making bridges, then India benefits. . . . The global Indian is a tool of 'soft power.' When the diaspora brings Bollywood, fashion, music, culture, and food to others, we are converting people to seeing India. . . . We need tentacles into the diaspora, because they are our cultural centers."[8] Similarly, Shefali Chaturvedi, CEO of the government-affiliated Overseas Investment Facilitation Center, spoke about the US diaspora as a uniformly impressive group that showcases the image of a successful, globalized ideal: "Many more vistas opened up with our global, affluent, capable, well-respected people doing so well throughout the world. . . . The dot-com boom very much contributed to 'brand India.'"[9] In other words, Indian government officials under the CEO MDR embraced elite emigrants' successes as a boost, rather than an embarrassment, for India's global image. This marked a stark shift from the geographically bounded definition of India guiding the Nationalist MDR. But it also marked a shift from standard accounts of transnationalism. *The CEO MDR's understanding of transnationalism for India was limited to elite emigrants, particularly those residing in the West.*

In the year 2000, the government formally accelerated its efforts to tap elite emigrants' social contributions by celebrating their immense social and political capital. It created a new NRI/PIO Division within the Ministry of External Affairs because, as the MEA noted in its Annual Report that year, "The Government felt that the approach to NRI/PIOs could not be merely investment centered. *A wider multi-faceted approach was needed,* including political, cultural, economic, consular and other matters" (Ministry of External Affairs 2001: 135).[10] The report singled out emigrants' "political and economic clout . . . in the USA, UK, and Canada"; their income, which the report claimed was "equal to India's GDP (approximately US$300 billion)"; their "advanced technical skills and expertise," which "ha[d] secured [their] global recognition"; and their "vast wealth and entrepreneurial skills" that enabled them to "contribute to India's development and India's socio-economic transformation to an advanced and modern

---

[7] Lok Sabha Debates, 6th Series, Vol. 7, No. 17, December 8, 1977, 142.

[8] Interview, January 25, 2011.

[9] Interview, January 20, 2011.

[10] Emphasis added by author.

economy and society" (Ministry of External Affairs 2001: 136). That year, the government also established a High-Level Committee to examine Indian emigrants (across classes and receiving contexts) and to suggest new policy and organizational frameworks.

Based on the High-Level Committee's 2001 report, the national government launched a series of initiatives designed to recognize the status of elite emigrants with 12 public awards. J. C. Sharma, a member of the Committee, explained, "Ego satisfaction was also key, so we set up the awards."[11] In 2003, the national government inaugurated an annual conference, Pravasi Bharatiya Divas, or Overseas Indian Day, a high-level, glossy event designed to foster state bonds with emigrants. The event has also become known for marking the annual Pravasi Bharatiya Samman Awards that the president of India bestows upon Indian emigrants in recognition of their technical, social, and political contributions to the country. It is notable that these awards are not given for financial contributions.[12] As Prime Minister Atal Bihari Vajpayee of BJP noted in his opening speech to the first Indian diaspora conference in New Delhi in 2003, "I have always been conscious of the need for India to be sensitive to the hopes, aspirations and concerns of its vast diaspora. We invite you, not only to share our vision of India in the new millennium, but also to help us shape its contours. We do not want only your investment. We also want your ideas. We do not want your riches; we want the richness of your experience. We can gain from the breadth of vision that your global exposure has given you."[13]

Two years later, Prime Minister Manmohan Singh of the Congress Party echoed his predecessor's sentiments: "I would like you to reach out and invest in a new India. Invest not just financially, but intellectually, socially, culturally and, above all, emotionally. . . . Come engage with India" (NDTV 2007). Such recognition included invitations to elite emigrants to return to work in and for the Indian government. Although suspicion and resentment toward elites abroad remained in place within the government, one official explained this as a matter of transition: "I think this is stupid pride. In a global world, why are we creating barriers for Indians to return?"[14]

---

[11] Interview, March 15, 2011.

[12] Contributions eligible for the award include tangible support for India's causes and concerns; building closer links between India, the overseas Indian community, and their country of residence; supporting social and humanitarian causes in India or abroad; fostering welfare of the local Indian community; philanthropic and charitable work; eminence in one's field or outstanding work that has enhanced India's prestige in the country of residence/work.

[13] For the full speech, see Government of India (2002).

[14] Gurucharan interview, January 25, 2011.

While the conference and the awards were subsequently extended to include poor emigrants across all countries, there is little doubt that the original impetus, as well as the ongoing structure and cost of the conference, was designed to target wealthy emigrants in the West. This focus was laid bare at the inaugural Overseas Indian Day conference, when the Indian government announced a sweeping change of citizenship regulations, allowing dual citizenship for Indians living in the United Kingdom, Canada, Australia, Finland, Ireland, Italy, the United States, the Netherlands, Singapore, Australia, and New Zealand, but not for Indians living in the Middle East (including the Gulf region), Africa, Latin America, or the Caribbean. Although the policy was extended in 2006 to allow dual citizenship for all overseas Indians who had migrated after 1950, the initial message of elite privilege was clear (Kudaisya 2006).

Channeling Elite Social Contributions

At a material level, elite emigrants' social contributions under the CEO MDR have been channeled into three areas within India: the private corporate sector, the private voluntary sector for social welfare, and real estate.

Expanding India's Private Services Sector (1970s–present)

Under the CEO MDR, the Indian government has tapped elite emigrants' social contributions (in the form of knowledge, ideas, linkages with external markets and networks) to help expand the country's private services sector. Elite emigrants' positions in private US-based service companies (as senior managers, founders, and CEOs) offered Indian capital and Indian elites a ready source of information when the government launched a private, globalized service economy. In particular, Indian Americans were tapped for their technical and business management expertise, and especially their valorization and understanding of privatization.

Over time, the CEO MDR has facilitated business exchanges and partnerships between Indian and emigrant capital and invited emigrant Indians to serve in key policy positions within the government—thereby creating a diffuse class of "global Indians" who traveled easily across the transnational sphere. The result has been a private service sector in India that represents not only the fastest growing but also the most export-oriented sector of the economy, making India the pioneer of a new development strategy known as "export-oriented services" which is contrasted to East Asia's wildly successful export-oriented industrialization approach (Kuruvilla and Ranganathan 2008). The class pact between domestic Indians and India's elite emigrants was fundamental to this rise. It is no coincidence that India's services sectors represent the very sectors that elites are employed in abroad, including medicine and (most notably) IT.[15] Despite India's relatively lower rates of EDI, India's software and financial service sectors are said to be more open to FDI today than China's sectors due to the partnerships forged between domestic and emigrant Indians (Ye 2016). And unlike Chinese EDI (which is 70% in manufacturing and 15% in real estate), Indian EDI is overwhelmingly geared toward the country's service sector, while some is also in real estate (Tsai 2010). Some scholars have even attributed the network effects of elite Indian entrepreneurs and professionals within US corporations to the fact that the United States is now India's largest trade and investment partner (Chakravorty, Kapur, and Singh 2017).

Efforts to tap elite emigrants' social contributions to build India's private service sector began in the early 1980s with a focus on science and medicine. In 1980, the Indian government launched two programs through its Council of Scientific and Industrial Research: Transfer of Knowledge Know-how through Expatriate Nationals, which operated through the UN Development Program, and Interface with Non-Resident Indians in Science and Tech, to attract elite emigrants to return to India and share their knowledge in science. In the mid-1980s, the government sought Indian Americans' expertise to build several large, lush, private medical institutes and hospitals in Indian cities. The most famous of these are the Apollo chain. These hospitals promised advanced equipment, expertise, diagnoses, and care, but because they were private they relied on a fee-for-service model and were thus geared toward elites in India and Westerners engaging in medical tourism. They were largely funded by a private-public partnership of Indian emigrants' funding and subsidies from the government in the form of cheap (sometimes free) land, water, electric power, telephone connections, and access roads. As well, the hospitals were staffed by emigrants in management and medical positions. When first built, these hospitals drew heavy criticism from the Indian population, who critiqued the use of state funds for goods that were inaccessible for most Indians (Lessinger 1992). But today they are valorized as exemplary of India's "world-class" medical services.

The mid-1980s also witnessed increased interactions between Indian Americans and India's emerging IT sector. Among the earliest initiatives was a system criticized as "body shopping" or the export of "techno-coolies," in which Indian software companies sent their IT workers to US firms to conduct

---

[15] According to the National Association of Software and Services Companies, which functions as the trade body and chamber of commerce of the industry, the IT and services industry is subdivided into four segments: IT services and software; IT-enabled business process outsourcing; hardware; and engineering services, R&D, and software products. For a detailed review of this sector in India, see Kuruvilla and Ranganathan (2008).

specified short-term projects. These projects lasted a few weeks to several months. The Indian company managed the export and return of these workers, and Indian Americans served as important intermediaries, connecting US-based companies with Indian companies, vetting Indian workers, and encouraging Indian workers to travel to the United States to become integrated into American companies. By 1988, 65% of Indian software production was said to be made through the export of their workers to US companies (Xiang 2011). Soon Indian Americans began a second initiative to connect Indians with American IT companies by encouraging their US employers to open a center in India and hire local Indians. The first such center was established in 1984 in Bangalore by Texas Instruments and General Electric. This model grew through the mid-1990s. Indian Americans often traveled to India to manage the centers. Transnational diaspora organizations, such as The IndUS Entrepreneurs and the Silicon Valley Indian Professional Associations were important bridges between elite emigrants in the United States and IT entrepreneurs in India. By 2002, India had become the preferred destination for the relocation of software production and IT-enabled services, capturing 24% of the global market. As a result of this practice, body shopping declined and by 2003 accounted for only 43% of IT exports—a significant drop from prior years (Saxenian 2005).

By the early 2000s, the elite class pact had begun to solidify between Indians at home and abroad. Indians had become a dominant ethnic group in the US IT sector. According to one study conducted in 2006, Indians founded nearly 16% of engineering and IT firms in California's Silicon Valley, which is more than immigrants from Britain, China, Taiwan, and Japan combined.[16] These Indians were highly educated, with 96% holding BAs and 75% holding MAs or PhDs. Importantly, many were recent arrivals and thus had fresh personal and emotional connections to India; 88% had earned their BA in India (relative to only 35% of Chinese BA holders working in the United States) (Kumari 2010). A significant share was in the United States on a temporary visa and were thus expected to return to India, where IT had become a dominant and fast-growing sector. According to another survey of elite returnees, although 90% did not hold the most senior management positions in the US IT sector, 44% found such senior positions in India's IT sector, and 61% said opportunities in India were better than in the United States (Kumari 2010). Therefore, many Indians in the United States returned to India to start new companies while maintaining their social and professional ties to the United States.

---

[16] For more citations of surveys on Indian American entrepreneurs in IT, see pp. 188–89 in Chakravorty, Kapur, and Singh (2017).

By tapping Indian Americans' social contributions and facilitating their exchange with Indian capital, the CEO-MDR used them as exemplars of successful private-sector professionals and entrepreneurs who were leading the world's most advanced, profitable service industries (especially in IT). Of course, Indian Americans also included middle-class small business owners of gas stations, motels, ethnic grocery stores, and restaurants. Although less glamorous and glorified than the jet-set crowd of elite Indians working in IT, this group also exemplified the CEO MDR's ideals of successful private-sector entrepreneurs. One study, for example, found that although Indian Americans did not have higher entrepreneurship rates than other ethnic groups, their business earnings far exceeded those of businesses owned by whites, Japanese, Korean, and Chinese, and many had expanded into franchise ownership (Chakravorty, Kapur, and Singh 2017: 190, Table 5.1).[17] As I detail in Chapter 8, the CEO MDR's widespread application to Indian Americans has shaped their fairly consistent support for liberalized global markets in India, despite their within-class differences.

In addition to facilitating business partnerships between Indian domestic and emigrant capital, the Indian government since the early 1980s has employed elite return emigrants in elite policy positions. In particular, emigrants have been invited to help reform Indian markets and facilitate the growth of private corporations. Unlike in the Coolie MDR (where the state exploited poor and educated emigrants) or the Nationalist MDR (where the state claimed to protect poor emigrants and ignore elite emigrants), therefore, *the state in the CEO MDR has orchestrated and joined the elite class pact that includes elite emigrants abroad.*

Rajiv Gandhi began this trend when he employed a group of emigrants, known as "lateral entrants," to serve in his cabinet and the Planning Commission to promote private business and policies that reduced government regulation (Kohli 2012; Shastri 1997). Several members of this group went on to hold extremely high positions in the government, including as prime minister and head of the Reserve Bank of India.[18] Perhaps most famously, Gandhi appointed emigrant entrepreneur Sam Pitroda as telecommunications minister, a move that is widely seen as spearheading India's private, export-oriented software sector (Kohli 2012; Ye 2016). Following this, Indian IT professionals and entrepreneurs in the United States served as key advisors to Indian policymakers interested in

---

[17] For a detailed study of these groups' entrepreneurial stories, see Chakravorty, Kapur, and Singh (2017: 188–89).

[18] This group included Montek Singh Ahluwalia, Manmohan Singh, Bimal Jalan, R. Venkitiraman, Jayanta Roy, Rakish Mohan, Shankar Acharya, Vijay Kelkar, Jairam Ramesh, Nitin Desai, and Madhur Srinivas.

promoting technology growth within India (Saxenian 2002). In 1999, Silicon Valley entrepreneur K. B. Chandrasekhar led the Committee on Venture Capital for the Securities and Exchange Board of India. The Committee's report developed a comprehensive vision for the growth of India's venture capital industry based on a survey of the global experience, and proposed a series of regulatory and institutional reforms to achieve this goal (Securities and Exchange Board of India 2000). Subsequently, the Committee brought together top policymakers and elite emigrants to discuss deregulation of telecommunications. Efforts such as these helped attract elite emigrant entrepreneurs.

Although at first these efforts to build a private corporate service sector were received with mixed feelings within India, by the 2000s the elite class pact of global Indians had solidified a majority of supporters within India's government and services sector. Every government official I interviewed celebrated privatization and global connections. Although the government has organized countless workshops and conferences to connect Indian Americans to India (in IT, hotel management, medicine, academia, and sciences), government officials always emphasized to me the involvement of the private sector in these initiatives. One official explained to me with brimming pride, "The focus has been on the nongovernment sectors. The real action is in the big corporations." He pointed to General Electronics' Research and Development Center in India as the largest one in the world outside the United States, housing 1,500 international PhDs, countless biotechnology and IT start-ups, and various university professor exchange programs. As an added bonus, he pointed to small companies in India that not only are private but also operate outside the sphere of state regulation in the informal economy. Rather than criticizing these small companies for avoiding government regulations designed to protect labor and the environment, he celebrated them for exhibiting free market principles, unhindered by state regulations.[19]

Expanding India's Private Voluntary Sector
(1970s–present)

The second area in which the CEO MDR has tapped elite emigrants' social contributions is the private sector of nongovernmental organizations (NGOs), which in India are more commonly called "voluntary organizations" (VOs). Like the corporate sector, VOs operate outside the government sphere. Unlike the private sector, VOs do not aim to maximize profit; rather they rely on philanthropic donations to perform activities that are usually nonprofitable. Since

[19] Interview, Gurucharan.

the late 1970s, the CEO MDR has fostered greater exchange between Indian Americans and Indian VOs, which has not only strengthened the elite class pact but has also helped legitimize its emphasis on private capital. As one leading Indian organization that is working to reform Indian VOs put it in its newsletter, "This is what is meant by *'vasudev kutumbkam'* the Indian mantra of universal family" (AccountAid 2011: 3).

Scholars have recorded that philanthropic giving and VOs have a long tradition in India (Bornstein 2012). Until the 1900s, these efforts were decentralized and uncoordinated and largely driven by family and religious motivations (Kapur, Mehta, and Dutt 2004).[20] But by the 1900s, philanthropy in India had become more regulated and systematized through registered foundations (Juergensmeyer and McMahon 1998). As a result, Indian VOs attained formal recognition and were subjected to greater state control. British colonists who felt threatened by Indian VOs, for example, enacted the Societies Act (which remains in place today), which stipulated new requirements on all VOs. The British also used their own large philanthropic trusts to promote missionary activities and political capital with businesses (Bornstein 2012). By the mid-1900s, Indians used VOs to contest the state—fighting colonialism and holding the postcolonial state accountable for development (in education, sanitation, cotton production, anticasteism, and decreased alcohol use). Indians also mobilized new funding sources for VOs by urging Indian companies to donate to temples, schools, and hospitals. Under the Fabian-Socialist state of the 1950s and 1960s, VOs were limited to small, local social welfare projects. And during the Emergency, Indira Gandhi suppressed VOs, viewing them as a threat to the state. She also neutered their primary funding source by instituting the 1976 Foreign Contributions (Regulation) Act (FCRA), which aimed to curtail foreign influence in Indian politics and controlled all foreign funding to Indian VOs.[21]

But in 1977, the Janata Party revived the role of private VOs in Indian development and the role of foreign financing of Indian VOs. In direct opposition to Gandhi, the Janata Party provided an incentive to India's corporate sector under Section 35 CCA of the Income Tax Act to donate to VOs involved in rural development. Rural Indian VOs had fought the Emergency and have been noted for helping the Janata Party win the historic 1977 elections.[22] Although these

[20] Also reiterated in author's interview with the director of Org 45, March 17, 2011.

[21] Interview, Sanjay Agarwal, FCRA, principal, AccountAid, January 18, 2011. The FCRA was enforced by the Ministry of Home Affairs. Under FCRA, for a VO to receive foreign funding, it must have FCRA clearance (which is a long, bureaucratic process), provide assurance of its charitable status, offer a tax deduction in the country of donation, and meet other permissions for currency exchange under the 1973 Foreign Exchange Regulation Act.

[22] Interview, Ajay Mehta, May 12, 2011. This is particularly true for Jayaprakash Narayan's rural-based Sarvodaya movement.

gains were promptly reversed when Gandhi returned to power in 1980, the Janata Party's actions set in motion the continued growth of VOs during the 1980s.[23] Rajiv Gandhi and subsequent coalition governments revived the voluntary chapter in the eighth and ninth five-year plans. In 1993, the government set up a voluntary action cell in the Planning Commission to promote the voluntary sector and shift VOs from being local welfare organizations to partners in planning and implementing large development projects. In subsequent years, the government pronounced the promotion of VO and NGO initiatives as a key goal, especially in rural areas, and it began holding formal consultations with VOs about development policy.[24] In 2007, the government, along with several leading VOs and NGOs, drafted a national policy for the voluntary sector that was widely seen to legitimize and institutionalize the voluntary sector.[25] The policy sought to accredit VOs and simplify their regulation.

Significant for this study is that during the post-Janata revival of Indian VOs, funding for VOs from NRIs was exempted from FCRA regulations that restricted VO funding from non-Indian foreigners.[26] Throughout the 1990s and 2000s, the Indian government remained suspicious of foreign funding for VOs. The 1976 FCRA, for example, was not amended until 2018, and in 2010 and 2015 the government canceled several VOs' FCRA licenses, thereby curtailing their foreign funding sources. But as in the corporate sector (see Chapter 5), NRIs offered a more palatable compromise: channeling foreign funding to the growing set of Indian VOs but retaining an "Indian" perspective. According to Sanjay Agarwal, head of an Indian organization called AccountAid, which helps VOs maintain their financial accounts, nearly 90% of the organized funding received by VOs in India comes from foreign sources: "It is total trash that most of VO funding comes from within India. We see their books. We know what is really going on. VOs just get around the FCRA."[27] While data on how much of this foreign funding comes from Indian emigrants is not available, Agarwal noted that VOs regularly tap their Indian emigrant friends and family members

[23] In 1980, Indira Gandhi's government took over all poverty-alleviation efforts in rural areas. In 1983, Gandhi instituted the Financial Act, which limited the funds VOs could receive from companies and removed the tax exemptions that the Janata Party had given to companies funding VOs. In 1986, Gandhi removed the tax exemptions on all income-generating activities of VOs, created national and state councils to oversee rural VOs, and instituted a code of ethics for VOs who join government councils. See Charities Aid Foundation (2010).

[24] Interview, Lalit Kumar, secretary, National Foundation for Communal Harmony, Ministry of Home Affairs, January 27, 2011.

[25] Interview, Lalit Kumar, January 27, 2011.

[26] Dual citizenship emigrants are treated as foreign and thus subjected to FCRA rules.

[27] Interview, January 18, 2011.

for funding simply because they are unregulated or because they can transfer funds when they travel to India.[28]

These initiatives during the 1970s and 1980s paved the way for the government to invest in motivating elite emigrants' interactions with Indian VOs even while living permanently outside India. Employing a rhetoric of "global citizenship," the government's High-Level Committee report on the diaspora recommended the government create a single point of contact in the form of a private foundation to receive and disburse diaspora philanthropy, simplify the FCRA to give second-generation and dual-citizen emigrants a special fast track, and create subnational government departments to connect the diaspora with Indian VOs. In January 2012, MOIA launched the India Development Foundation of Overseas Indians (IDF), a registered trust that is exempt from FCRA, to raise funds from emigrants. Aarthi Krishna, who was tasked by MOIA to lead IDF "due to her impressive connections," described it to me in terms that fit Indian Americans' demographics and ideals of transparency: "These will be small accounts from retail donors . . . middle-class people. There are no administrative costs involved. And we give accountability and credibility to where the money is being spent. People can specify exactly where to spend the money, or we can pool it to provide a bigger sum."[29] Krishna, the daughter of a prominent minister, had lived in Washington, DC, for a decade before returning to India. In DC she served as an important link between the Indian Embassy and Indian Americans, answering their questions about Indian polices on visas, landownership, marriage, and gender. "I gave NRIs a human face," she said proudly.[30]

Indian Americans were well-placed to draw upon their own experiences managing and growing VOs in the United States, a land where VOs have a long history of being celebrated. Together, Indians in India and abroad celebrated the growth of a voluntary sector in India as "a powerful alternative to government" (Viswanath 2000: 28). Agarwal explained VO reliance on foreign funding as a need for ideological support: "The Indian state gives money, but that is to implement some scheme. So that is 'money to do,' not 'money to talk.' The discourse here is dominated by foreigners as a result."[31] As well, during the 1990s some Indian VOs opened offices in the United States to secure diaspora donations

[28] VOs also avoid FCRA regulations by routing foreign funds through a VO who has been registered to receive foreign funds. Interview, January 2018.

[29] Interview, March 21, 2012.

[30] Interview, March 21, 2012. Krishna had returned to India to try her hand at politics. But in the meantime, MOIA asked her to launch the IDF. Although she managed to attract 10 pledges from emigrants in Canada, the United States, and the Gulf in her first three months on the job, IDF was shut down under the next government.

[31] Interview, January 2018.

that are tax-exempt under US law.[32] These offices, which I detail in Chapter 8, were headed by Indian Americans.

A key aspect of Indian VOs' interactions with Indian Americans was channeling funding away from detached, impulsive, and informal giving (a practice derogatorily referred to as "charity") and toward "philanthropy," which is characterized by involved donors who are "rational" and systematic in their giving and attached to their recipients. Some scholars have argued that philanthropic giving since the 1990s offers a way for capitalism and the increased wealth that has resulted for some Indians (within India and abroad) to weaken resistance and protest movements (Bornstein 2012). Some Indian activists I spoke with bemoaned it as "un-Indian" and thus doomed for failure.[33] Nevertheless, the Indian government, elite emigrants, and many Indian VOs celebrated it.

Priya Viswanath, ex-CEO of Charities Aid Foundation, recalled the excitement around NRI's philanthropic giving during the early 2000s, "There was [a feeling] that something new was going to happen."[34] It was the first time that NRIs began to give in an organized way for tax purposes (Viswanath 2000). They drew on early examples, such as when Parameshwara Rao returned to India and set up the Bhagvatula Charitable Trust in Andhra Pradesh in 1967 to fund innovative philanthropy programs. In 1999, the Rejuvenate India movement began in the United States and quickly grew to 400 members. Similarly, Kanwal Rekhi mobilized a network to raise US$1 billion to upgrade the world-famous Indian Institutes of Technology, which had trained so many Indian Americans.[35] The Indian NGO, Child Rights and You, built a center to systematically get donations from NRIs in the 1990s and eventually opened a US chapter for these purposes.[36] In 2006, India was one of the few countries recognized at the Bellagio meeting on the voluntary sector for the India Literacy Project, which channels $1.5 million of diaspora donations each year to 22 NGOs across India to support literacy (Bakewell 2007).

In addition, the Indian government worked with elite emigrants and Indian VOs to revise India's regulatory framework and tax regulations to systematize philanthropic giving and model its voluntary sector on that of the United States. Efforts included creating new codes of conduct for VOs, instituting formal grades similar to those for financial institutions, and unpacking and reorganizing regulations and categorization of different types of organizations. In 2000, the government's Planning Commission worked with Charities Aid Foundation to

---

[32] Interview with official from Charities Aid Foundation, January 25, 2011.

[33] AccountAid held this view.

[34] Interview, March 18, 2011.

[35] This eventually became the organization Friends of Indian Institutes of Technology.

[36] Interview, Amita Puri, Charities Aid Foundation, January 25, 2011.

improve the credibility of India's voluntary sector by engaging in a validation program of all VOs. The aim was to encourage Indian emigrants to engage with Indian VOs and overcome their suspicions. As Harsh Jaitli, CEO of the Voluntary Action Network India, a network of 370 development NGOs, explained, "A major problem that [Indian emigrants] face is: Who should they give to? There is no accreditation, no public accounting, no charity commissioner here. The absence of all this is creating a gap with individual giving. So we worked with the Planning Commission on the National Law on the Voluntary Sector. We wanted a single law for registration with a national accreditation concept."[37] This need for accreditation as a way to attract diaspora funds was repeated by several leaders and experts on the voluntary sector.[38] Jaitli reiterated what Indian VOs were learning from the United States: "After 9/11 there was a tightening of the voluntary sector in the US, and we are doing the same here. We are all learning from each other."[39]

Sampradan is another Indian-based organization that is helping Indian VOs learn from the US model. Its executive director, Pradeepta Kumar Nayak, explained to me, "Indians today already give quite a bit of philanthropy, but not in the institutionalized way that the US is doing it. We are trying to institutionalize it." To this end, Sampradan has created "community foundations," a concept that was pioneered in Cleveland, Ohio, in 1914. As Nayak proudly explained, "They grew in the 1980s and have been very successful in the US, Canada, and Europe. But India is lagging in this. Sampraddan [sic] is the only organization in India currently working on this."[40] Community foundations, according to Nayak, help to organize individual philanthropy. "We believe that the best form of change for civil society is the community foundation. We have to involve people to create their own destiny. Although people have always given in India, we are asking them to give to an organization, lead that organization and manage that organization."[41] Despite his best efforts to institutionalize philanthropy, however, Nayak admitted that success has been quite thin.

In 2016, the BJP government passed a historic Finance Bill that amended the FCRA to make it easier for political parties to accept foreign donations for the first time in India's postcolonial history. This was a true testament to the shifting ideology against foreign involvement in Indian politics. In 2018, the government made further amendments by exempting political parties' foreign funding from scrutiny by the government and opposing parties. These changes opened the

[37] Interview March 17, 2011.
[38] Interview, Lalit Kumar, January 27, 2011.
[39] Interview, March 17, 2011.
[40] Interview, January 13, 2011.
[41] Interview, January 13, 2011.

doors even wider for Indian emigrants to participate in Indian politics. While more research is needed in this area, existing reports have found that emigrants send more money to India in election years, suggesting the contemporary Indian state may even use emigration to circumvent democracy (Nyblade and O'Mahony 2014).

Swelling India's Private Real Estate Market (1990s–present)

A third area in which the government has tapped elite emigrants' social and ideological contributions under the CEO MDR has been in real estate. Throughout my interviews, Indian Americans were repeatedly credited (and criticized) for the boom in Indian land prices. In Punjab, the rising land prices have been recorded since the 1970s (Kessinger 1974; Taylor, Singh, and Booth 2007). And since the 1990s, other Indian states have been experiencing a similar phenomenon. Government officials in Andhra Pradesh, for example, blamed the housing bubble in Hyderabad on Indian emigrants in the United States, particularly third-wave emigrants working in the US IT sector. N. V. Ramana Reddy, special secretary for political and NRI affairs, explained that since the mid-1980s software explosion in India, Andhra Pradesh has had a large number of mostly middle-class, urban, educated software engineers emigrate temporarily to the United States. "They really support the real estate boom, especially after they return," said Reddy. "I would say the entire rise in prices of real estate in Hyderabad can be attributed to NRIs' speculation and investment."[42] Real estate experts believe that in Delhi, 20% of all property worth over US$250,000 was bought or funded by NRIs (Chishti 2007). Similar claims have been made about the rise in land prices in Punjab since the 1970s (Chishti 2007).

In addition to spurring a market for land speculation and a housing bubble, Indian Americans' real estate investments in India are shaping Indian middle-class tastes, aspirations, and desires for exclusiveness. This can be seen in the growth of so-called Western-influenced condominium projects that cater to the assumed tastes of Indian American consumers. Much has also been said of Bollywood films and television programs catering to Indian American sensibilities in recent years (Bose 2008). There has been a notable increase in opulence and investments in distinction in areas where Indian emigrant investments in real estate have been high, such as in the states of Punjab, Gujarat, and Kerala. Such investments include the construction of mansions, communities marked off by gilded gates, massive temples, and water tanks in the

[42] Interview, May 23, 2011.

shapes of eagles, airplanes, and footballs (Osella and Osella 2000; Ramji 2006; Taylor, Singh, and Booth 2007).

These efforts to attract Indian Americans have helped create a group of idolized, highly successful, mainly professional doctors, engineers, accountants, business entrepreneurs, IT workers, academics, and scientists, whose assumed tastes, interests, and financial capacity local Indians can and should emulate (Bose 2008). As well, they confirm findings from other sending countries that contributions from emigrants tend to reproduce local structures in the place of origin (Portes, Escobar, and Radford 2007).

Drawing from the Gujarat MDR

The Gujarat government has pioneered state recognition of elite emigrants and has served as an important model for the national government. As Ravi Saxena, Additional chief secretary in Gujarat's Department of Science and Technology, explained with some irony, "The Gujarati diaspora are more Gujarati than Gujaratis! But American Gujaratis look to Gujarat for recognition from the government."[43]

The Gujarat government's efforts to build a shared identity with its largely middle-class emigrants began in the early 1990s under the Congress Party, when the state's chief minister visited the United States and held large conferences in Gujarati. But it was Narendra Modi (then chief minister of Gujarat and now prime minister of India) who inflated these efforts to a new level. Under Modi, the diaspora conferences were filled with calls for investments and covered with symbolic, cultural embraces. In 2011, in time for the state's global investors conference, known as Vibrant Gujarat, Modi built an enormous convention center, called Mahatma Mandir (Temple of the Great One), after Mohandas Gandhi, who not only comes from Gujarat but represents the nation's most famous migrant returnee. Modi described the building as a place for negotiating world peace. To inaugurate the building on the 50th anniversary of the founding of Gujarat, he invited Gujarati emigrants from around the world to bring soil and water from their host countries to pour into the foundation of the Mandir. More than 3,000 Gujarati emigrants from 40 countries came to perform the ritual; all were self-financed.[44] The participants then returned to their host countries with pots of soil from Gujarat that they were asked to spread across different regions in their host countries.

[43] Interview, March 12, 2011.
[44] Interview, March 12, 2011.

In addition to building a shared cultural identity, the Gujarat government has tapped emigrants' social contributions. Within Saxena's Department of Science and Technology, for example, is a unit for administrative reforms and training that works on issues concerning Non-Resident Gujaratis (NRGs). The unit keeps an updated directory of all NRGs across the world, offers an NRG identity card that grants discounts on businesses in Gujarat, and helps Gujaratis getting married to partners living abroad by providing them with information on laws as well as cultural assimilation issues. The preface of the *NRG Directory* notes, "The incentive [to invest in India] need not be merely financial, but even in the form of social currency recognition by the Homeland" (Government of Gujarat 2013: 1).

The Gujarat government also tried to systematize emigrants' philanthropic donations for development. The *NRG Directory* lists all NRG-funded phil-anthropic projects, something the national government still does not do, explaining, "These donations are the result of what the Chinese call the *qiaoxiang* ties (Diasporas' ties to their ancestral hometowns) and have played a very sig-nificant role in filling certain missing gaps in the rural and urban infrastructure" (Government of Gujarat 2013: 3). Indeed, within India, Gujarat (and Punjab) have the largest number of hometown associations. I visited several villages in Gujarat that were entirely funded by diaspora money, including a cutting-edge glaucoma hospital, knee replacement hospitals, meditation center, water filtra-tion system, and retirement homes for NRGs.[45] As Saxena explained, "We find the socioeconomic investments and cultural investments in the villages [are] much greater than business investment, which is much less."[46] Gujarat is also often credited for spurring Indian American philanthropic donations to India due to the government's ability to channel aid after the devastating 2001 earth-quake in the state.

Cementing the New Dominant Ideology among Poor Emigrants

The late 1970s and 1980s forged an elite class pact of "global Indians" that cemented elite consent for privatization, voluntarism, and globalization within India. But the CEO-MDR's elite class pact never articulated poor Indian

---

[45] For example, Kansar Village in Anand District is the result of a UK-based NRG who developed a water supply pump in his home village. Thamana in Thasra Taluka is an example of an NRG who moved back to his village, where he paved all the roads. Dharmaj Village provides another example of NRG-funded development.

[46] Interview, March 12, 2011.

emigrants as an ideological or social resource for India. This raises questions on how the elite class pact is reproduced among poor emigrants. Rather than tapping poor emigrants' unique social contributions, the CEO MDR, since the 2000s, has worked to build poor emigrants' consent for elite emigrants' ideals by constructing a single cross-class category of "emigrants," which in turn occludes the class-based differences in emigrants' needs and interests.

Constructing New Government Institutions for All Emigrants

A key avenue through which the government has tried to secure poor emigrants' consent and construct a cross-class migrant identity has been a set of new emigration institutions that the government under the CEO MDR launched in the 2000s. These institutions were designed to improve (and eventually replace) the notoriously slow and corrupt Protector of Emigrants (PoE), which had been regulating and protecting "vulnerable" Indian emigrants since the colonial era. In contrast to the previous PoEs, the CEO MDR's new institutions not only promise more modern and efficient services; they also offer services to both poor and elite emigrants.

Unlike the PoE, which operated under the Ministry of Labor, the new institutions operate as their own cabinet-level ministries or under the MEA, thereby divorcing the category of "emigrants" from "labor" (as it had earlier been understood). On one hand, the new emigrant institutions have often been headed by Kerala government officials, who have represented the interests of poor emigrants since the 1970s. On the other hand, the new institutions draw from and appeal to the very characteristics that elite emigrants have been promoting since the 1970s. Specifically, and in explicit contrast to earlier emigration institutions, the new institutions celebrate high-tech modernity, private-sector development, entrepreneurship, and self-sufficiency.

The prime example of the CEO MDR's new emigrant institution was the Ministry of Overseas Indian Affairs, established in 2004. MOIA represented the culmination of Prime Minister Vajpayee's (BJP) efforts to alter the Indian government's institutional approach to emigration. Although Vajpayee had launched the NRI/PIO cell within the MEA in 2000, and soon after agreed to create MOIA as its own ministry, it was Prime Minister Manmohan Singh of the Congress-led coalition that officially launched MOIA, marking the first time the Congress Party celebrated emigration. MOIA was billed as a "service ministry" and a "one-stop shop" for all emigrant issues. It established India as one of a handful of countries to have a cabinet-level ministry entirely devoted to issues of emigration.[47] It comprised four units: Diaspora Services, Financial Services, Emigrant Services, and Management Services. While Diaspora Services targets

[47] The original name was Ministry of Non-Resident Indian Affairs. As a result of MOIA, the MEA annual reports no longer addressed emigrant issues from 2004 to 2015.

elite emigrants and Emigrant Services targets poor emigrants, the remaining two units service both classes of emigrants simultaneously.

In 2015, Prime Minister Modi (BJP) folded MOIA back into the MEA, making it the Department of Overseas Indian Affairs (DOIA) as part of his mission to "minimize government and maximize governance" (Ministry of External Affairs 2016: 206). Despite losing its position as an independent ministry, DOIA continues to have its own identity and still serves as the face of India's emigration regime.[48] Like MOIA, DOIA expresses itself as the representative of all classes of emigrants. In its inaugural report, it emphasize its mission to not only "invite overseas Indians to contribute to India's growth story" but also to offer "special attention to ensuing welfare and protection of vulnerable" emigrants (Ministry of External Affairs 2016: 206). Interestingly, in 2015, the very year that Modi disbanded MOIA, the number of government clearances provided to poor emigrants began to progressively fall for the first time since the 1980s, from 781,000 in 2015 to 334,000 in 2019.[49] To explain this drop, Deputy Secretary Rajeev Sharma of the new Department of Overseas Employment under the PGE in the MEA pointed to poor emigrants' rising education levels rather than a fall in labor demand, as many argue. According to Sharma, the data among Indian embassies in receiving countries indicated the number of Indians in the Gulf was, in fact, increasing. But since educated emigrants did not require clearance, the drop in clearances represented a fusing of poor and elite emigrants.[50]

A key goal of MOIA (and later DOIA) is to replace the PoEs' slow, corrupt, bureaucratic image with a new image of the national government as an efficient facilitator and protector of economic growth through modern technology and private-sector development. Importantly, this image draws from characteristics that have come to define India's elite emigrants but, through these new institutions, now extends to poor emigrants as well. To this end, MOIA (and later DOIA) celebrates modern technology. Under much fanfare, Prime Minister Singh created Insta Remit, an electronic management system designed to enable poor and wealthy emigrants to instantly remit money to 14,500 settlements in India. In 2010, MOIA began a new online system, called E-migrate, to streamline emigration procedures for poor emigrants and better regulate recruiting agencies. E-migrate was continued under DOIA. In my conversations with government officials, they repeatedly extolled MOIA's/DOIA's high-tech projects

[48] Although many also critiqued the disbanding of MOIA. See, for instance, *Free Press Journal* (2019).

[49] Figures drawn from Ministry of External Affairs, Annual Reports, 2015, 2016, 2017, 2018, and 2019. The 2020 Annual Report did not include the number of emigration clearances due to the COVID-19 pandemic.

[50] Interview, January 4, 2019.

as an ideal representation of India's liberalized, efficient, and modern governance structure. To many, technology promised to eliminate the human error and
corruption that the government's emigration practices had been criticized for in
earlier MDRs. As Sharma said, "E-migrate was actually devised to promote migration and to make it transparent. It offers a common platform for emigrants,
recruiting agency, and employers. . . . It is really unique in the world. The PGE
spent a lot of time on this. It completely removes the human interface. It offers
complete technology."[51] E-migrate was also noted for meeting emigrant organizations' demands for more updated data on poor emigrants.

As well, MOIA's (and DOIA's) services for both poor and wealthy emigrants
explicitly promote and celebrate private-sector development. Although MOIA
was a government ministry, its offices were furnished to look like corporate
offices, complete with polished floors and massive leather couches. Dr. Singh,
secretary of MOIA, proudly explained to me, "MOIA is small and compact—
only thirty people. The entire format is based on outsourcing."[52] That government
business is being outsourced to the private sector did not seem problematic to
Singh. Similarly, although the Overseas Indian Facilitation Center, which aimed
to help elite emigrants invest in India, was funded by the government, it did
not employ government workers; rather it was housed in the Confederation of
Indian Industries and had a staff of three. The Center's CEO, Shefali Chaturvedi,
was equally proud to underline the unit's commitment to privatization. "It is all
outsourced," she stated.[53]

Attached to MOIA/DOIA are several subsidiaries, which also proudly
present themselves as independent from government or private enterprise.
Gurucharan, whose title is CEO of two of these subsidiaries (namely, the Indian
Council of Oversees Employment and the India Development Foundation of
Overseas Indians) prides himself on being "efficient" and thus different from
typical bureaucrats. In the course of one year, I watched him grow his office with
impressive speed. He spoke passionately about emigration and was brimming
with ideas on how to fit it into India's development plans. When I first met him,
he related a long list of programs the government had started to assist poor
emigrants on their outbound and return journeys. These included media education campaigns, migrant resource centers that disseminate information, skill
development programs, and international certification efforts. And almost all
of them relied on the private sector. As Gurucharan explained with pride, "We
don't do the actual training. We hire an independent, international certified,
private company to do the training." He spoke about shifting poor emigrants'

[51] Interview, January 4, 2019.
[52] Interview January 19, 2011.
[53] Interview, January 20, 2011.

economic contributions to be more similar to those of elite emigrants: "We are also launching programs for financial inclusion to transform workers from giving just remittances to becoming investors."[54]

Interestingly, although these new emigrant institutions purport to offer services to poor emigrants, they have also enabled the national government to engage in what Wang (2016) has called "the politics of concealment" with regard to the state's attention to poor emigrant workers. Just as the 1983 Emigration Act helped cover up the government's lack of protection for poor emigrants, MOIA's launch in 2004 took the topic of emigration out of parliamentary debates. Government officials repeatedly referred those who raised emigration issues in parliamentary sessions to MOIA's annual reports. MOIA's programs, however, were more symbolic than material, and funds were rarely disbursed. Whenever MOIA was held accountable for the lack of implementation of emigrant programs, its defense was that emigration welfare was a state subject, and the national government was thus unable to do much. As a result, despite poor emigrants' enormous financial contributions to the Indian economy in the form of remittances, they have remained invisible in Indian policy discussions under the CEO MDR.

Reframing (Male) Emigrant Workers as Entrepreneurs

Underlying the government's progressive liberalization of poor emigrants under the CEO MDR has been an offer to free vulnerable male workers from the control of government officials, recruiters, and employers and enable them to protect themselves—by investing in and owning their own human capital.[55] To attain poor emigrants' consent for this approach, the national government has redefined "vulnerable workers" as high-quality "entrepreneurs" who can own their own human capital and become self-employed, especially upon their return to India. As Gurucharan proudly noted, "We are beginning to see a shift from Gulf returnees being workers to deploying capital themselves."[56] This redefinition deflects attention from the important class differences between poor and wealthy emigrants.

To institutionalize this reframing, the national government eliminated the Ministry of Labor from emigrant affairs, and instead deemed the Ministry of Small and Medium Enterprises as a key partner of MOIA. As well, the government redefined its own role, from being a protector of labor abroad (which

---

[54] Interview, January 25, 2011.

[55] Ministry of Labor, Standing Committee on Labor and Welfare, 1998–99, Demand for Grants, 10th Report, Parliamentary Debate, Vol. 6, No. 2, December 1, 1998.

[56] Interview, March 20, 2012.

was a long-held and unmet demand among emigrant workers) to being a protector or manager of the market for businesses (including those of emigrant entrepreneurs).[57] In 2006, the government began discussions to amend the 1983 Emigration Act, and in 2009 a replacement bill, aptly named the Emigration Management Bill, proposed to provide poor workers with skills training and upgrades and predeparture orientation. The Emigration Management Bill, which was still pending as of 2021, specified that the MEA would be the nodal ministry for emigration, and only two other ministries would have representation: Ministry of Home Affairs and the Ministry of Human Resource Development.

The Emigration Management Bill received massive support from government officials, as well as emigrant activists. Vayalar Ravi, then head of MOIA and a longtime emigrant rights activist from Kerala, stated in a parliamentary session, "The proposed new Bill is aimed to transform emigration into a simple, transparent, efficient and humane economic process, facilitate legal migration, prevent illegal migration/human smuggling, enable ethical recruitment practices, and enhance protection and welfare of emigrant workers."[58] With these words, the government erased labor rights and the threat of labor exploitation from the regime of emigration and instead subjected Indian workers to the market-oriented forces of efficiency in the name of protection.

To foster this new identity among poor, male emigrant workers, the Indian government has helped create an enormous industry for teaching, training, and certifying Indian emigrant workers. Based on these programs, these workers are marketed as "more qualified" than "the unprofessional" Nepalese workers. These efforts parallel the highly reputed and globally ranked tertiary educational institutions in India that already certify the skills of elite emigrants in the United States. In 2016, the government launched a new program to train potential emigrant workers "in line with international standards to facilitate overseas employment . . . focusing on sectors that are in demand in ECR countries [i.e., countries that are demanding Indian immigrant labor]" (Ministry of External Affairs 2018: 227). This program, known as Pravasi Kaushal Vikas Yojana, was launched by DOIA and the Ministry of Skill Development and Entrepreneurship under the ministry's "Skill India" mission.

---

[57] In the late 1990s, the Vajpayee government announced that it would consider emigrant workers' long-standing request to streamline personnel in the Indian missions abroad (which operate under the Ministry of External Affairs) to also include a representative from the Ministry of Labor, who could be solely responsible for handling emigrant complaints of exploitation and malpractice by employers and recruiting agents. But this request was never implemented.

[58] Overseas Indian Affairs, Question and Answer, December 9, 2009, Question No. 3236, 1.

Unlike elite emigrants' certifications, many of which come from publicly funded tertiary institutions, most of the skills training and certification programs for poor workers are offered through the private sphere. Some are conducted by the recruiting agency itself, others by a third-party private institution. Either way, workers bear the costs of the training as an "investment in their future earnings." Some of these programs are fraudulent; all are costly. Recruiters repeatedly explained to me, however, that they are necessary because employers in the Gulf countries base their recruitment of migrant workers not only on numbers but also on "quality." Because verifying migrants' quality or qualifications is difficult, employers rely on building relationships with recruiters. Recruiting agencies test workers' skills before recruiting them, verify their certifications, and sometimes provide additional training before departure. Interestingly, the government has funded some seed programs for more educated workers in poorer regions of India. For example, MOIA piloted a program in northeast India that trains and certifies potential migrants to work in the healthcare and hospitality sectors of Europe.[59] But as Basant Kumar Potnuru, a research officer at the Indian Council of Overseas Employment, was quick to point out, "Once the program goes pan-India, it will be self-pay." As well, the program aims to foster a "public-private partnership model" by relying on an interdependent international agency to certify the standards of the government training.[60]

At the subnational level, the Kerala government has attempted to channel migrant remittances into industrial investments since the early 1980s. In 1984 the state's minister of industries announced in the legislative assembly the formation of an investment company to mobilize Keralites in the Gulf to invest in industries in Kerala. In 1986, it proposed to start small and medium-size industries that would employ returnees. According to a survey of return migrants, these efforts did not yield much success (Nayyar 1989). Still, the Kerala government, which established the Department of Non-Resident Keralites Abroad (NORKA) to institutionalize government welfare policies and funding for poor emigrants, continued to pursue similar projects in the subsequent decades. In 2002, it created NORKA-Roots with three subdivisions: welfare, research, and entrepreneurship and economic activity. When the 2008 financial crisis sent tens of thousands of poor Keralite emigrants in the Gulf back to India, the Kerala government offered them financial support in the form of small loans to start small businesses. But most interviewees noted that very few people have taken advantage of these programs. Still today, government programs provide subsidized low-interest loans to help return migrants launch small-scale businesses in animal husbandry,

[59] To qualify for this certification program, workers must have completed 12 years of schooling and have some work experience.

[60] Interview, March 20, 2012.

dairy, retail, vegetable and milk vending, taxis, and IT.[61] NORKA also holds seminars to educate returnees on how to start such small-scale businesses.

The Limits of Entrepreneurship

The government's promotion of entrepreneurship has pushed many poor migrants to pursue such opportunities upon their return to India. In a survey of over 2,000 return migrants conducted in 1990, 25% of employed returnees were self-employed (Nair 1991). In another survey of emigrants' occupations before and after migration conducted across three years (in 2003, 2008, and 2011), self-employment represented the biggest occupational shift, especially among male migrants. In 2011, for example, while 10% of males worked as self-employed entrepreneurs before migrating, 26% were self-employed upon return (Kumar and Rajan 2014: Table 3.17).[62]

Although in my interviews with poor migrant organizations none critiqued the governments' programs to promote self-employment and entrepreneurship in principal, all mentioned that the programs have so far had minimal effect. Starting a business is not easy, especially for those who have meager business management skills, networks, and resources. As Kadakkal Ramesh, vice chairman of the Kerala state NRIs Coordination Council, explained, starting a business became too risky, especially when the economy began to taper in the Gulf around 2008. So instead, those with resources turned to speculative investments, such as gold and real estate. "The price of land [and gold] went up like [a] rocket. . . . Nobody has got the confidence to start a new business. They thought that it is safer to invest in land. . . . Ordinary people like us cannot buy even one piece of land in Kerala now!"[63] In other words, the earnings from remittances went into what many felt were nonproductive assets (consumption and land) rather than industry and agriculture, which were still held up as the ideal options for development. K. Satish Nambudiripad, ex-CEO of NORKA, explained that the migration income "was consumption-driven": "So the land price also increased. We were all living on a false sense of plenty which was backed neither by agriculture or investment."[64]

Moreover, self-employment efforts have been more effective for elite return migrants than they have for poor return migrants. Joseph Thomas, vice president of a migrant organization called AKGRO, returned to Kerala at the age of 55 after working as an electrical engineer in the UAE for 31 years.

---

[61] Interview, K. C. Joseph, Minister of NORKA, March 22, 2012.
[62] Self-employment absorbed only 1% to 2% of female migrants.
[63] Interview, August 3, 2012.
[64] Interview January 11, 2017.

Because of his age, he was not able to find a job when he returned, so he began his own business doing electrical repairs for air-conditioning units and other small machines. He was even able to hire a few contract laborers. He expressed the advantages of having his own business in terms of the time and freedom it entails for him, "being his own boss" and "taking care of matters at home if needed." However, he also noted that he did not have to rely on the business for his household income because his wife was a teacher, and that he did not rely on the government for assistance in starting his business. In other words, for well-resourced workers who are not reliant on income from a new business and are able to take the risks involved, entrepreneurship offers a viable path. But for the tens of thousands of poor emigrants who return to India with few resources, entrepreneurship has offered a limited path to upward mobility, let alone daily survival.

Launching Paternalist Welfare Programs and the Return of the "Vulnerable" Migrant

The limited ability of entrepreneurship to foster self-sufficiency among returnees has forced the government to legitimize the CEO MDR and retain poor emigrants' consent by instituting emigrant welfare programs. At the national level, the rhetoric (although not necessarily the material delivery) around these welfare programs has noticeably accelerated since 2016.

Part of the government's impetus to offer welfare stems from the historically cemented electoral expectation of state protection for workers. But an additional push comes from the CEO MDR's particular reliance on temporary or circular migration, which has been increasingly preferred by receiving countries. As a result, the Indian government has inadvertently committed itself to accepting and incorporating emigrants upon their return to India. This contrasts with earlier MDRs that warded off return migration. Irish ministers and civil servants in the 1950s, for example, feared return migrants would bring with them "unemployment . . . leftist ideas about state welfarism . . . and unmentionable contagious diseases" (Bartlett 2010: 474).

At the state level, the Kerala government has instituted welfare programs that have had important significance, especially in recognizing poor emigrants' economic contributions. Although Kerala's programs served as the blueprint for the national-level programs, the latter have been paternalist rather than rights-based, which has revived earlier notions of the "vulnerable migrant" and undermined the CEO MDR's professed ideals of self-sufficiency. While I will elaborate on poor emigrants' experiences with these welfare programs in the next chapter, let me review these programs from the government's perspective here.

Emigrant Welfare and Recognition in Kerala

As early as October 1983, more than two decades before the national government started its first emigrant welfare program, the labor minister of Kerala launched a new welfare scheme to assist poor emigrants from Kerala to educate their children, settle income tax disputes, conduct lawsuits, reduce air and train transportation costs, and buy land for housing construction (Nayyar 1989). In 1996, during the Iraq invasion of Kuwait, thousands of Indians were sent back to India, and the Kerala government set up NORKA to help them. Nambudiripad, ex-CEO of NORKA-Roots, explained to me, "Expatriation and migration [are] under the [national government], not the state. So, therefore, the Kerala state government could only give welfare."[65]

Since its start, NORKA has expanded considerably. In addition to its impressive office in Kerala, it has offices in Delhi, Bombay, Chennai, and Bangalore to help Keralites living in or emigrating out from those major cities. As well, its emigrant welfare has been institutionalized at the state government level. In 2008, the Kerala government under Chief Minister V. S. Achuthanadan of the Communist Party of India–Marxist passed the Kerala Non-Resident Returnees Welfare Act, and in 2010 the government established the Non-Resident Keralites' Welfare Board, which offers a contributory pension to emigrants' families in the event of an emigrant's accident or death, educational support for emigrants' children, support for medical expenses, support for emigrants' daughters' weddings, and interest-free loans. Keralites living abroad, return migrants who worked outside Kerala for at least two years, and return migrants who work and live within India but outside Kerala for at least six months are eligible to become members of the Welfare Board. The Board is funded by emigrant member fees and government funds.[66] To date, the Boards have 90,000 members, governed by a 15-member governing board of seven government officials and seven private citizens (often wealthier emigrants). The minister of NORKA is an unofficial member of the Board, and the NORKA secretary is the director. The Welfare Board follows a long tradition in India that has been used for unprotected workers domestically (Agarwala 2013).

While NORKA's track record in delivering emigrant welfare has been spotty, its existence has been significant. It was the first government department in India explicitly designed to meet the needs of nonresident Indians. In 2001, Chief Minister of Kerala A. K. Antony of the Congress Party appointed

[65] Interview, January 11, 2017.

[66] To join the Board, emigrants must pay a fee of Rs. 200. Foreign emigrants must pay Rs. 300/ month for five years to get pension payments after age 60; domestic emigrants and returnees must pay Rs. 100/month for five years to get pension payments after age 60.

a minister of emigrants to head NORKA, elevating emigration's status in the state's political and policy arena. These efforts served as a role model for other state governments, as well as the national government. State governments in Tamil Nadu, Punjab, and Gujarat studied the Kerala model and followed suit with their own state-level departments of emigrant affairs. NORKA "was a small department, but we got so many phone calls to come see our department and our work," beamed K. C. Joseph, minister of NORKA.[67] Indeed, Kerala's efforts single-handedly inspired the national government's welfare programs, as well as institutions, such as MOIA.

The most significant feature of Kerala's welfare programs is that they recognize poor emigrants' contributions to the economy, something national government programs still do not do. In my interviews, Kerala government officials repeatedly justified their welfare programs by underlining the massive economic benefits India attains from its poor emigrants. Indeed, nearly 20% of India's total remittances go to Kerala, making it the largest remittance-receiving state in India (Reserve Bank of India 2018). In a passionate appeal for increased welfare for emigrants in 2002, Kerala's member of Parliament Ramesh Chennithala exclaimed, "The contribution of Indians to convert this desert into heaven is laudable. The mutual cooperation of the two countries have definitely helped in promoting peace, amity and development in the entire Middle-East."[68]

Consistent with most studies on remittances, however, Kerala government officials rarely credited emigrants' financial contributions for catalyzing local economic growth. For example, Nambudiripad, the ex-CEO of NORKA-Roots, reiterated a common complaint that emigrants merely contribute to consumption and not investment: "They are bringing so much money into Kerala. But there is no scope for industry in Kerala, the credit-deposit ratio is so low . . . so the money sits idle. It's used for consumption, which creates inflation and unproductive construction and housing. . . . The land price also increased so much."[69]

Other Kerala officials I spoke with framed emigrants as a safeguard against economic crises. Ravi Vayalar, previous MP from Kerala and then the minister of MOIA, credited Gulf emigrants' financial assistance during the 1991 economic crisis as the inspiration for the national government's interest in emigrants: "Dr. Manmohan Singh in 1991, when he was the finance minister, appealed to overseas Indians to help. India's gold reserves were taken to the UK. It was extremely embarrassing for India. So Singh appealed to the Gulf workers to put money in Indian banks. They changed the restrictions on currency convertibility. Through this experience, he became inspired to look at overseas

[67] Interview, March 22, 2012.
[68] Parliamentary Debate, Vol. 29, No. 16, December 11, 2002, 284.
[69] Interview, January 11, 2017.

Indians. He sees them as a major potential to be tapped."[70] Similarly, although Chief Minister of Kerala Oommen Chandy described the Kerala's welfare programs as a form of "generosity" and protection, he was also quick to acknowledge emigrants' contributions to Kerala and thus as deserving recipients: "There *are* problems [with emigration]. But [when] there was a major drop in prices in all agriculture, this was a serious crisis for Kerala. . . . The economy survived only due to remittances."[71] Minister Joseph similarly admitted, "Our economies [i.e., India's and those in the Gulf] are totally linked and dependent. . . . Remittances are thirty percent of our state income. . . . Migration is our major stabilizing force."[72]

Incorporating the Private Sector in Kerala

Interestingly, the Kerala government's public recognition of poor emigrants' financial contributions has enabled it to place the CEO MDR's fascination with private-sector development within the state's tradition of democratic responsibility for its laborers. When the Kerala government created the quasi-governmental entity NORKA-Roots, it called its head a CEO, took in funding from private donors, and put private emigrants on its board. Despite this private structure, NORKA-Roots operates under the government body NORKA, produces publicly available annual reports, and reports to the state's chief minister, who is the chair of its Board.[73] Its mission is to implement NORKA's policies, assist in emigrant recruitment and return, disburse emigrant welfare, and serve as an interface between emigrants and the Kerala state government. Today, NORKA, the Emigrant Welfare Board, and NORKA-Roots reside together in a sleek and shiny new building with large, sparkling glass windows and well-made furniture inside. The building took six years to construct and was completed in 2011. Noyal Thomas, CEO of NORKA-Roots at the time of my interview, expressed pride that it "did not look like other government buildings."[74]

Kerala government officials vehemently defended this quasi-governmental organizational structure. Nambudiripad proudly explained, "It was me that made that decision [to register as a nonprofit company], and it was me that came up with the name 'Roots'. . . . I wanted it to have meaning."[75] He further explained,

[70] Interview, May 19, 2011.

[71] Interview, March 22, 2012.

[72] Interview, March 22, 2012.

[73] Interview, Noyal Thomas, CEO of NORKA-Roots, March 13, 2012.

[74] Interview, March 23, 2012.

[75] Interview, January 11, 2017. The name "Roots" was drawn from American Author, Alex Haley's 1976 award-winning book, *Roots: The Saga of an American Family*.

"The government doesn't have money. Roots is funded by private shareholders and rich Malayali NRIs. Some are in the Gulf itself, like Yosef Ali. They are also members of the Board with the chief minister. These people like the prestige they get."[76]

Kerala's efforts to embrace a private-sector image through its emigration institutions has not undermined its public responsibility toward emigrants, especially relative to national-level efforts. For example, NORKA provides orientation programs and training certificates to migrant construction workers, as well as links with banks to facilitate remittances. In addition, it certifies the courses and training programs that have exploded in the private sphere in recent years. The government stamp is viewed by foreign employers as more trustworthy than private programs. According to Thomas, "*This* is what makes money for NORKA."[77] He said they use this income to help run the Welfare Boards, which do not earn enough through members' fees or government contributions to cover operations. The certification helps ensure emigrants receive a higher salary, and thus send higher remittances. Kerala government officials complained that the national government was not keeping up with other country governments' emigration work. As one NORKA recruiter stated, "Sri Lanka and Nepal have reintegration certificates to acknowledge the skills learned abroad. We don't have such a certificate [from the Indian government]. We only have certificates given by private institutions."[78]

National Welfare Programs

In the late 1990s, Prime Minister Vajpayee and the BJP-led government finally followed Kerala's lead and instituted several national-level welfare programs for poor emigrants. The first, which were announced by the MEA in 2003, included educational quotas in Indian schools for children of Indian emigrant workers in the Gulf and Southeast Asia, a fund to sponsor the repatriation of a dead body and assistance for disability incurred at work, and an insurance scheme required only for poor emigrant workers (called Pravasi Bharatiya Bima Yojana) (Ministry of External Affairs 2004). In 2008, MOIA launched the new Overseas Workers Resource Center and a 24-hour help line in eight languages for existing and prospective emigrants. In 2009, the Indian Community Welfare Fund was established in all Indian missions abroad to assist emigrants in need, and by 2020 it had extended assistance to 156,000 Indians (Ministry of External Affairs

---

[76] Interview, January 11, 2017.
[77] Interview, March 23, 2012.
[78] Interview, March 23, 2012.

2021).[79] That year, the National Committee for Women became the coordinating agency with MOIA for overseas employment, indicating the government's commitment to emigrant women. In 2012, MOIA launched the Mahatma Gandhi Pravasi Suraksha Yogana, a welfare program that provided emigrants with life insurance, pensions, and savings for return and resettlement.[80] In 2013, for the first time in India's history, the Presidential Address to Parliament mentioned the government's various welfare programs for emigrants. Stated President Pranab Mukherjee, "My Government is deeply committed to promoting the interests and welfare of overseas Indians."[81] And in 2016, the national government's annual report on overseas Indians made a striking shift by first detailing its national welfare programs for poor emigrants before turning to its programs for elite emigrants (Ministry of External Affairs 2016).

Although these national-level welfare programs have helped legitimize the government's claims to protect poor emigrants in the context of liberalization, they have been heavily paternalist and consistently failed to acknowledge poor emigrants' contributions to India. This stands in sharp contrast to Kerala's welfare programs. Moreover, they have not yielded much in material terms, ironically undermining poor emigrants' ability to meet the government ideal of becoming self-sufficient. First, disbursements from the national government's welfare programs have been woefully thin. In my meeting with R. Shahul Hameed, the finance manager of the Emigrant Welfare Board, it was clear that activity was low. The shelves in his office were nearly empty, and he had very little information to give. In 2012, about one year after it began, the board had 85,000 members; 33 families had received the Rs. 30,000 death allowance for the death of their family member at work; 50 more death allowances were pending at the time of the interview. Only one person had received the medical benefit, and 25 medical benefit applications were pending. Members were eligible to receive medical and death benefits upon joining, but since pension benefits require five years of contributions, none had received the pension at the time of my interview. An important weakness in the emigrants' Welfare Board is that, unlike Indian welfare boards for domestic construction workers (Agarwala 2013), it does not mandate financial contributions from employers, nor is it required by law in every state. Several organizations expressed extreme frustration with the government's pension scheme for migrants because of this, and because it offers a very low contribution from the government.

[79] This was only a small increase from the 145,000 it had assisted by 2019. Given the extraordinary circumstances of 2020 with the COVID-19 pandemic, the 2020 figure is rather low.

[80] This program was shut down in 2017. The government retained the Pravasi Bharatiya Bima Yojana, the mandatory insurance scheme, but this only covers accident or disability, *not* natural death.

[81] Lok Sabha Debates, 15th Series, Vol. 31, 13th Session, February 21, 2013, 54.

Second, despite national government officials' proud claims that they are protecting their fellow Indians, they did not take much responsibility for protecting poor emigrants and repeatedly reminded me that emigrant rehabilitation was actually the responsibility of subnational state governments. MEA Deputy Secretary Sharma suggested, "The PGE is more concerned with getting emigrants out than rehabilitating them upon return." Unless a migrant is trying to return under duress, Sharma explained, migrant return is the responsibility of state governments, not the national government.[82]

Finally, unlike in Kerala, where welfare programs have been offered as a response to workers' immense financial contributions to India, national government officials repeatedly emphasized what the government gives poor emigrants, while underplaying what the government gains from them. Potnuru, the research officer in the government think-tank for emigrants, said, "Wages are not that great in [the] Gulf. And the quality of living and work is too low for trained people. The exploitative nature of Gulf work makes [the Indian government] more responsible for protection of Gulf emigrants. While for the US emigrants, [the Indian government] can focus on reaping benefits."[83] Implicit in this statement is that there are no benefits to be gained from poor emigrants.

Similarly, a joint secretary in the Overseas Indian Affairs Division of the MEA stated, "This government is clear, we need to take care of the vulnerable people."[84] He contrasted the government's "caring" and protective attention to poor emigrants to "the think-tank circuit [that] likes to talk about the dollar diaspora [i.e., wealthy, elite emigrants]."[85] He did acknowledge the financial benefits from wealthy emigrants, but prided himself on having a more moral focus on vulnerable workers. Sharma also downplayed the financial benefits attained from poor emigrants to instead frame government welfare in terms of a moral commitment: "The government doesn't only look at migration from the remittance point of view. Each person is a precious individual, who we need to protect. . . . The poor chaps come from the poorest areas and they need more protection. . . . We do this protection for the brotherhood of our fellow Indians."[86]

Let us now examine how the CEO MDR is experienced by the migrants themselves.

[82] Interview, January 4, 2019.
[83] Interview, March 20, 2012.
[84] Interview, January 4, 2019.
[85] Interview, January 4, 2019.
[86] Interview, January 4, 2019.

Poor Emigrant Organizations and Migrant Recruiters

This chapter begins our analysis of how India's contemporary CEO MDR is experienced by migrants. An important unintended consequence of the CEO MDR is that it catalyzed formal organizations among poor and elite emigrants. This chapter analyzes the strategies and demands of poor emigrants' organizations and migrant recruiters, while the next chapter examines the organizational strategies and demands of elite emigrants.

A key point made in Chapter 5 was that poor workers had long demanded the liberalization of emigration and were thus instrumental in legitimizing the CEO MDR. As well, poor emigrants have long demanded rights-based protections from the state. But the CEO MDR has failed to meet this demand. Instead, it celebrated the right to seek job opportunities abroad and restricted the emigration of a subset of poor workers in the name of state protection. As detailed in Chapter 6, the CEO MDR has also offered poor emigrants a chance to emulate elite emigrants' ideals of self-sufficiency, "hard work," and entrepreneurship, while offering some welfare to retain its legitimacy. But the enterpreneurship and welfare programs have had minimal impact on migrants' material needs, and have ironically resuscitated the image of the "vulnerable migrant" that the Nationalist MDR had earlier produced and the CEO MDR had tried so hard to eradicate.

This chapter shows how poor emigrants have mobilized new organizations to hold the state accountable for their material and symbolic needs under the CEO MDR. Given the temporary nature of their emigration (mostly to the Gulf countries), poor migrants in India demand support for their departure, their time away from India, and their return. They target the national and subnational governments for the increased liberalization of their emigration, rights-based protection, data, and dignity. And to get the government's attention they wield

The Migration-Development Regime. Rina Agarwala, Oxford University Press. © Oxford University Press 2022.
DOI: 10.1093/oso/9780197586396.003.0007

their structural power as voters and as economic heroes who protect the nation's foreign currency reserves.

But despite these impressive efforts, poor migrants have largely consented to the CEO MDR's underlying elite class pact that deflects attention away from wage labor and labor organizing. This chapter examines how and why poor migrants articulate this consent through their uneven experiences with entrepreneurship and government welfare, and the reasons for their lack of radicalism. Finally, this chapter examines how the CEO MDR has ironically also undermined private recruiters, a class actor that the CEO MDR legitimized and legalized with the 1983 Act.

The Unintended Formation of "Return Migrant" Organizations

The legalization of emigration under the 1983 Emigration Act was an important victory for the poor workers who had been demanding such legalization since the 1970s. An unintended consequence of this legalization was that it catalyzed the formation of officially registered organizations among poor emigrants. The first of such organizations emerged in Kerala in the late 1980s, shortly after the 1983 Act was enacted. At the same time, labor demand in the Gulf was plateauing, and the first set of poor emigrants was approaching retirement age. As a result, these emigrants were denied renewed emigration visas to the Gulf and were forced to return to India. The dismal economic conditions they faced upon their return forced them to start organizations designed to gather returnees, build solidarity, and lobby the Indian government for assistance and welfare.

As a result of these conditions, migrant organizations in Kerala (and India more broadly) have several unique features. First, because most poor emigrants from Kerala go to the Gulf, and emigrants in the Gulf are so strictly monitored and forbidden to organize politically, almost all organizations among poor emigrants are registered in India.[1] Second, because poor emigration from India to the Gulf is temporary, Indian migrants' political organizations comprise what are known in India as "return migrants" or "returnees." Some return migrants are in India temporarily while they wait to become eligible for another job abroad, and others have returned home permanently. In Kerala, emigrants reside abroad for an average of six to eight years before returning, and many emigrants conduct multiple migration cycles (Kumar and Rajan 2014: Table 3.18). As a result,

---

[1] The few organizations that Indian migrants have in the Gulf focus exclusively on social and cultural issues (at least officially).

although poor emigrant organizations in Kerala assist emigrants in all stages of their out-migration (recruitment, predeparture, and while abroad), a major focus has been to assist them when they return. Thus, today emigrant organizations in Kerala are often referred to as "returnee organizations."

The vast majority of India's poor return migrants come from the Gulf. While many are skilled in their trade, they either failed to retain a job abroad or aged out of employment options. Returnees face resentment from nonmigrant Indians (who often assume all emigrants are financially wealthy), and they lack access to employment information and networks within India.[2] As a result, return migrants have become known for their high unemployment levels (Amjad 1989; Zachariah, Kannan, and Rajan 2002). According to one of the only large-scale surveys of Indian returnees, emigrants face higher unemployment upon return than before emigrating; among 2,749 returnees, 60% were unemployed upon return to India (Nair 1991).

One of the first returnee organizations to form was the All Kerala Gulf Returnee Organization (AKGRO), which was launched by Mr. S. Ahmad in 1988. Ahmad had worked with the same company in Saudi Arabia for 10 years, Oman for 10 years, and the UAE for 5 years. He began organizing AKGRO during his three-month return trips to India between jobs. While the members of AKGRO are mostly poor emigrants, the founders and current leaders are wealthier, midlevel return migrants from the Gulf. The general secretary, Kadakkal Ramesh, for example, is a software technician who worked in the Gulf for decades, and the vice president, Joseph Thomas, was an electrical engineer and worked in a supervisory role in the UAE from 1979 to 2010. Today AKGRO operates in 14 districts in Kerala and has 15,000 members, only one-fifth of whom are women. At the start, AKGRO charged members Rs. 10; today the membership fee is Rs. 100. Each member receives an identity card.

Under the CEO MDR, organizations similar to AKGRO grew in number throughout the 1990s and 2000s. Like AKGRO, they are membership-based (with fees and identity cards) and are registered as NGOs or as affiliated branches of political parties. Despite their membership, very few are registered as trade unions. All the organizations in my sample were led by middle-class migrant returnees. The organizations were almost entirely male in leadership and

[2] As many have shown, the Indian development dream of absorbing its mass labor force into full-time, formal jobs in manufacturing has not borne out in the contemporary era. Manufacturing growth in India has been dismal and unable to compete with that of China (Ghose 2016). Instead, informal, insecure, and unprotected jobs in urban construction and services have shown the greatest growth in employment in recent years (Agarwala 2019). In rural areas, continued land grabs have dispossessed the peasantry of agricultural income sources (Levien 2018). Some have even pointed to the dismal return of "pauperism" among India's rural and urban poor (Breman 2016).

membership. A few exceptions notwithstanding, women were included as family members rather than as emigrants. Finally, most leaders and members were over 40 years old, since returnees are usually approaching retirement. Many leaders spoke of how young, able bodies are utilized abroad, only to be returned home after they are less attractive as workers.

Poor Emigrants' Demands: Targeting the Government

Since the Nationalist MDR and still today, returnee organizations in Kerala have targeted the national- and subnational-level governments for help. In my interviews, organization leaders consistently critiqued the government (at both levels) for its exploitation of emigrants, inadequate protection, and lack of recognition of emigrants' contributions to India's economy. Yet they still depicted the government as a key site for a solution to emigrants' problems. This approach is typical in India, where the democratic legitimacy of the state as a protectorate of "the people" remains strong, especially among the poorest, most vulnerable and marginalized populations (Agarwala 2013). In the case of emigrant workers, the state holds an even higher degree of accountability, given their employers operate abroad and thus outside the legal reach of the Indian government.

Poor migrants in Kerala target both the national and state governments for increased recognition. But beyond that, organization leaders explained the division as follows: since the national government is responsible for restricting their free movement abroad, the Kerala government is responsible for the consequences of those restrictions. Within India's federalist structure, state governments are responsible for disbursing welfare to vulnerable populations. Therefore, migrant demands to the national government focus on increased deregulation and data on poor emigrants, while their demands to the state government focus on improved state welfare for them and their families. As well, migrant organizations agitate for seats in government schools abroad that are designed for NRIs and reservations in government jobs in India (similar to those given to military and defense personnel).

In my interviews, it was clear that migrant organizations seek government attention as much for the symbolic value it still holds in India as for material support. Leaders spoke with pride about their ability to attract government officials to speak at their events, since it gave their organizations legitimacy and prestige. Leaders of the Kerala Pravasi Welfare Association (KPWA), for example, recounted their star guest speakers at their annual meeting: State Minister of Labor Shibu Baby John of the Revolutionary Socialist Party and various members of the state legislative assembly. KPWA began in 2003 and currently has 22,000 members and is independent from any political party. Nevertheless, having political speakers was expressed as a point of pride. Even organizations that take no money from the government and rely only on private sponsors call on government officials, rather than the private sponsors, to distribute the funds.[3]

Demanding Deregulation of Poor Emigrants at the National Level

As already noted, poor workers began demanding the national government liberalize their emigration in the 1970s. But even after the legalization of their emigration under the 1983 Act, they have continuously pressured members of Parliament to lift the remaining regulations, vehemently contesting state claims that these regulations are protective. Migrants argue that the tedious bureaucratic paperwork and the onerous government fees (official and unofficial) underlying emigration regulations have inhibited poor workers' free movement and disempowered them. Migrants have also lobbied the national government to hold Indian embassies in the Gulf accountable for helping them address problems with living and work conditions abroad and with visas. As M. P. Achuthan, member of Parliament for the Communist Party of India (CPI) and president of Kerala Pravasi Federation (KPF) candidly put it, "Being a Member of Parliament, the embassy people will respond."[4]

Demanding Government Welfare at the State and National Levels

In material terms, migrant organizations in Kerala have demanded the state government provide welfare assistance. As shown in Chapter 5, poor workers' demands for liberalization never excluded their simultaneous demands for rights-based state protections. Although the CEO MDR tried to reframe state protection as merely the right to seek employment abroad(), its liberalization of emigration for poor workers relied on a fundamental contradiction. That is, it relied on receiving countries' growing preference for temporary or circular migration, which has legitimized poor emigrants' continued demands for state protection, especially upon their return.

Migrants' demands have included assistance for their families in India (such as education funds, healthcare packages, loans for housing), for emigrants

---

[3] Interview, August 3, 2012.
[4] Interview, August 10, 2012.

while they are working abroad (such as insurance in case of accidents at work, funding to transport bodies home in case of death, and reduced airline ticket fares for migrants traveling the government-owned airline, Air India), and for return migrants (such as pensions). As Najeeb Mohammed, Trivandrum District president of the Kerala Muslim Cultural Center (KMCC) noted, the temporary nature of poor emigration in India has held the state government accountable: "That earning target is never achieved. . . . Even then, they are forced to come back. . . . Now it is a question for the Kerala government—how to rehabilitate these people."[5]

In particular, organization leaders repeatedly spoke of the health consequences of work in the Gulf, pointing to the harsh physical conditions of working in the desert and living in labor camps, where migrants must take care of themselves. Unlike China's "dormitory regimes" (Pun Ngai), food, cleaning, and laundry are rarely provided in the Gulf labor camps. Organization leaders also noted the mental strain of being away from family and familiar food and culture. Unlike in the United States (see Chapter 8), Indian emigrants in the Gulf have been unable to reproduce their own cultural communities abroad.

Nearly all the organizations I interviewed also spoke about the need for the government to control the ticket prices of Air India, an airline that was publicly owned until 2021. These demands for reasonable airfare mirror earlier labor demands for mass public transport within India (and elsewhere). Migrant organizations coordinated joint protests at Air India offices and demanded the national government stop Air India's labor strikes during peak seasons when most migrants return home for holidays. As part of this strategy, the organizations frame Air India as an enemy of the migrants. Joseph Eugine, state president of the KPWA, exclaimed, "I think that all the airlines are like dacoits! Plundering the savings of poor *pravasis* [migrants]."[6] Eugine went on to exclaim, "Without any reason, they [Air India] simply declare [a] strike during the peak time. That gives golden opportunity for international airlines to hike the charges according to their wish, and the [Indian] government won't take any action."[7] Although Eugine was quick to defend the workers' right to strike, he argued that Air India workers were conspiring with foreign airlines and the Indian government against poor workers. He painted a grim, albeit unverified picture: "They [the government] cannot prohibit striking. It is [workers'] legitimate right. . . . But we feel this is a planned drama between the international airlines and Air India and the political system here. Why? International airlines will hike airfare . . . [and] get their share. Air India can show their

[5] Interview, August 12, 2012.
[6] Interview, August 11, 2012.
[7] Interview, August 11, 2012.

hands, telling . . . we are on strike. The government can say we are not charging. So I think this is a collective conspiracy."[8]

Demanding Government Data on Poor Emigrants

Almost all organization leaders I interviewed spoke about the need for greater government data on poor emigrants. There is no official count of Indian emigrants residing abroad or of return migrants.

Under the CEO MDR's 1983 Emigration Act, the government began collecting data on all poor workers who received clearance to legally emigrate. Despite repeated demands from migrant organizations to present this data by state, it is available only at the aggregate or national level. Those who do not require clearance (due either to their education level or their country of destination) are not counted by government's emigration offices.[9] For years, the government justified its imbalanced data collection as a form of protection that needed to focus on the most vulnerable emigrants requiring clearance. But in reality, the system also omitted the millions of poor workers who emigrated illegally or without clearance (often because they were convinced by a recruiter to avoid the costly government clearance fees). Moreover, as the government alters the criteria for clearance, relieving more workers from those requirements, the data on poor workers is thinning further.

The government also maintains no information on poor migrants after they return home to India. S. Ahmad, founder and president of AKGRO and chairman of Kerala's NRI Coordination Council, said, "The government doesn't know anything about who the returnees are. We [migrant associations] are not on the board of NORKA or the Welfare Board. People don't even know about our organizations. NORKA knows only me, and they send everyone to me."[10]

Many organization leaders described this lack of data as a problem for poor emigrants' visibility. To improve the situation, Abdul Khader, general secretary of Pravasi Sangham (Communist Party of India–Marxist [CPM]), called on the government to "take a census and then give them [migrants] all identity cards."[11] In addition to its symbolic value, such recognition would be a way to increase the number of return migrants accessing government welfare benefits. Some, such as Mohammed of the KMCC, expressed it as a way for the government

---

[8] Interview, August 11, 2012.

[9] India's Intelligence Bureau, as well as receiving countries, may have data on educated emigrants, but this data is not collected or maintained by India's emigration-related offices, nor is it made publicly available.

[10] Interview, March 23, 2012.

[11] Interview, August 16, 2012.

to learn about migrants' work in order to capitalize on those experiences and help migrants find a job upon their return. Others view the need for recognition as a matter of security. Many leaders complained about the ignorance of Indian embassies relative to those of other sending countries. V. S. Sunil Kumar, member of the state legislative assembly (CPI) and former secretary of KPF, complained, "If you put a question to [India's] central government—no answer, there is no statistics. [It's a] very dangerous situation. Malaysia knows how many Malaysian citizens [are] in Dubai . . . so, any citizen facing a problem . . . [the Malaysian] embassy will interfere. But if an Indian is in jail, nobody will come. . . . Nobody will care."[12]

Data and visibility were also expressed as a way to alter existing misconceptions about poor emigrants. During and after the Coolie MDR, emigration was associated with a loss of dignity. Under the CEO MDR, however, public conceptions about emigrants swung to the other extreme. President Achuthan of KPF explained, "There was an impression in Kerala that Gulf NRIs were minting money there because when they came back they would have the perfumes, good shirts, and they look as if they are well off. But when we went there, we saw the plight of people there, the vast majority of them are underpaid laborers, and many of them are not able to visit their families once in five or six years because they won't have the money to get air tickets." He spoke empathetically about the decrepit living and working conditions, the exploitation by recruiters, and the high cost of the visas that force them into bankruptcy or into illicit, risky migration.[13] Maintaining government data on emigrants' lives was viewed as a way to publicize information on their plight.

Asserting Emigrant Dignity

Finally, emigrant leaders expressed a deep commitment to elevating emigrants' reputation within India. As noted in Chapters 5 and 6, the CEO MDR has tried to reframe emigration as an economic opportunity available to all. In reality, and unsurprisingly, poor emigrants face myriad economic pitfalls on their migration journeys. Nevertheless, migrant organizations expressed a need to assert emigrant dignity *even* when emigration fails to bring sustained economic benefits.

Returnees I interviewed consistently extolled the social benefits of emigration, consistent with other scholars' findings. According to the 1991 survey by Nair (1991), 80% of returnees felt their friends and relatives held them in "great esteem." As many scholars have noted across countries (including India), a large

---

[12] Interview, July 30, 2012.
[13] Interview, August 10, 2012.

share of migrants' financial remittances is used in conspicuous consumption that explicitly aims to increase emigrants' reputation within their local communities. Such consumption patterns include basic comforts (such as a solid roof or floor or toilet), as well as sheer opulence (such as the purchase of TVs, an ornate gate, or home expansion). As detailed in Chapter 1, debates abound on whether such consumption spending has benefited sending-country development by creating chain effects (such as creating employment in residential construction) or lifting people out of abject poverty or has hindered development by drawing away from investment spending (Massey 1988; Walton-Roberts 2014). In many cases, consumption spending is not sustained. But few scholars deny that migrants' consumption spending has increased their social standing within their communities.

Migrants also spoke to me about the ideas they brought home to their local communities. These included more "modern values" toward their children (both boys and girls), more favorable opinions about education, greater aspirations regarding their future employment and social status, and more freedom to choose their own career. Indeed scholars have repeatedly shown that migration has increased the incentive to attain education in India (Khadria 2007). Some have argued that male returnees are more willing to share household duties with their spouses and are more receptive to family planning (Nair 1991; Osella and Osella 2008). Not surprisingly, "modern values" are replete with contradictions, especially when they interfere with economic accumulation. For example, scholars have shown that migration actually exacerbates existing gender hierarchies and institutions such as dowry giving, which is used by families seeking to fund their sons' emigration (Walton-Roberts 2014). In an ironic twist on "modernity," educated boys are considered "of greater value" and can thus demand higher dowries.

In my interviews, several leaders reflected upon the "superior" worldview of migrants (relative to nonmigrants) due to their migration experiences. That the government did not recognize this made their invisibility more frustrating. P. T. Kunhimohammed, founding president of Kerala Pravasi Sangham (CPM), spoke passionately about how his migration to the Gulf helped release him from the colonial inferiority that he had absorbed and been taught in the English-inspired Indian school system: "[With migration] a new world opened. When I went to Gulf, then only I understood I am Indian. . . . Now I say that I am a Keralite. I have no inferiority on all these things. I think I am equal to any other nation's citizens: American, or France, or any other. I am also culturally equivalent, linguistically. . . . From migration, you become more confident."[14] Kunhimohammed worked in the UAE in the personnel department of a French

---

[14] Interview, August 8, 2012.

and Lebanese construction company from 1974 to 1984. After returning to India, he helped found and led KPF, became a member of the state legislative assembly, and is now a filmmaker; one of his recent films is about the torn identity of a middle-class migrant worker.

Similarly, Priyadas G. Mangalath, founder of the World Malayali Council (WMC), viewed the work of his migrant organization as addressing the social deficits in Kerala, which is known for its high literacy and low mortality rates. Mangalath spoke proudly of his ability to build global social competence among Indian return migrants, appealing to a Western sensibility, fluency in English, the internet, public speaking, communication skills, and "proper" dress. Drawing from his own migration experience, he trains young new migrants to cultivate the cultural capital he has attained: "I need not be ashamed, I need not shy away, I need not feel different. That is what I am telling [the students]. . . . We are asking the students to become globally competent."

Poor Emigrants Wield Structural Power: Vote Banks and Economic Heroes

To draw government attention, returnee organizations underline emigrants' citizenship as their only power to make demands since they do not work for Indian employers and Gulf employers are absolved of legal responsibility toward their workers. As Kunhimohammed noted, "These people are forgotten by all organizations and governments of the world. But poor people think [of] their own country always, because they have no citizenship power [in the Gulf]. They have their own citizenship in their own country. So they love their country."[15] In other words, migrants' demands for government assistance in India are framed as an expression of loyalty to their home country and a demand for due citizenship rights in return. In my interviews in Kerala, migrant organization leaders described their ability to win government attention by framing emigrants as (1) a key vote bank or block of votes and (2) economic heroes who are saving the nation's foreign reserves.

The Emigrant Voter

In Kerala, the sheer mass of poor emigrants has enabled migrant organizations to successfully attract the attention of almost every political party there.

---

[15] Interview, August 8, 2012.

By mobilizing poor emigrants, therefore, the organizations have inadvertently created a vote bank or block of votes for politicians.

That I attained access to the chief minister due to my study on migration was reflective of the importance of this topic for the state government. At a similarly high level, Minister K. C. Joseph of NORKA explained, "Emigrants in Kerala influence elections, the economy, public opinion. Communications between them and the government are high."[16] K. Satish Nambudiripad, ex-CEO of NORKA-Roots, said of state support for welfare for returnees, "Both parties support it. They have to. . . . This is a vote bank issue. Politicians can't say no to these people. It's all political symbolism. . . . No party can avoid the migration issue in Kerala. It is very important"[17] J. C. Sharma, a member of the High Level Committee on the Indian Diaspora and former secretary of the Ministry of External Affairs, concurred, suggesting the attention emigrants receive from the Kerala government is "due to the large Malayali community in the Gulf. So [their] total focus is on the Gulf with an eye on Kerala elections."[18]

But unlike domestic informal workers who also wield their structural power as voters (Agarwala 2013), migrant organizations have not retained their organizational autonomy from political parties. Rather, they are deeply intertwined with political parties, which has enabled parties in Kerala to control them. Today, every political party in Kerala has its own affiliated migrant organization.[19] KMCC, for example, is affiliated with the Indian Union Muslim League, which has periodically enjoyed political power in Kerala. KMCC began in 1982 as the Chandrika Readers Forum to hold religious classes and social and cultural activities in the Gulf. Like other migrant organizations affiliated with Indian political parties, KMCC has tapped its emigrant members to offer social and cultural activities in the Gulf, while also addressing political issues in India. In 2012, when the League served as a ruling front partner in the Kerala government, KMCC started a sister organization, the Pravasi League, to lobby for and assist return migrants in Kerala. KMCC's membership fee is Rs. 500, and as with other migrant organizations, its leadership comprises middle-class return migrants. The KMCC's president, Najeeb Mohammed, for example, is a schoolteacher in the Sharjah Indian school in the UAE.

Similarly, Kerala Pravasi Sangham formed in 2001 as an affiliate of the CPM, which alternates with the Congress Party as the state's dominant party in power.

---

[16] Interview, March 22, 2012.

[17] Interview, January 11, 2017.

[18] Interview, March 15, 2011.

[19] Pravasi Sangam is affiliated with CPM; Pravasi Federation is affiliated with CPI; Kerala Pradesh Returnee Congress is affiliated with the Congress Party; Pravasi League is affiliated with the Indian Muslim League, and Pravasi Sangh is affiliated with the BJP.

It, too, works through cultural organizations based in the Gulf, as well as political organizations in India. Like others, its members are middle-aged and older. Unlike most migrant organizations, however, it addresses female emigrant issues, and nearly one-third of its members are women. KMCC has a women's subcommittee to assist female emigrants with issues of harassment and sexism in the Indian embassies in the Gulf, where their forms and claims are consistently ignored. Membership in KMCC is much lower than in other organizations at only Rs. 10 per year.

Even the independent organizations whose members I interviewed had strong links with elected officials and political parties. Leaders of both independent and politically affiliated organizations were often elected government officials. For example, the president of the CPI-affiliated KPF is a member of Parliament in the upper house (Rajya Sabha), and the former secretary of KPF, Sunil Kumar, is a member of the legislative assembly in Kerala. Although KPWA spoke proudly of its unique independence from any political party, its Kollam District president, K. Raju, is a member of the legislative assembly in Kerala from the CPI.

Some political parties formed organizations to lobby for migrant welfare programs, such as the Migrant Welfare Boards, in order to get votes. As S. Ahmad bluntly put it, "Each political party has a returnee organization. Why? They do this for votes. Each panchayat [village level government] gets 325 votes from returnees."[20] Even Noyal Thomas, the director and CEO of NORKA-Roots, said, "The Welfare Act is more of a politically motivated act. It is not financially sound. Every government just wants to score points."[21] Nambudiripad reiterated this point, arguing that including domestic migrants on the Welfare Board makes no sense since they have completely different issues and concerns (for example, bringing a dead body home from another state in India is not nearly as difficult as bringing one from another country). "But this is a vote bank issue. Politicians can't say no to these people. It's all political symbolism. . . . No party can avoid the migration issue in Kerala. It is very important."[22]

Other political parties formed their migrant organizations only after the state government had set up the migrant welfare programs and boards. The CPI-affiliated KPF is one such example. According to Sunil Kumar of the Kerala legislative assembly and former secretary of KPF, they formed to assist workers in joining and accessing the Emigrant Welfare Fund and other government programs. In this way, they could be seen as assisting workers in attaining welfare. Although KPF was among the last of the party-affiliated organizations to form, it has 30,000 members today.

[20] Interview, March 23, 2012.
[21] Interview, March 23, 2012.
[22] Interview, January 11, 2017.

Ironically, however, poor emigrants are often denied the right to vote. As Kumar explained, "They [migrants] have no voting rights here [in India]. Because they are the citizens of India they have passports, but their names are not put in the ration card [for public food subsidies]. Therefore, they are not getting the election identity card from India. . . . So we are proposing to central government that enactment is very necessary because all the Indian people, whether they are staying inside India or outside India, they have the right to elect their representative."[23] Although the government has now expanded the right to vote to migrants who are in India at the time of enrollment, migrant groups are pressing the government to allow Indians abroad to also vote. Otherwise, for the majority of emigrants who are stuck in endless circular migration, the power to vote remains a distant one. On the attraction of emigrant organizations as a vote bank, Kumar exclaimed, "It's a question of right of citizen. . . . So, only because of that we decided to organize the Pravasi."[24] As Nambudiripad noted, "The government's attention and efforts with NORKA and NORKA-Roots came due to this unique situation of 'migration without citizenship.' This is the mother of all problems. This was the guiding light for Roots."[25]

Because migrants are legally forbidden to vote while abroad, they often do not see themselves as voters. Therefore, organizations spend substantial energy building voter identity among poor emigrants. Eugine of the KPWA, explained, "The government is always bothered about those who are staying in the state because they are the vote banks for the politicians. For the *pravasis* [emigrants], it is not possible for them to come and cast their votes during the election. So the politicians are least bothered about their rights, their welfare, their settlement, their rehabilitation. So for the last ten years or more, we are working to mobilize the expatriates . . . those who are staying outside to make them aware of their rights, to unite them, and to demand their legitimate rights from the government!"[26]

The Economic Hero and Protector of Foreign Exchange

In addition to depicting themselves as potential voters, migrant organizations draw government attention by framing poor emigrants as "economic heroes" who contribute to India's development through their financial remittances and foreign currency. In return for their contributions, they argue, emigrants

---

[23] Interview, July 30, 2012.

[24] Interview, July 30, 2012.

[25] Interview, January 11, 2017.

[26] Interview, August 11, 2012.

deserve government assistance. This strategy has been particularly effective at the state level.

Eugine proudly noted, "The money sent by the *pravasis* changes the face of the country. Poverty has been eradicated by the *pravasis*. Our home country has been reconstructed. High buildings, roads, industries, huge shopping malls, are all the contributions of the *pravasis*. And *pravasis* are the main bloodline for the foreign currency reserve of the government of India as well as the government of Kerala."[27] Similarly, President Achuthan of KPF emphasized the structural power migrants have in the economy through the financial sector: "Migrant remittances contribute to thirty-two percent of the GDP in Kerala. So it's actually the *pravasis* [that] are helping the central government to ... narrow the gap of the foreign reserve. So, our contention is that the government is bound to help them because it is such an important segment of our economy."[28]

To fortify their claims, organization leaders compared poor migrants to other actors who currently receive government assistance in return for their contributions to the Indian economy from their work abroad. For example, some leaders compared migrants to exporters who are given a 6.5% refund of the foreign exchange they bring in through exports as an incentive to grow their business. Similarly, migrant organizations have demanded a percentage refund of their remittances and their emigration clearance fees.[29] The Kerala government has also long demanded the national government refund emigrants' unclaimed security deposits to fund subnational or state-level relief programs for returnees. But the national government has repeatedly refused, noting that statewise emigration data on clearances is (conveniently) not collected in India.

Other leaders compared emigrants to military workers. Kumar pointed to how much the government provides for the families of military personnel who have to go abroad for their work: "[Migrants] are doing the same thing for the country! So, that is why we are organizing."[30] Similarly, Kadakkal Ramesh, vice chairman of the Kerala State NRI's Coordination Council and general secretary of AKGRO, said, "[The government] can keep some reservation [quotas] in the government job sector for returnees. There is already a reservation [for jobs] for the defense people. ... They are the protectors of our land, whereas the NRIs are the protectors of our foreign reserve fund. We are helping the nation to stand ahead, in front of other nations in the world. We are the protectors of the economy of our nation. ... So it is the moral responsibility of the government ... to protect

[27] Interview, August 11, 2012.

[28] Interview, August 10, 2012.

[29] Interview, Sudarsan Kesavan, State Vice President of Kerala Pravasi Welfare Association, August 11, 2012.

[30] Interview, July 30, 2012.

their interests, to provide jobs . . . to provide housing . . . so that they can stand with their head straight in front of others!"[31]

Embracing the Land of Entrepreneurs in the Universal Interest

A striking feature of poor emigrants' politics in India is its distinction from domestic workers' politics. In Kerala, relations between migrant organizations and workers' unions are tense. Rather than joining domestic trade union efforts to demand government welfare and recognition and organizing emigrants as workers, returnee organizations have embraced the national government's attempts to reframe poor male emigrant workers as entrepreneurs (alongside the CEO MDR's corresponding ideals of individualism, self-sufficiency, and self-employment outlined in Chapter 6). To this end, they have worked hard to inculcate an entrepreneurial identity among poor migrants, especially upon their return to India. This entrepreneurial identity blurs the material distinctions between poor and wealthy emigrants by reconstructing all classes of emigrants into a single and joint cross-class category. This finding stands in sharp contrast to informal workers' organizations in India, who have similarly been left out of most union organizing efforts but who have nonetheless launched alternative unions with a worker identity (Agarwala 2013).

Poor migrants' acceptance of a new entrepreneurial identity is striking given its limited material outcomes (see Chapter 6). Returnee organizations in the contemporary era thus exemplify what Gramsci famously noted: the power of ideology lies in its ability to appeal to universal interests (Gramsci 1971).

Among officials of migrant organizations, none that I spoke with framed poor emigrants as workers. Leaders instead repeatedly framed workers as domestic and relatively privileged. As Ahmad of AKGRO put it, "Trade unions are a political class. They are of a trade. We are of people doing work!" Several leaders reiterated unions' failure to organize emigrants. Kunhimohammed of Kerala Pravasi Sangham (CPM) said this was the reason they began organizing migrants: "Because it is Kerala . . . people are organized in almost all sectors. . . . Only this sector was not organized before. So, because of that, nobody was caring [for] them."[32] To underscore the distinction, some leaders harked back to the Nationalist MDR to depict domestic workers as protected by Indian law, while equating poor emigrants to slaves. Kunhimohammed, for example, explained

[31] Interview, August 3, 2012.
[32] Interview, August 8, 2012.

emigration as "a new phenomenon that capitalism likes, because they are getting rootless laborers. Rootless means those who are plucked off from their home and don't have rights or their own culture, language, music. . . . They have a slave. They are not under unilateral acts, this is not applicable. . . . Even trade unions are not at all involving these poor people's problems."[33]

Rather than depicting poor emigrants as workers who deserve protection, migrant organizations depicted them as capital-owning "entrepreneurs," especially upon return. Abdul Khader, general secretary of Pravasi Sangham (CPM), said, "We have now decided to create a culture of self-employment and we want to start more institutions in the local area. . . . The social atmosphere is that."[34] The values of individualism and self-sufficiency underlying this push reflect 18th-century artisan values of self-discipline and self-help combined with a sense of community purpose from the culture of the "respectable" working class, which also spread among European labor during the Industrial Revolution (Abercrombie, Hill, and Turner 1980: 112). For example, Mangalath of WMC spoke of a project he initiated to train educated youth to be globally competitive and confident in service professions. But part of the program trains youth to become coconut climbers or provide live-in elderly care in return for housing. Mangalath explained, "I am training them to become more creative and friendly. [I tell them] don't clamor for rights unless and until you do your duty. . . . Accept, recognize, respect the dignity of labor. . . . Due to our caste system . . . many things are considered menial here. So, in order to change that social phase and psyche, I am doing these trainings." Mangalath attributes the unemployment among return migrants to their arrogance toward manual work and a lack of humility and obligation. But his interest in professional labor prevents him from organizing emigrants alongside manual workers.

To promote self-employment among return migrants, migrant organizations have demanded the government offer interest-free loans to start businesses. Unlike government initiatives, however, migrant organizations have made these demands *in addition to* rather than in place of demands for welfare and for government assistance in getting returnees wage jobs in the government or in the private sector. Along with demanding government support, almost every organization has provided its own support for migrants' self-employment. In 2012, the Congress-affiliated Kerala Pradesh Pravasi Returnees organization launched the Kerala Pravasi Cooperative Society to assist returnees (especially women) in starting their own businesses in livestock and agro-processing. Together with the ruling Congress government, the Society hosted a one-day seminar

---

[33] Interview, August 8, 2012.
[34] Interview, August 16, 2012.

to provide information and invited delegates from the agricultural department, small-scale industry department, and the hatchery (bee-keeping). Salim Pallivila, the Society's district president, expressed his faith in the potential for self-employment to assist poor returnees: "Land is there, and we would like to take that for the Society and cultivate vegetables. Kerala is facing [a shortage in] natural, organic vegetables. Everything is from other states . . . [and] all chemical. . . . We would like to take this opportunity . . . and use that land and the help of government, and from our part we can help with financial support and very low interest rate."[35] The Society also supports migrants in starting businesses in the Gulf (through private funding rather than government funding). Similarly, the community-affiliated Kerala Pravasi Sangham offers classes to help members start their own businesses. They have also started a *pravasi* college (with 13 staff members in Malappuram District), a small bank called the Pravasi Cooperative Society (with 10 staff members) to channel all government assistance, and a coconut-based small-scale industry in Trissur District (20 employees). The KMCC is also starting a new cooperative bank society in Mallapuram District.

Migrant organizations' efforts to channel returnees toward self-employment has affected trade unions, which show no interest in organizing emigrants. When asked to explain why, union leaders framed emigrants' interests as distinct from domestic workers'. Several union leaders assumed emigrants have more capital than domestic workers have. For example, A. D. V. Subodhan, treasurer of the Kerala office of the Indian National Trade Union Congress and head of Kerala's Construction Workers Congress, acknowledged that return migrants do not show much upward mobility: "Labor will always be labor." But he added, "Gulf workers need help with travel problems from the Gulf. They don't need money. . . . They return in financially high status and do not join construction again when they return. That is why we are not connected to them. They will marry their daughters and invest earnings in property and do petty business and get income from assets. And [they will] act as mini contractors."[36] In other words, although return migrants remain poor in social and financial terms, their new identities in contradictory class positions, as self-employed entrepreneurs and rentiers with enough capital for consumption and investments, separate them from domestic workers.

K. O. Habeeb of the Confederation of Indian Trade Unions in Kerala expressed a similar disinterest in organizing emigrants. His organization "is not taking on the issue of the Gulf . . . because many of the Gulf migrants are contractors and engineers, not just labor."[37] Rather than targeting the laborers among the

[35] Interview, August 9, 2012.
[36] Interview, March 22, 2012.
[37] Interview, March 23, 2012.

migrants, Habeeb lumped migrants under one cross-class identity that was, by definition, not suitable for union organizing. He also expressed a common resentment non-migrant workers feel toward returnees: "When they return they are no longer workers. They think they are better [than us]. . . . They spend all their money and have a miserable life [upon return]."[38] Although Habeeb was uninterested in organizing migrants as workers, however, he acknowledged their working-class needs. But he noted that his political party, CPM, rather than his union addresses the exploitation they face from employers, their low pay, broken promises, lack of accident compensation, vulnerable status as foreigners and as manual laborers, and even their unemployment.[39]

One interesting source of unions' disinterest in emigrants stemmed from Kerala's location as a migrant-sending state at the global level, but a migrant-receiving state within India. This was especially apparent in unions' views toward migrant welfare boards. As I have illustrated elsewhere, Indian unions have long fought for welfare boards for workers employed within India (Agarwala 2013). While Subodhan of Kerala's Construction Workers' Union celebrated domestic-level workers' welfare boards, he disparaged Kerala's migrant welfare board as a product of the ruling CPM in West Bengal trying to assist domestic Bengali workers *immigrating* into Kerala. Subodhan explained, "Many Bengalis come to Kerala to work. The migrant board gives Rs. 50,000 for death of the worker and they send the body to the family and cover funeral expenses. So this was to please the West Bengal voters."[40] In other words, from Subodhan's perspective, the ethnic differences between Bengalis and Keralites trumped both groups' class similarities, and global emigrants (even if from Kerala) were simply free-riding beneficiaries of a domestic political battle.

Government officials acknowledged the resentment between local workers and emigrants without trying to alleviate it. Ooman Chandy, chief minister of Kerala (INC) at the time of my interview, noted, "Some social tension is natural when [migrants] return due to [their] financial gain."[41] In other words, Chandy supported the assumption that migrants earn large sums while abroad but did not underscore the risks and costs they bore as a result. Others explained the social roots of the resentment. As Nambudiripad, ex-CEO of NORKA-Roots, noted the first migration streams to the Gulf were mainly poor Muslims: "They started buying out the [Hindu] upper castes. This created resentment. There are even remnants of that now. . . . The richness of the Muslim community is very visible."[42] Although Nambudiripad led Kerala's government institution

---

[38] Interview, March 23, 2012.
[39] Interview, March 23, 2012.
[40] Interview, March 22, 2012.
[41] Interview, March 22, 2012.
[42] Interview, January 11, 2017.

to support migrants, he himself disparaged emigrants' families within India, pointing to their conspicuous consumption: "[Migrants] are totally exploited by their own family. The family is getting money doing nothing, just having a cushy life. Driving a Honda motorbike."[43]

Instituting and Experiencing Government Welfare Programs

Kerala's migrant organizations take full credit for the existing emigrant welfare programs in Kerala and at the national level. For example, AKGRO leaders recalled how in the 1980s, they lobbied the chief minister of Kerala, Sri E. K. Nayanar (CPM), to form a department to take care of poor emigrants (while abroad and upon return). In 1990, the Iraq-Kuwait War flooded Kerala with masses of return migrants, forcing the Kerala government to pay more attention to AKGRO's demands for rehabilitation assistance. S. Ahmad, president of AKGRO and chairman of Kerala's NRI Coordination Council, attributed legitimate goodwill to government officials: "We had a left front government under Chief Minister I. K. Nayar, and he wanted to do something for them [returnees]."[44] So the state government set up a small office under the leadership of Dr. Veno in the government secretariat, called the "Kuwait Cell," that assisted returnees. Within six months, the cell was broadened into the "Non-Resident Keralite (NRK) Cell," and in 1996, under the next government, Chief Minister A. K. Anthony (UDF) elevated it to the department level in the state government and appointed a minister, M. M. Hassan.

Ramesh of AKGRO recalled how his organization lobbied Minister Hassan for increased assistance for migrants: "We presented a lot of things, we advised the government what to do, how to help the poor nonresident Keralites by providing them rehabilitation schemes for education of their children. Pension was the most important thing. . . . We put pressure [for it] to be implemented." AKGRO also demanded support for medical expenses and migrant daughters' marriages. "After struggling for nearly ten to fifteen years, all these schemes were implemented one by one," said Ramesh proudly. "Our members say because of the continuous pressure from the leaders of AKGRO, the state government and the center government have implemented several schemes for the welfare of the Gulf returnees who are a main source of foreign currency deposit for the government of Kerala."[45]

---

[43] Interview, January 11, 2017.
[44] Interview, March 23, 2012.
[45] Interview, August 3, 2012.

Similarly, Pallivila of the Kerala Pravasi Cooperative Society attributed the government's pension scheme for returnees to the pressure that his parent organization, Kerala Pradesh Returnees Congress, placed on Ooman Chandy (Congress Party) when he was the leader of the opposition. Along with other organizations trying to build mass support for the Congress Party, Kerala Pradesh Returnees Congress formed in 2008 as a Congress Party affiliate. Today it operates in all 14 districts of Kerala and has 23,000 members, 90% of whom are male. Once Congress won the state elections and Chandy became the chief minister, Pallivila recalled, his organization held "powerful agitations [to] seek the attention of the government. . . . With the help of Ooman Chandy and eight of our [legislative assembly members] . . . we submitted a notice . . . then [Chandy] announced a subcommittee meeting of legislative assembly, legislators, three members of legislative committee. . . . They studied the matter in light of our demands, they suggested [to] the government . . . and then they approved our demands and accepted the *pravasi* returnee welfare. That is the actual story."[46] Whether this is or is not the actual story, it is significant that migrant organizations claim credit for the government's existing welfare programs.

Once in place, the state government welfare programs spurred new migrant organizations to emerge to spread information about the programs and to connect more migrants to the relevant government agencies disbursing the welfare. According NORKA's Minister Joseph, local associations have now formed in all districts of the state, and they are very active. Ramesh Chennithala, president of the Kerala Pradesh Congress Committee, explained, "NORKA and local migrant associations work together with self-help groups to hand-hold migrants and expose them to new technology."[47] Kumar credited migrant organizations for the reach of welfare programs: "When we passed this Act, we expected more than two hundred thousand people to enroll. But after two years, the statistics show only seventy-five thousand people enrolled." He credited migrant organizations for the few enrollees they do have. "Our challenge is how can we organize them? This is a very difficult task."[48]

At the same time, nearly all leaders I spoke with complained that the emigrant welfare programs pale in comparison to emigrant workers' economic contributions to India, and that the implementation of government welfare programs has been woefully inadequate. Some leaders pointed to the legislation itself, noting the 1983 Emigration Act does not sufficiently call for the protection of emigrants or stipulate enough funding for welfare.[49] Migrant

---

[46] Interview, August 9, 2012.
[47] Interview, March 22, 2012.
[48] Interview, July 30, 2012.
[49] Interview, P. T. Kunhimohammed, August 8, 2012.

organizations have joined together to demand higher contributions from the government for migrant welfare. And almost all migrant organizations spoke about the patronizing way that government officials implementing the welfare boards treated migrants and the difficulties migrants faced in getting the required documentation and certification of their time and income abroad from local authorities. Eugine of the KPWA accused authorities of giving migrants the runaround and demanding money in exchange for documents: "The government, they don't believe the people. The people, they don't believe the government. This is the plague going on. The people don't want to believe government, because the promises of government are in vain. The government thinks that the people will bring fake documents to avail the programs the government gives."[50] Similarly, Khader of Pravasi Sangham lamented the Kerala government's failed attempt to support return migrants after the 2008 financial crisis by providing loans to start small industries under the Kerala Financial Corporation: "Only some people took that opportunity. . . . There are just too many documents to fill!"[51]

Fostering Nonradical Migrant Organizations

Despite poor emigrants' authentic demands, articulate mobilization frames, and intermittent successes (deregulating their emigration, facilitating some self-employment among returnees, and attaining some welfare programs), they have largely failed to hold the national government accountable for their needs. One key reason for this failure is that their organizations have been mostly nonradical due to their (1) close relationship to political parties and (2) cross-class membership and leadership. Together, these features have left poor migrant organizations unempowered, especially relative to elite emigrants (see Chapter 8).

A Partisan State-Migrant Relationship

Organization leaders spoke of their relationship to state government officials as close and collaborative rather than conflictual. For example, Chennithala of the Kerala Pradesh Congress Committee displayed a close relationship with Minister Joseph of NORKA. AKGRO leaders also spoke highly of NORKA and of their relationship to the government (at the national and state levels), and indeed AKGRO was one of the few migrant organizations that the Kerala

[50] Interview August 11, 2012.
[51] Interview, August 16, 2012.

government officials knew about. Kadakkal Ramesh of AKGRO recalled with pride their early interactions with NORKA: "Our organization was very close to the government of Kerala and to the NORKA department and the NORKA minister, Mr. Hassan. He was very helpful for us."[52] Ramesh was complimentary of the government's programs, proud that AKGRO's pressure had paid off: "We are happy with the performance of both the government [at the state and national levels]. And the members of our organization are also happy."

Underlying the close relationship between migrant organizations and the Kerala government is political party involvement, which has made migrant politics in Kerala highly partisan. As a result, victories are often unsustained across elections. Party-affiliated organizations consistently traced their growth to periods when their parties were mobilizing support as the opposition, and their victories to periods when their parties were in power. As well, leaders' critiques of government often targeted periods when their opponents were in power. For example, Pallivila of the Congress-affiliated Kerala Pravasi Cooperative Society presented a neat and clear narrative of civic action leading to a government response for migrant pensions when Congress won power. But he was as quick to critique the subsequent left front government for stalling the process. In other words, democracy works, but politics stalls.

The partisan nature of emigrant organization was also described as a deterrent to joint action across organizations, despite organizations' remarkably similar demands. This is a familiar trope in India and is often stated as a problem with traditional workers' unions. For example, Achuthan of the KPF described how organizations affiliated with the ruling parties would not critique the government as much as those tied to the opposition. He added, laughing, "Everybody has got political interest. It is fine and good if we visualize that every *pravasi* is organized under one umbrella. But it is wishful thinking. It will be impossible. We don't have a single platform where different *pravasi* organizations can work together."[53] In the early 2000s, Ahmad of AKGRO launched a Coordination Council (of which he is the chairman) to bring together the different migrant organizations: "[AKGRO] was the first organization, but then suddenly there were thirty-six organizations just in Kerala alone. . . . Now there are one hundred twenty!"[54] But AKGRO's Ramesh was less enthusiastic about its prospects: "We are working from different angles. . . . Everybody's demands are the same . . . there is no disagreement. But we don't take a united move for pressurizing the government."[55]

[52] Interview, August 3, 2012.

[53] Interview, August 10, 2012.

[54] Interview, March 23, 2012.

[55] Interview, August 3, 2012.

Cross-Class Membership and Leadership

Another contributor to migrant organizations' inability to affect radical change is that their membership and leadership often comprise a cross-class coalition of migrants, ranging from very poor laborers to midlevel professional workers to wealthy managers, business owners, politicians, and even recruiters. This cross-class character of migrant organizations fits well with the CEO MDR's approach to promoting a cross-class identity among emigrants (see Chapter 6).

All the organizations whose members I interviewed were founded and led by professional return migrants who had operated at midlevel jobs in the Gulf, such as electrical engineers, personnel managers, business owners, and teachers; some had begun doctoral programs in literature and philosophy and one was president of a software development company. They spoke with great pride about their accomplishments. Organization leaders often blamed rich migrants in the Gulf for poor emigrants' exploitation. For example, Kumar blamed rich Indian migrants for charging high fees in the Gulf's Malayali schools. Others blamed rich Indians in the embassies, "who don't pay attention to uneducated, poor migrant workers," and the rich Indian emigrants who don't invest in industries at home, as Chinese emigrants did.[56] Aside from these complaints, however, I found no instances in which organizations mobilized to hold wealthier migrants accountable for poor migrants.

Rather, organizations more often tried to capitalize on wealthy migrants' financial and cultural capital by forming cross-class coalitions with them. The KMCC's Mohammed, for example, spoke highly of Youssef Ali, founder and owner of the LuLu supermarket chain, and his contributions to the medical centers that KMCC and the Indian Union Muslim League built in Kerala. KMCC's strong presence in the Gulf has enabled it to collect money from wealthy migrants there (including from Yosef Ali) to use in Kerala. With these funds, KMCC has built medical centers, offered education scholarships and housing, and built wells in rural areas. At the time of interviewing, they were planning to hold a marriage feast where they would give Rs. 100,000 to 13 poor couples (not only return migrants), who would be selected based on age and income. Additionally, they would offer to take one or two of the grooms to the UAE for a job. With their private donations, KMCC also offers emigrants in the Gulf their own social security scheme in the event of death (3 to 6 lakhs, depending on the country); it is a contributory scheme only for KMCC members (100 dhirmas/year). They also help with job placement, provide tickets to return to India for visits and passport services for a fee. Mangalath of WMC spoke proudly of his most famous and largest project, a village adoption program in which wealthy emigrants in the

---

[56] Interview, July 30, 2012.

Gulf adopted a village in each district of Kerala. Mangalath himself gave 10% of the profits from his software development company to the village he adopted.

Through these cross-class coalitions, almost all organizations generated private support to assist migrants with day-to-day problems within their own families, as well as with community members, local authorities, or recruiters. Services include legal advice on employer or recruiter malpractice, help with land disputes, and information on regulations in the Gulf. Organizations used their networks to access local lawyers, as well as wealthy Indian emigrants in the Gulf. These contacts provide philanthropic funding to organizations, in-kind donations to migrant families (such as school bags, books, wheelchairs), as well as welfare-type packages (such as education awards and partial medical treatment packages). For assistance in the Gulf, they help migrants fill out forms and navigate court cases, assist those who are jailed abroad, and organize dead body returns to families in India.

Although these efforts are laudable, the cross-coalition of reliance on wealthy migrants undermined the radicalism of migrant organizations' demands. Several leaders proudly distinguished their approach from the more revolutionary civil society approaches that are familiar to Kerala's history. Mangalath described how he dismantled WMC in 1998 just as it was taking off with nearly 2,000 members. He had formed WMC in 1995 in New Jersey among emigrants living in the United States. In 1996, WMC welcomed return migrants living in Kerala and formed offices in all 14 districts. Mangalath explained, "But I understood in due course that this is just degenerating into an organization which is militant in nature, like any of the organizations in Kerala. Because they have existence only to go and fight against other people. Fight for your rights. Because the mindset in Kerala is very much leftist. Even know I am [supportive] of leftists, but at the same time, I am not ready to take up the methodology that they have adopted. I am bringing in a new methodology in my latest activities."[57] Mangalath attributed this decision to his need for and commitment to a cross-class coalition along ethnic lines. "All these rich people are known to me. They helped me . . . and the original goal of WMC was two things. One was Malayalis for Malayalis. Means, through networking, Malayalis all over the world should benefit. They needed a platform, and this is the platform. Secondly, the overall development of Kerala, which is the birthplace of all the Malayalis. Now, it is not the economic development which I am talking about. It's the social, it's the spiritual. And we initiated a few projects."[58] Instead, he turned to philanthropic approaches, such as village adoption by wealthy expats and youth employability

[57] Interview, August 15, 2012.
[58] Interview, August 15, 2012.

enhancement programs. A more recent project that began on January 9, 2009, ALTIUS, aims to "make the students of Kerala globally competent and socially competent."[59] Explained Mangalath, "It's basically a training course. This year we have started interfering in the social context of Kerala. . . . We want people to be positive, friendly, and creative. When I say this, the youth presently is not. Because if they have a problem, immediately they just go out of the college campus and just throw stones at the buses and stop everything. This type of destructive activities."[60]

The Rise of Private Recruiters under the CEO MDR

In addition to legitimizing migrant organizations, the CEO MDR's legalization of emigration for poor Indians legitimized and catalyzed growth in the number of private recruiters. While precise estimates vary (from 50% to 90%), there is little doubt that recruiters are responsible for the majority of poor Indian emigrants in the Gulf today (Abella 2004; Shah and Menon 1999).[61] As Manollo Abella (2004: 201) writes, profit-seeking intermediaries are "probably more responsible than any other factor for increasing the speed of emigration and determining the direction of the outward flows."

Despite their central role in the migration industry, however, private recruiters today represent an understudied class actor.[62] My own interviews with recruiters expose an important contradiction in the CEO MDR's push for privatization and entrepreneurship, which ironically does not cleanly apply to private recruitment entrepreneurs.

The Vilified Business of Recruiting

The business of recruiting consists of connecting Indian workers to Gulf employers and helping workers emigrate according to Indian government regulations. For employers, recruiters ensure they receive the type of worker

---

[59] Note the launch date is the date of Pravasi Bharatiya Divas (Overseas Indian Day). Altius is drawn from the Olympic motto: "Higher, faster, stronger." See ALTIUSyouth.com and altiusyouth. org.

[60] Interview, August 15, 2012.

[61] Other channels of migration to the Gulf include family sponsorship (especially among migrants who first arrived through a recruiter) and direct contracts with employers (usually reserved for professionals) (Shah and Menon 1999).

[62] Buckley (2012) offers one of the few analyses based on interviews with recruiters.

they are seeking in terms of skills, age, health, and even religion. For workers, recruiters help them find employers; organize their job interviews; certify their skills and sometimes provide skill-improvement training; provide medical tests, passports, airline tickets, and visas; and (most important) fill out the government's emigration clearance papers and attain the coveted stamp allowing them to leave India. None of the recruiters I interviewed worked with the migrants upon their return. Explained one recruiter, "I am not in the business of knowing what they do when they come home. I can only send them out again."[63]

In return for their services, all recruiters charge migrants a hefty fee. Although government regulations under the CEO MDR have capped that fee, almost all recruiters admitted they have to charge more unofficially to cover their expenses and make a profit. But recruiters differ on their fee structures for these services. The majority of private recruiters charge emigrants for all the above services. In some cases, employers pay for the airfare, visa fees, and medical certifications, and a minority of government recruiters fund free skills-upgrade training and a predeparture orientation.

Recruiting agencies also differ in their operational structure. A small number of the recruiters I interviewed had large, corporate-looking, shiny businesses with in-house testing centers to certify migrants' qualifications and provide skills training (for a fee). An even smaller number of recruiters I interviewed operated simultaneously as employers in the Gulf, managing affiliated construction companies there. Some I interviewed operated officially as travel agencies, while running an unlicensed recruiting agency in the back office (although this practice is slowly declining with increased government regulation). But the vast majority of the recruiting agencies I visited were tiny outfits that focused only on recruiting, operating out of half-finished buildings, located in back alleys, with a small staff. In all cases, the small size of the business gave me easy access to the managing directors. Despite their shabby physical structures, they all maintained a professional online presence, with glossy and up-to-date websites, which were required by law in order to retain their registration licenses.

Almost all the recruiters I interviewed represented lower- to lower-middle-class small business owners and entrepreneurs. None had been raised in English-medium schools (a hallmark of class in India), and all had sons or nephews who were involved in and planned to take over the business (a typical multigenerational trajectory in middle-class business families in India). Most of them began their businesses in the 1980s, after the 1983 Emigration Act legalized emigration.

---

[63] Interview, Asloob Khan (Yawar), January 13, 2007.

But some began by smuggling poor workers out of India in ships during the early 1970s, when emigration was still illegal and rare. As K. M. Jamaluddin, proprietor of Hiba Exports India, recalled, "The ship's timing or date was not fixed. So we had to also house and feed the workers for a few days at the port, so we were ready when the ship came. We arranged the ship ticket. We had to advise them about the ship and the laws and the passports, et cetera. Twenty-five percent would die on the way."[64]

Given these features, we might expect private recruiters to be supported by the CEO MDR. Throughout my interviews with almost every actor in the migration industry, however, it became abundantly clear that recruiters are the most despised. In addition to being a large and profitable industry of small businesses, it is exploitative. As one recruiter admitted to me, "Look, this is a *big* money game. The bottom line is that the poor, uneducated workers will spend any amount of money if there is a light at the end of the tunnel. So it is easy to charge them money to go through that tunnel."[65]

But more than other exploiters in the industry, such as Gulf employers, private testing centers, and airline operators, recruiters are consistently viewed as *illegitimate* exploiters. Almost every actor I interviewed (including government officials, academics, journalists, migrants, and even recruiters themselves) viewed recruiting agents as the biggest villains of the migration industry. Irudaya Rajan, a highly regarded scholar at Kerala's Center for Development Studies who has tracked emigration to the Gulf for two decades, eloquently pointed out that migrants "are going to the Gulf to sell their labor, but they have to pay to sell their labor. There's something wrong here" (quoted in Kamat 2015). The perceived illegitimacy of recruiters' profits served as an excuse for other actors to continue their own exploitation. For example, Abhay Pathak, general manager (commercial) Northern India of Air India, explained why Air India has not met migrant demands for reduced airfare to the Gulf: "We have a reduced price for tourist groups. But not for migrants. Migrants buy individual tickets and are not coming together to make a group price. Usually recruiters don't have to pay the [airfare], so they are not trying to get the group price. In fact, they are usually trying to make money off the migrants by taking a fee for the higher plane fare. It's all an employment racket. And why should we help the [recruiting] agents with reduced fares?"[66]

[64] Interview, November 18, 2015.
[65] Interview, Varun Khosla, Dynamic Staffing Services, November 20, 2015, emphasis in original.
[66] Interview, November 15, 2015.

Recruiters and the 1983 Emigration Act

As noted in Chapters 3 and 4, private recruiters have been profiting off poor emigrants since the colonial era. Under the Nationalist MDR, when the state criminalized poor workers' emigration, private recruitment operated extralegally, making it an extremely exploitative, high-risk, high-profit industry. Therefore, when poor workers demanded the legalization of their emigration, they also demanded the government replace private recruiters with state-based recruiting services. But the government did not meet poor workers' demands. Instead, under the 1983 Emigration Act that legalized poor workers' emigration under the CEO MDR, the Indian government recognized, registered, and licensed private recruiting agents, claiming to regulate them and prevent them from exploiting poor emigrants.

This new system of registering and licensing private recruiters fit the privatization ideal of the CEO MDR. But it also increased private recruiters' ability to exploit poor emigrants. As a result of the new system, private recruiters say that they earn more money placing poor workers than they do placing professional workers (Rajan, Varghese, and Jayakumar 2011).[67] First, the 1983 Act stipulated that all poor emigrants requiring government clearance must use a government-licensed private recruiter, thereby making poor workers even more dependent on private recruiters' services. To ensure that emigrants had no other option, the government repeatedly refused to replace private recruiters with a government entity, arguing the government does not have the capacity to out-compete private recruiters. The government also discouraged foreign employers from directly recruiting emigrants by requiring employers to attain a recruitment permit. Second, the new government clearance fees provided recruiters with a new profit stream; recruiters became notorious for charging poor emigrants a fee to avoid the costs of emigration clearance and instead emigrate on tourist or pilgrimage visas for Hajj and Imran.

To retain its image as a "protector" of vulnerable workers in this context of recruiters' continuing exploitation, the government under the CEO MDR vilified private recruiters. The 1983 Act, for example, explicitly turned the government gaze from exploitative foreign employers to exploitative Indian recruiters. Throughout the parliamentary debates on emigration during the CEO MDR, recruiting agents were repeatedly highlighted as the "main culprits," the "most greedy," and the "most villainous" actors in the industry. They were deemed worse than the employers abroad (who were granted exemptions within the Act) and worse than the "corrupt" government Indian officials. To control recruiters' exploitation, the government capped licensed recruiters' fees

[67] This statement was also confirmed in my own interviews with recruiters.

and promised to punish violating recruiters with a fee, imprisonment, and loss of registration. Finally, the government required each recruiter to pay a hefty bank deposit to the government for each migrant client, which it would use to address worker complaints against recruiter exploitation.

For decades, these government regulations of private recruiters were rarely enforced. As Krishna Kumar and Irudaya Rajan (2014: 25) write in their examination of Indian emigration and their policy recommendations for the future, "Regulating the recruitment industry in the 21st century has to imply something more than giving it a bad name and failing to hang it." Unregistered recruiters thus continued their operations; a large share of poor emigrants remained undocumented; and the risky, exploitative, high-profit, extralegal migration industry continued to flourish through the 1990s. Poor young females, who were still legally forbidden to emigrate, pay private recruiters additional fees to facilitate their emigration. But in recent years, the government has increased its regulatory attention to recruiters.

The CEO MDR's Failure to Protect Small Businesses

Although all the recruiters I interviewed supported free-market entrepreneurship, they all bemoaned the increasing regulatory weight the government was placing on their businesses. And they argued these regulations favored large corporate recruiters over small recruiting businesses, as well as elite migrants over the poor.

All the recruiters I interviewed displayed an impressive adaptability to the changing political parties in power and corresponding changes in migration policies, regulations, and institutions. One leader relayed, "Congress started e-migrate, [and] BJP is implementing it. . . . Before we answered to the Labor Ministry, then MOIA, then MEA. . . . There is no difference for us. Now they don't know anything about labor in the MEA. But slowly they will learn. No big thing."[68] Despite their adaptability, almost all recruiters voiced negative opinions about the national government, which they saw as "useless," "ignorant," and focused only on elite emigrants. One recruiter exclaimed, "MOIA doesn't do anything. They have given one stop to NRIs [or elite emigrants in the West], but NRIs are so different [from Gulf migrants]! MOIA won't even meet recruiting agents or the Gulf migrants. But an NRI from the US and UK can get a meeting immediately."[69]

[68] Interview, Yawar, Asloob Khan, January 13, 2007.
[69] Interview, Bandhu Travels of Sunil Kumar Kushwaha, Managing Director, November 23, 2015.

At the core of recruiters' distaste for government officials was a critique of government regulations that interfere with free, competitive markets. Recruiters blamed government regulations that aimed to protect poor emigrants (such as the minimum wage, bank deposits, and employer certifications) for slowing the process of attaining emigrant visas and thus undermining labor demand from Gulf employers. As business owners of human "exports," recruiters viewed the minimum wage requirements as government interference in export pricing, which undermined their competitiveness in the global market of labor supply. As one recruiter said, "We are competing with other countries. So this is not practical. We are asking the GOI [government of India] to be more practical."[70] Echoing a common critique of labor protections, recruiters complained that employers are recruiting labor from other countries with fewer requirements (an accusation that was not supported by emigration officials, who claim that labor demand from the Gulf is actually increasing). Recruiters accused the government's increased regulations of being performative, protecting India's global image more than workers. As one recruiter explained, "GOI is an international figure. So they have to show they are protecting their workers."[71] Another noted, "The regulation is higher because of the international shaming."[72]

More than any other new regulation, recruiters at the time of interviewing complained about the government's new digital system, e-migrate, designed to organize, register, and regulate them (see Chapter 6). In particular, recruiters argued that the requirements of e-migrate hurt small recruiters, who cannot afford to meet the conditions of registration.[73] "Our government is stopping us," said one recruiter.[74] Recruiters also complained that e-migrate requirements were attempting to formalize their small businesses to replicate corporate entities. In addition to maintaining up-to-date, professional websites (which all agencies I interviewed maintained), the government (along with the International Labor Organization) has demanded that agencies reorganize with separate departments and clear job delineations of who is the director, head of human resources, head of recruitment, and so on. One recruiter of an agency that his father started in 1952 laughed at the request: "We have such a small company with a small income. How will we create all this staff and departments and organizational charts?"[75]

[70] Interview, Construction Consultants, Apar Singh, founder and owner, January 12, 2017.
[71] Interview, Yawar, Asloob Khan, January 13, 2007.
[72] Interview, Al Mansoor, Imran, January 12, 2017.
[73] Interview, Al Mansoor, Imran, January 12, 2017.
[74] Interview, January 13, 2007.
[75] Interview, Capital Travels, Gurvinder Singh, November 23, 2015.

Only one recruiter was complimentary about e-migrate. That he had the largest agency in my interview sample was not a coincidence. He described e-migrate as a response to recruiters' earlier complaints against corrupt government officials: "In the past, when we would apply for a visa for our workers, the companies would call me and say, 'Varun, we really like you and we want to hire through you, but the embassy is insisting we use a different agent.' So I would have to go the embassies and make relations with the ambassador and promise him some bucks. I had ambassadors calling me directly on my cell phone saying, 'I want a TV.' So recruiting agencies would spend a lot of time making relations with the embassies. But now it's finally centralized with e-migrate. And we have the same principles and rules for every country. This has decreased the power of the embassies. This is the first excellent initiative by the ministry."[76]

Recruiters were quick to separate their dislike for e-migrate from any wrongdoing on their part. One recruiter complained that his business will have to shut down due to the new regulations, but he admitted, "[Regulation] is good for the employee and for taking away smuggling. For the decent agencies, there is no big difference due to e-migrate. If you were doing something bad, then now [the government] will catch you."[77] But by the end of our interview, this recruiter was agitated and defended his attention to emigration restrictions against young women and household labor: "And let me tell you—I have never ever sent a single woman or a single driver for a household. I am not getting involved in all that. I do my work honestly. I might earn less. I will die with empty hands, the way I was born. But I will go in peace."[78]

Instead, recruiters claimed that e-migrate was offending Gulf employers. One recruiter explained, "These Arabs think they are doing some huge thing when they just sign one paper. Why would they bother with all these requirements?"[79] Many recruiters stated that it was "unreasonable" to demand Gulf employers complete paperwork, wait in line at the Indian Embassy to provide information, pay workers a minimum wage, and be forbidden to keep workers' passports. One recruiter complained, "GOI is trying to make the lives of the Indian worker good, but they are not looking at the employer's needs." He added, "And the government is making their policies so rudely. They don't know anything. Skeikhs feel that no one can rule over them. But GOI thinks they can just make these rules and the sheikhs will listen?!... The companies are furious!"[80]

[76] Interview, Varun Khosla, Dynamic Staffing Services, November 20, 2015.
[77] Interview, Yawar, Asloob Khan, January 13, 2007.
[78] Interview, January 13, 2007.
[79] Interview, January 13, 2007.
[80] Interview, Capital Travels, Gurvinder Singh, November 23, 2015.

Recruiters also repeatedly (and correctly) noted the discrepancy between the government's increasing labor regulations regarding emigrants and foreign employers versus its decreasing labor regulations within India. Indeed, in the context of the contemporary era of increasingly liberalized markets within India, it is surprising to hear business owners complain about increasing regulations. Ironically, like many government officials of the CEO MDR, recruiters framed migrant regulations as a barrier to poor people's right to work. "If I could, I would tell the government to relax their rules. Let people go and work!" said Asloob Khan.[81] Another recruiter pointed to the lack of jobs in India and migration as the only alternative for the poor: "If you don't want Indian workers to go abroad for a job then why don't you give them a job here?! The poorest are the ones being hurt. And you will hurt the foreign exchange and GDP of India."[82] One recruiter scoffed at Prime Minister Modi's campaign "Make in India," which tried to increase domestic jobs by attracting foreign manufacturers to India: "Who is going to come here? No one! . . . No one has jobs in India. GOI needs to be serious with Indian labor. But instead, Modi went to the UK and asked for more student visas! He wants to send more money abroad. He wants to take foreign exchange out! We are trying to get more jobs for Indians and get foreign exchange in!"[83]

To voice their critiques, recruiters have formed associations and a federation of associations. The MEA now sets aside a day to meet with individual recruiters or associations. The Federation of Indian Chambers of Commerce and Industry has held meetings with the International Labor Organization, government officials, and recruiters' associations to discuss policies and concerns around the migration industry. However, most of the recruiters I spoke with did not feel the associations were representative of small businesses.

Nevertheless, recruiters' associations took the government to court to demand the government explain how it determined the minimum wage. One recruiter complained about the unreasonableness of having a minimum wage that was not determined by the market: "GOI's rule makers are not part of this business. They have no idea. They cannot say what the minimum wage should be! They should ask us what the wage scale should be. The wage is what the market says it should be. These rules are unenforceable. If they enforce it, Indians will be kicked out of the jobs."[84]

---

[81] Interview, January 13, 2007.

[82] Interview, Capital Travels, Gurvinder Singh, November 23, 2015,

[83] Interview, Capital Travels, Gurvinder Singh, November 23, 2015.

[84] Interview, Pamposh constructions, Sandeep Sadhu, Director, November 20, 2015.

Increased Invisibility

In part, these expressions of frustration indicate that regulations over recruiters *are* being enforced. As is common in India, however, enforcement of regulations has inadvertently increased extralegal and illegal activity. Most recruiters were open about the need to operate extralegally. One recruiter admitted, "We all need subcontractors. So of course we do it illegally. Everyone does and everyone knows."[85] Subcontractors in this case are local contacts recruiters use to enter villages. Almost all recruiters admitted to charging fees that exceeded the government cap (which at the time of interviewing was Rs. 20,000). One recruiter claimed, "We have to collect money illegally. We don't want to, but what to do? We have to do this to make ends meet."[86] Another recruiter said illicit cash "exists *because* of the government rules themselves."[87]

Nowhere was the increased illegal work more apparent than in the recruitment of poor female migrants. All the recruiters I interviewed stated that they never work with women because it is illegal. Some noted that recruiting women for domestic work was too risky to bother with. "Domestic maids have many complaints. Even for the smallest of things. So I don't want the risk of recruiting women. It's too risky," explained one recruiter.[88] "Risk" was a word repeatedly and consistently used when speaking of recruiting women workers. In short, government regulations had turned women into a business risk. However, recruiters were equally open about the fact that they send women through informal channels. One recruiter who told me he does not work with women kept a stack of applications on his desk from female workers. Another said, "We can't send [female] domestic workers legally, so our agents [i.e., subcontractors] take the domestic workers."[89]

Reframing Recruiters as Emigrant Representatives

Most scholars familiar with migration are familiar with recruiters' role in producing, commodifying, and selling low-wage emigrants by finding, training, marketing, and (most notoriously) indebting them through high recruiter fees. Every recruiter I interviewed was aware of their reputation as immoral, greedy exploiters; some even agreed the reputation was justified.

---

[85] Interview, Construction Consultants, Apar Singh, founder and owner, January 12, 2017. (

[86] Interview, Construction Consultants, Apar Singh, founder and owner, January 12, 2017.

[87] Interview, Varun Khosla, Dynamic Staffing Services, November 20, 2015.

[88] Interview, Bandhu Travels, Sunil Kumar Kushwaha, Managing Director, November 23, 2015.

[89] Interview, Al Mansoor, Imran, January 12, 2017.

However, recruiters also framed themselves as the only real representative of poor emigrants' interests. In some cases, return migrants, such as the vice president of KPWA, Sudarsan Kesavan, became recruiters. These recruiters said they understood migrant experiences in ways that government officials never could. Other recruiters claimed their profit structure aligned their interests with those of migrants. Although no recruiters mentioned return migrant organizations, they critiqued trade unions for abandoning emigrants. As one recruiter said, "Unions are just political. We are the ones that care. It's our business. Our livelihood. Unions don't care."[90] Another recruiter presented a rose-colored win-win situation that he felt his work creates with migrants: "I do this business because of the good that it does. Our work has a 'trickle effect.' The guy who goes abroad gets [paid] at the most basic level. And most of that goes to his wife and kids because it is all net savings . . . it is tax free, and there is no cost for housing, food, travel, or medical."[91]

While these claims of joint interests between recruiters and emigrants appear far-fetched against the real experiences of most emigrants, recruiters used these claims to explain why the government (in their opinion) has shifted all responsibility for migrants' welfare onto recruiters. At the same time, recruiters expressed frustration with this responsibility. For example, under present law, recruiters are not allowed to employ subcontractors and must take full responsibility when workers face abuse by employers. This requirement contrasts with the domestic environment, where subcontractors are widely used, even by public-sector entities. Because employers are foreign citizens and not held liable by Indian law, the government has placed all responsibility on recruiters. As one recruiter noted, "Sometimes an employer goes bankrupt and then they can't pay. Now the GOI wants the recruiter to bring the worker back. How can we?! The Protectorate Generate of Emigration is the one who should check the employers' ability to pay before giving clearance, no? But they don't take responsibility after that. India is getting seventy-two billion dollars in remittances every year from this business. . . . The government pays nothing. They are just benefiting. But the government does nothing to help."[92]

Asserting Cultural Capital through Emigration

Like poor emigrants, recruiters praised the increased cultural capital they earned from their involvement in emigration. Many asserted with pride that they are

[90] Interview, Construction Consultants, Apar Singh, founder and owner, January 12, 2017.

[91] Interview, Varun Khosla, Dynamic Staffing Services, November 20, 2015.

[92] Interview, Construction Consultants, Apar Singh, founder and owner, January 12, 2017.

well-traveled and have thus learned new ways of thinking and being. All intended to send their sons (more often than their daughters) abroad to study and work.

And at the same time, recruiters expressed strong nationalist views toward India and its workers. This is not surprising, given recruiters' need to market Indian workers relative to workers from other nations. As well, recruiters' location in the migration process puts them in a subservient position to employers abroad, which often leads them to offer strong critiques of Gulf citizens (particularly the employers). Echoing the same sentiments of government officials in the CEO MDR, Asloob Khan noted, "[Gulf employers] look down on Indians. They see them as poor people. But now India has top technology. They favor Indians because of that. . . . You will never find a country in the world that has as many good people as India. Pakistan is useless. They can't send any workers!"[93]

Demanding Recognition as Economic Heroes

Like emigrants, recruiters describe themselves as vital but underappreciated exporters in India's globalizing economy.

Many recruiters pointed to the contributions they make to India's economy, providing employment and foreign currency. One recruiter lamented, "Everyone thinks recruitment agents are terrible. No one respects us. But who else has given three hundred thousand jobs to people? I have done that! This should be recognized as an export industry. And agents should be recognized as service exporters. But the government treats us like we are untouchables."[94] Similarly, another recruiter explained, "Our industry of manpower recruiting is India's biggest industry with foreign exchange. . . . We do so much. But we can't do anything to change the government policy [against us]."[95] Several recruiters demanded government recognition of "manpower recruitment" as an industry. One stated passionately, "We want to get industry benefits. So we are demanding to be recognized. Let's see if anything happens. . . . I don't think we will see industry recognition in our lifetime!"[96]

Several recruiters argued that their businesses are no different from most. One noted the double standard placed on them compared to domestic recruiters for Indian corporations: "Infosys is offering cheap Indian labor through outsourcing and overcharging for that labor. They are making a huge profit, and the Indian worker is earning much less. But they are not considered thieves like [we] agents

---

[93] Interview, January 13, 2007.

[94] Interview, K. M. Jamaluddin, proprietor, Hiba Exports India, November 18, 2015.

[95] Interview, Yawar, Asloob Khan, January 13, 2007.

[96] Interview, Construction Consultants, Apar Singh, founder and owner, January 12, 2017.

are. Infosys is just getting richer, GOI is getting more taxes, but not the workers. Why are they not seen as *chors* [thieves]?"[97]

Still another demanded that recruiters (like other businesses) receive recognition awards for success and good behavior, rather than only punishing recruiters who "misbehave": "We have had no registered complaints against us in six years. People don't even believe me when I tell them that. And we should be recognized for that. There is no ranking for example of recruiting agents."[98]

[97] Interview, Capital Travels, Gurvinder Singh, November 23, 2015.

[98] Interview, Varun Khosla, Dynamic Staffing Services, November 20, 2015.

Elite Emigrant Organizations

This chapter continues our analysis of how India's contemporary CEO MDR is experienced by emigrants—this time turning our gaze to the organizational strategies and demands of elite emigrants in the United States. As with Chapter 7, which focused on poor migrant organizations and group-based experiences with the CEO MDR, this chapter examines elite emigrants' group efforts through their transnational diaspora organizations rather than their individual experiences.

A key point made in Chapter 5 was that the CEO MDR has tried to tap elite emigrants' financial contributions to India in the form of remittances, savings, investments, and bonds. To attract these contributions, the Indian government has offered financial incentives to save and invest in India and appealed to the racial and ethnic bonds that emigrants share with India. But these efforts have been costly and yielded mediocre and volatile flows. Chapter 6, therefore, explored a second resource the CEO MDR has gotten from elite emigrants: their social and ideological contributions in the form of ideas, ideals, tastes, networks, and technical expertise. To attract these social contributions, the CEO MDR has employed a currency of status recognition, appealing to a particular image of Indian Americans as successful, hard-working, professional, and entrepreneurial elites whom domestic Indians can and should emulate. This has forged a *powerful class pact between elites* in India (within the government and business) and elite emigrants in the West.

This chapter illustrates how Indian Americans have built hundreds of transnational diaspora organizations throughout the United States to help channel their financial and social remittances to India. Indian Americans' transnational organizations address a diverse range of topics and have differing visions for India. But nearly all their group-based efforts support, rather than critique, the CEO MDR's underlying development ideals of privatization, self-sufficiency, and globalization. Nearly all also reflect exactly the portrait of the elite global Indian that the CEO MDR idealizes (a portrait that, in fact, masks the community's

The Migration-Development Regime. Rina Agarwala, Oxford University Press. © Oxford University Press 2022.
DOI: 10.1093/oso/9780197586396.003.0008

more layered heterogeneity). Doing so not only empowers Indian Americans to help shape India's future; it also valorizes their own status within the United States and India and thus affords them material and symbolic benefits in the process. As my interviews indicate, Indian Americans' social remittances continue to face resistance in some sectors of India, highlighting the role that Indian Americans play in *building consent* for these ideals within India. But my interviews also underscore the remarkable similarity in the ideals purported by Indian Americans' transnational organizations and those shared by business and government elites in India—a similarity that underscores the elite class pact framing the CEO MDR.[1]

The Development of Elite Emigrant Organizations

The majority of elite Indian emigrant organizations in the United States have emerged during the CEO MDR. Of my interview sample of Indian American transnational organizations, 30% began in the 1970s and 1980s, and 70% emerged after the 1990s.

This can be attributed to several factors. First, scholars of other diasporic groups in the United States have shown that immigrants are most likely to form transnational organizations with their home countries only after they are assimilated in their host countries, in terms of culture and employment (Portes, Escobar, and Radford 2007). The story of Indian Americans supports this finding. The post-1965 second wave of professional Indians and their families first launched transnational organizations in the United States in the late 1970s, and the larger, third wave of IT professionals created a new round of organizations after the late 1990s. The younger, third-wave cohort of IT professionals (age 25 to 40), many of whom are on temporary visas, are more active than the older, second-wave cohort of traditional professionals who have immigrated permanently (age 50 and older). This, too, is consistent with research showing that circular migrants are more likely than permanent migrants to retain connections with the homeland (Lucas 2005).

Second, Indian Americans' transnational organizations emerged alongside the aging of their children. Almost all leaders I interviewed said a primary mission of their organization was to build bridges with India so their American-born children would feel more connected to their home country. Despite leaders' desire to connect their children to India, however, these transnational organizations

[1] The findings in this chapter often refer to my inventory of transnational Indian American organizations. For more details on the inventory, see Chapter 2.

are dominated by first-generation immigrants (a trait that is typical of other immigrant transnational groups in the United States). In my sample, religious and development organizations noted some second-generation participation.

Interestingly, several older, second-wave leaders who arrived in the United States during the 1960s and 1970s also mentioned the need to preserve traditional Indian cultures, languages, arts, and habits that were dying within India due to growing "Western influences" under contemporary globalization. The dilution of yoga and classical Indian dance and music into Bollywood forms are prime examples. Second-wave leaders also singled out as part of the problem the third wave of Indian immigrants who arrived in the United States in the 1990s and 2000s to work in the IT sector, underscoring potential rifts within the Indian American population. One leader equated third-wave Indian immigrants to second-generation Indian Americans: "They are the same, because India is a Westernized country. . . . I am worried about India."[2] Another second-wave leader agreed: "The new guys are the problem. They are young, but their ideas are totally different. They don't know anything about this country [i.e., India]. They don't know what to do, but they want to be members [of our organization]. Eventually they come to leadership. But some of them don't have the same values and respect [as older members]."[3]

Given Indian Americans' interest in educating the second generation (and even young Indians) in traditional notions of India, it is not surprising that the vast majority of their transnational organizations self-identify as "cultural." As shown in Table 8.1, 70% of organizations in my inventory self-identify as "cultural" (organizing around subnational religion, ethnicity, and art), while only 30% identify as "noncultural" (organizing around development, profession, or alumni status).[4] The vast majority of cultural organizations mobilize around subnational ethnic, linguistic, and religious lines, while most of the noncultural organizations mobilize around pan-Indian identities. As I have written elsewhere, religious organizations are the most common form of Indian American transnational organizations (Agarwala 2015a), totaling over one-third (205) of the 624 organizations in my inventory. Even those that identify as "arts" or "ethnic" (some of which claimed to eschew religion) organized and mobilized around religious traditions, practices, and assumptions. Leaders across religious identities repeatedly expressed the fluidity between migrants' religious and cultural identities, and many noted the difficulty in separating the two.

---

[2] Interview, Organization 1, April 19, 2011.

[3] Interview, Organization 2, April 22, 2011.

[4] Types were self-reported. Multiple categories were allowed, but were mainly used by religious organizations.

Table 8.1 Distribution of Organization Type in Interview Sample vs. Inventory

Organization Type	Number in Inventory	% of Inventory Organizations	Number Interviewed	% of Interviewed Organizations
Religious/religious combination	205	32.8	24	34.8
Ethnic/caste/linguistic/identity	166	26.6	12	17.4
Development/health/education	119	19.1	10	14.5
Professional/alumni	51	8.2	13	18.8
Arts/cultural	50	8	5	7.2
Human rights	17	2.7	3	4.3
Political	16	2.6	2	2.9
Total	624	100	69	100

Note: "Religious combination" refers to organizations that combine religion with another aim, including development, arts, linguistic identity, human rights, political, and alumni.

Most Indian American transnational organizations are small. My interviews indicate 70% have fewer than 1,000 members, and 75% have an annual budget under US$1 million.[5] Most organizations are also local. Two-thirds operate in a single city, while the remaining one-third operate at the national or international level with several local chapters. Approximately 10% serve as umbrella organizations. The vast majority appeal only to ethnic Indians, while only one-fourth recruit some non-Indian members, volunteers, staff, donors, and/or board members. Over 70% of them have no paid staff and operate solely with volunteers. This is significant, given that most Indians in the United States work full time and long hours. My interviewees all displayed enormous dedication and commitment to their entirely unpaid work with transnational organizations.

A Portrait of the Ideal "Global Indian"

Despite the diversity of organization types, Indian American transnational organizations overwhelmingly mirror the image of elite Indian emigrants that the CEO MDR glorifies.

In fact, they helped create the image in the first place. Almost all Indian American organizations are led by the most educated, integrated, elite diaspora members. As noted, IT professionals are especially active. As well, the nearly exclusive involvement of first-generation Indians reflects the CEO MDR's reliance on elite emigrants with fresh emotional and personal connections to India. Meanwhile, the 6% of working-class Indian taxi drivers, factory laborers, newsstand operators, and farmers, as well as the approximately 200,000 undocumented Indians in the United States, are not well-represented in the membership or leadership of Indian transnational organizations (Ministry of External Affairs 2000; Terrazas and Batog 2010).[6] To the extent that working-class Indian immigrants in the United States are organized, my interviews indicate they participate in the religious rituals offered by transnational religious organizations or organizations mobilizing for their rights within the United States, and are thus less involved in transnational efforts to shape India's development.

Strikingly, Indian American transnational organizations are dominated by men, a feature that also defines the CEO MDR (as noted in Chapter 5). Women are nearly absent from leadership positions; in my sample of 73 organization interviews, only eight (11%) were female-led (in arts and development). And over 60% of my interviewees said their organizations have almost no female

[5] For organizations that do not have members, we used the number of volunteers or donors.

[6] This finding may be partly attributed to interviewees' attempt to present a particular image of Indian Americans. Survey questions on education level, English proficiency, and occupation were found to be the most sensitive. Further study of this group of Indian Americans is needed.

members. The small share of female participation that does exist was explained by interviewees as a function of women's role in the family—as helpers in a family business, wives with wealthy husbands who allowed them to start an organization, or participants in a family-based membership. Some also pointed to a younger generation of leaders (raised in India and the United States) who were more open to gender equality, although my findings show males also dominate the organizations located in American universities. One leader explained, "We try to involve more women, but they have to attend board meetings that are out of state. It all depends on the husbands in our community."[7] Several organizations said their counterparts in India were more equal in terms of gender.

The male-dominated nature of Indian American transnational organizations is consistent with studies on male-dominated Latin American hometown associations in the United States (Goldring 2001). Scholars argue that women gain power through migration and are thus more inclined to invest in their host countries, while men lose power and thus look "homeward," where they intend to return and regain their higher gendered status (Grasmuck and Pessar 1991; Jones-Correa 1998; Milkman 2018). Scholars of professional Indian immigrants have similarly argued, "Women enjoy more career mobility in the U.S./Canada compared to India . . . and do not want to go back and face societal pressures about their careers. For men, the increasing opportunities created by the growing Indian economy could be a reason for their wanting to move back in greater numbers" (Chand 2009: 13).

Indian Americans' Interest in Indian Development

My interviews show that all Indian transnational organizations—whether they identify as "cultural" or "noncultural" or as a "development" organization or not—are deeply committed to shaping India's development, particularly in the economic sphere. As I argue elsewhere, this is an important corrective to common assumptions, especially among Indian government officials, that discount cultural organizations as "nondevelopmental" (Agarwala 2015a).

Indian Americans consistently expressed emotional, psychological, and cultural motivations for their involvement in Indian development, thereby upholding the CEO MDR's attempt to appeal to their racial and ethnic bonds to India. As well, almost all my interviewees credited India's liberalization policies for catalyzing Indian American involvement in India's economy. Some also credited the growth of India's IT sector.[8] But as I illustrated in Chapters 5

[7] Interview, Organization 3, September 29, 2011.

[8] A few interviewees pointed to natural disasters, such as the 2004 tsunami that devastated parts of southern India and the 2001 earthquake that hit the state of Gujarat. While these events

and 6, the causal arrow could just as easily be pointed in the opposite direction, crediting Indian American involvement in India for strengthening India's liberalization efforts as well as the growth of its IT sector. As S. Kannan of the Confederation of Indian Industries in India's IT hub city of Hyderabad, said, "Hyderabad was created by the NRIs," not the other way around.[9]

I argue, therefore, that the CEO MDR *created the conditions for* Indian Americans to mobilize group-based efforts to influence India's economic development. Indian American organizations offered the Indian government an organized vector through which it could tap elite emigrants' financial and social resources and cement domestic acceptance for privatization and globalization within India. Therefore, most Indian American organizations" development efforts *support and help constitute, rather than critique, India's contemporary economic development ideology.* Among my interviews, I found little to no criticism of the Indian government's economic policies among Indian emigrants' *group-based* expressions (although, as I will elaborate, I did find criticism of the government itself). As I detail at the end of this chapter, minority religious organizations provide an exception in offering some critiques of the current Indian government.

This finding on Indian Americans' group-based attitudes on Indian development should not be equated to their individual attitudes toward the current Indian government. For example, a 2020 survey of individual Indian Americans found approximately half of those surveyed were critical of some to many of Indian government policies (Badrinathan, Kapur, and Vaishnav 2020). This difference between Indian Americans' individual and group-based opinions may reflect the fact that critics of Indian government policies are channeling their views not through immigrant organizations but through issue-based organizations. The difference may also reflect individuals' growing criticisms of the current Indian government, which has only recently dropped in popularity, while group-based expressions by organizations reflect longer, more sustained opinions that supersede the ebb and flow of partisan politics. Finally, it might reflect Indian Americans' overwhelming support for India's economic policies of globalization and liberalization, but their more diverse views on the government's stance toward Hindu nationalism (which I elaborate on at the end of this chapter).

An important turning point in the interactions between elite emigrants in the United States and the Indian government occurred in the early 1970s, just as an economic crisis was looming over India, the Nationalist MDR was beginning

certainly spurred new organizations to form, they occurred several years after the major rise of Indian American transnational organizations.

[9] Interview, May 24, 2011.

to fade, and the population of elite Indian migrants in the United States was growing. In this context, Gopal Raju, an immigrant from South India living in New York, launched a diasporic newspaper called *India Abroad*, which helped catalyze a fresh approach to Indian emigrants' organization in the United States. The newspaper's name reflected an attempt to construct a nation outside the state (Shukla 2003). As with most ethnic diaspora groups, the growing numbers of Indians arriving in the United States after 1965 had created a need for them to not only gather together over familiar food and rituals but also to articulate their new identity within the context of their host country. But in addition to helping Indians assimilate within the United States, *India Abroad* tried to build a bridge between Indian Americans and the Indian government, particularly in the economic sphere. As Sandhya Shukla (1999: 26) writes in a history of the newspaper, "The material interests of Indian capitalism were well represented; in article after article of early editions of *India Abroad*, one can see alongside the economic stirrings of immigrants for individual betterment, the clearly articulated needs of the Indian nation-state. Investment in India was the *raison d'etre* for many *India Abroad*–sponsored activities."

India Abroad thus served as a powerful space in which the Indian government could communicate its emerging interest in attracting elite emigrants' economic contributions to India. Articles "throughout the 1970s touted the stability of developing Indian enterprises, with advice about how to invest in India . . . and specifically underscored the favorable climate for investment in India" (Shukla 2003). In 1974, the Indian Embassy in the United States and the director general of the Indian government's Council of Scientific and Industrial Research of India[10] sponsored a series of seminars in the United States that were devoted, as *India Abroad* (1974) opined, to "help India meet her needs." Specifically, the newspaper noted that the Indian government wanted to convince Indian American scientists to return to India (Shukla 1999: 26). At the end of the year, the chairman of the Federation of Indian Export Organizations[11] visited the offices of *India Abroad* in New York (Shukla 1999: 27).

By the 1980s additional immigrant newspapers emerged, such as *News-India* and *India Monitor*. Like *India Abroad*, they displayed an intense interest in the Indian economy as well as Indian politics, and they all underlined the cultural connections between emigrants and the homeland. Also like *India Abroad*, they offered the Indian government a communication channel to Indian Americans. This strategy of spreading information on investment opportunities in India

---

[10] The Council is an autonomous organization that started in 1942 but is mainly funded by the Indian Ministry of Science and Technology.

[11] The Federation was set up jointly by the Indian Ministry of Commerce and private trade and industry in 1965.

to elite Indians abroad by drawing on shared cultural connections can still be found today, not only in immigrant publications but also in Indian government publications, such as the *PD Magazine*.

It was in this context that Indian Americans set up their first transnational diaspora organizations. These organizations moved beyond just communicating information about individual investment opportunities in India to pool social and financial resources from members to support dying arts, schools (usually the alma maters of diaspora members), NGOs (whose funding resources were thinning), poverty-alleviation efforts in a hometown or home region, religious institutions, and industries in India.

Economic and Social Ideals: To the Right

Despite their diverse range of organization types, and a handful of exceptions which I will discuss later, almost all Indian American organization leaders in my sample displayed remarkably consistent moderate to center-right views on social issues (especially regarding class, gender, and caste inequities) and on the economy.[12] This finding should not be read as an indication of political party affiliation, which is contingent on nationally defined spectrums.[13]

Although many organization leaders expressed disinterest in formal politics and refused to voice support for a particular political party in the United States or in India, almost all expressed strong views on economic issues such as government involvement in markets, privatization, ideal market models, and global trade. Most organization leaders and members I interviewed celebrated unfettered capitalism and open geographic borders for trade and migration. For a majority of organizations (although not all), religion served as an effective motivator for development-oriented giving, as well as geopolitical power. Most organizations also worked to expand private, rather than public, funding from individuals and corporations, as well as private, rather than public, service delivery in India.

Indian Americans' consistent lack of organization around issues of social inequity (along lines of class, caste, and gender) was also notable (again, a few

---

[12] This finding does not represent all Indian Americans, but rather the subset who have invested time, labor, and money into establishing formal transnational organizations, projects, and interactions within India. As noted, this group is dominated by first-generation, highly educated, professional male Indians.

[13] Because political party spectrums differ across countries, the "left-right" distinction loses some meaning at the transnational level. One survey, for example, indicates that Indian emigrants largely favor the left-leaning Democratic Party in the United States, but the right-wing BJP in India (Badrinathan, Kapur, and Vaishnav 2020).

exceptions notwithstanding). This finding, which I expand on at the end of this chapter, is consistent with other studies on Indian diaspora philanthropy (Sidel 2005). In the noncultural realm, professional emigrants donate to highly specialized tertiary medical care or to elite higher education institutions in India, usually their own alma maters, such as the publicly funded Indian Institutes of Technology and the private Indian School of Business in Hyderabad, Andhra Pradesh.[14]

Despite the long history of left parties and labor activists in India, almost no Indian American organization in my sample reflected upon class-based approaches to alleviating poverty or overturning inequalities. In fact, most organizations expressed disdain for leftist approaches to development. One engineer who also leads an arts organization that performs Hindi-language plays explained that most Hindi-language theater is "left-leaning, about how the rich are sucking the blood of the poor . . . but they are extremely crude . . . crass and silly. . . . The average Hindi play will have a typical guy who is rich and bad. He will control a lot of resources, like oil. His own son will consume the oil and get sick and die and [the father will] say to himself, 'I should be good to the people.' "[15] Vernacular theater has long served as a form of protest and advocacy in India, and this leader himself identified as a "left-leaning guy." But his organization took a strong stance against political theater. He asserted, "I will never do any advocacy for a cause through theater. I will forbid it. In that way I am a free-market guy. As long as people are ready to give money, we will stage plays that entertain and appeal to them."[16]

Similarly, although India's left-wing parties fought hard to liberalize emigration (see Chapter 4), they are absent among Indian American transnational organizations. In contrast, the right-wing BJP has a large following in the United States, and the Congress Party is also present. None of these groups tried to tap Indian Americans for help in overturning social inequalities in India. Rather, they focus on using Indian Americans to encourage stronger military, political, and business relations between the United States and India.

Among the handful of organizations that identified as "progressive" or "left-leaning," their leaders said they receive more support and funding from non-Indian Americans and American-born Indians than they do from first-generation immigrants. One leader lamented, "We target the Indian community, but most of our fundraising comes from white people. Indians care, but they do

---

[14] Of the 7,827 Indian Institutes of Technology alumni whose addresses are known, fewer than half (3,832) are in India; 3,412 are in the United States; 298 in the United Kingdom, Canada, and Australia; and the remaining are scattered in 56 countries (Kapur, Mehta, and Dutt 2004).

[15] Interview, Organization 5, May 15, 2011.

[16] Interview, Organization 5, May 15, 2011.

not contribute."[17] A leader who organizes Dalits (members of the lowest caste in the hierarchy of India's caste system) to raise awareness against caste inequities explained, "Ninety-five percent of our donors are [non-Indian] American. Indians are very well-to-do in the US, but they are not convinced of helping their own people. They don't believe in their own system. . . . Sixty percent of Dalits in the US are professional. The remainder are sponsored by their families, but they are still middle class. But they are useless. They don't want to identify themselves as Dalit. On the other hand, [non-Indian] Americans on social security are giving money to make a difference in the lives of Dalits. Can you imagine? And Indians are willing to do nothing."[18]

Promoting Private Provisioning of Development

The most consistent development ideal that Indian American organizations expressed to me was their faith in private, rather than government, funding and service delivery for development. This ideal fits the CEO MDR's valorization of the private sector described in Chapter 6.

Although they worked with the Indian government to grow private businesses in India and to transmit new development ideas, leaders across organization types expressed a deep lack of trust in the Indian government's ability to deliver development. This finding is consistent with a recent survey that found over one-third of Indian Americans believe "government corruption" is the single biggest challenge facing India today (Badrinathan, Kapur, and Vaishnav 2020). Rather than relying on the government or addressing government corruption, therefore, Indian American transnational organizations unequivocally promote the private sphere—be it generous individual donors, NGOs, or private corporations—to grow India's economy and to soften (rather than eliminate) inequalities at the bottom extreme. This view echoes exactly the development ideals valorized by the Indian government under the CEO MDR (see Chapter 6). And they stand in sharp contrast to the views of poor emigrants who continue to hold the government responsible for delivering development promises (see Chapter 7).

Like poor emigrants, elite emigrants acknowledged the deep political power the Indian government retains in controlling India's economy, and the symbolic power Indian government officials still hold in facilitating development projects. Explained one leader whose organization targets high-net-worth Indians in the United States, "On the India side we keep away from politicians. But we do need

---

[17] Interview, Organization 6, February 17, 2011.
[18] Interview, Organization 7, April 13, 2011.

to retain our connections to get anything done . . . and because we have to do things for our trustees that impress them. . . . For example, they got a VIP tour of the Golden Temple, but we had to keep repeating that this is the same service given to Bill Clinton and Manmohan Singh. . . . Every time a new [political] party comes in, we have to think out of the box on how to . . . reestablish a relationship."[19]

Also like poor emigrants, elite emigrants expressed frustration with their failed efforts to work through the Indian government. One related, "I was involved in creating the [Pravasi Bharatiya Divas] conference. . . . But none of them [i.e., government officials] are interested in substance [i.e., poverty alleviation and development work]."[20] Another leader explained, "The government is not much help. They always say 'yes,' but then they don't do anything. . . . So we try our best to do the work ourselves." Others downplayed the Indian government's ability to handle private donations for development: "The Indian government wants to create a foundation for NRIs to give money. But why would any Indian who hasn't lost his mind give to the Indian government?! They don't understand how any of it even works!"[21]

But unlike poor emigrants who, despite their frustrations, continue to target the Indian government for support, elite emigrants have turned entirely to the private sector. As a result of their lack of faith and trust in the government's ability to deliver on development, nearly all organization members I interviewed (including the minority of left-leaning organizations) worked to *rechannel India's development efforts from public to private funding sources*, such as large donations from a few high-net-worth individuals, smaller donations from a mass base (known as retail philanthropy), and corporate funding. Corporate funding for development was especially sought by human rights organizations and development organizations, as well as some professional and alumni organizations. Donating corporations included Indian businesses (such as Tata) and US-based multinational companies that employ a large number of Indians (such as IT companies, pharmaceutical companies, Ogalvi, NASA, Boeing, and Marriott).

Given the professional composition of the Indian American community, it is not surprising that their organized giving relies on individual and corporate philanthropy. It also helps explain the absence of critical approaches to capitalism among Indian American efforts (including even the minority of left-leaning organizations). Most organizations did not express any concern about tapping corporate donors for development funding. Rather, they were explicit about using Indian American professionals to pressure their corporate employers

[19] Interview, Organization 8, May 17, 2011.
[20] Interview, Organization 6, February 17, 2011.
[21] Interview, Organization 8, May 17, 2011.

to give to Indian NGOs. Only one organization voiced some trepidation and emphasized that only 3% of their funding comes from corporations and that those corporations must share the progressive vision of the organization. This leader explained, "We do not take money from pharmaceuticals, or Coca-Cola. But we have applied for Yahoo Foundation and eBay where they fund education."[22] Interestingly, and again not surprisingly given the large presence of Indians in IT, IT corporations are uncritically billed as ethically moral.

Despite their faith in private funding, however, every organization leader I interviewed acknowledged its multiple challenges, particularly its unpredictable and cyclical nature, noting the flood of funding they received from Indian Americans during the IT boom of the early 2000s and its rapid decline after the 2008 financial crisis. Leaders also noted the difficulty of working with Indian American donors who distrust not only the Indian government but also NGOs. Organization leaders repeatedly complained that donors fear that organizations (in the United States and in India) will misuse their donations. As a result, donors refused to pay overhead or staff salaries, forcing most organizations to be very small and driven by an unreliable volunteer base. Organizations also expressed frustration over diaspora donors' micromanagement of funds to a particular state, community, or topic. Finally, organizations noted that although diaspora donations are higher than those of Indians in India, diaspora donors had unrealistic expectations of what could be done with their money (relative to Indian donors), and organizations had to spend considerable time managing these expectations.[23] One activist in India who has long supported diaspora philanthropy said Indian Americans' distrust of NGOs surprised many Indians who had assumed the NGO culture in the United States would have ensured that they were more "comfortable giving through organizations than Indians in the Middle East, who tend to only give back to their families."[24]

Nevertheless, no Indian American interviewee suggested scrapping private philanthropy as the primary mechanism of development funding. On the contrary, diaspora organizations have tried to convince NGOs in India to turn more to private philanthropy and practice the organizational austerity that philanthropy is said to ensure. For example, one US organization leader explained how they chose an Indian organization to fund: "They looked like an organization that warranted the money and was using it well. . . . All of [the workers in the organization] are volunteers. That is really something that took my students' and my fancy. If that is the case, no one is getting paid. That was something that we really liked."[25] One organization leader in India said in frustration, "The diaspora

[22] Interview, Organization 8, May 17, 2011.

[23] Interview, Organization 9, January 25, 2011.

[24] Interview, Organization 9, January 25, 2011.

[25] Interview, Organization 10, April 25, 2011.

mistrusts Indian NGOs. But somehow Indian NGOs don't mistrust them. They still seek their funds."[26]

To increase private funding for development in India, diaspora organizations have worked closely with Indian government officials to reform India's tax system in ways similar to the US system. Despite India's long tradition of private giving practices (for a nice review, see Bornstein 2012), Indian Americans spoke of the need to "teach Indians" the art and culture of "organized" giving. As noted in Chapter 6, the Indian government has been receptive to working with elite Indian Americans to institutionalize and regulate private philanthropy, which does not alter the structures that created the inequalities in the first place, but rather relies on the precarious and voluntary goodwill of those at the top to soften the differences.

Asserting a US Model

Nearly all Indian American leaders I spoke with attributed their ideals of private provisioning of development to the values and practices they had learned in their own histories as immigrants. The United States, therefore, served as a model to be exported to India, and immigrants served as a willing vector of transmission.

Leaders consistently said they first learned about philanthropy when they came to the United States. One exclaimed, "The US and UK are unusual in understanding the power of private sector philanthropy!"[27] Said another, "The US is the only country where philanthropy is a value and is supported by the tax system. This is how we created role models like Carnegie, Warren Buffet, Gates, Clinton, et cetera. Ninety percent of Americans give. Nowhere else will you find this. . . . When I came here, I learned this and I wanted to inculcate this value and practice of giving. I didn't know anything about this giving culture before arriving."[28]

To justify their promotion of private philanthropy, leaders appealed to the ideal of self-sufficiency—another hallmark of the CEO MDR—and spotlighted themselves as exemplars. Interviewees consistently recounted their own "rags-to-riches" immigration stories, in which (in their account) they had managed to move out of India and achieve high-status lives in the United States completely on their own. Almost none acknowledged their relatively elite class background in lower-middle to middle-class families in India, or their privileged positions

[26] Interview, Organization 11, March 18, 2011.
[27] Interview, Organization 12, July 20, 2011.
[28] Interview, Organization 6, February 17, 2011.

in the Indian caste system.[29] Although several leaders acknowledged their excellent public education in India and expressed their deep gratitude toward their teachers (as well as guilt for having left India), they did not *attribute* their success to their Indian public education or promote expanded public education in India (see below).

As well, leaders defined voluntarism, an approach tied to private philanthropy, as an American ideal. As one leader put it, "I was curious why this country [the United States] ticks. Then I learned there is commitment to your community and society [in the United States]. In India it is commitment to your own values and own social life. It is about your personal time. Everybody keeps their house clean, but the streets are not clean. I have learned from being here [in the United States] that you have an obligation to your own community or institution. I feel that very strongly. We got free education and top-notch education from India, so we want to give back."[30] Despite this leader's appreciation of his own publicly funded quality education, however, he echoed Indian Americans' distrust of the Indian government's ability to provide social services—be it education, healthcare, credit, or employment.

Instead, Indian Americans' transnational organizations valorized an American-style commitment to the private sector, voluntarism, and self-sufficiency as social goods. Thus, their transnational organizations aim to *shift* India from a past (that they ironically benefited from) to a new ideal that replicates the "American dream."

Defining Development

Armed with their strong faith in private provisioning, self-sufficiency, and voluntarism, alongside their personal credibility as elite workers, Indian Americans address development projects in several areas—all of which provide financial and ideological support for the CEO MDR's underlying development agenda. By far the favorite development topic among Indian Americans is education, followed by poverty alleviation. These groups cite traditional philanthropic desires to uplift and give back to their communities. A minority of organizations seek to develop Indian private businesses, citing a desire to assist while also gaining from India's growing economy. An even smaller group works to improve Indian-American bilateral relations, citing desires to create a global Indian

---

[29] One leader acknowledged that his middle-class background had shielded his exposure to and awareness of issues of class inequality, which he came to understand only after arriving in the United States. Interview, May 2, 2011.

[30] Interview, Organization 13, August 1, 2011.

identity. As noted, these development efforts were pursued by a range of organization types, including religious, arts, ethnic, alumni, and professional organizations, as well as development.

Education: An Invitation to the Elite Class Pact

The most popular development cause among Indian American transnational organizations is education in India (Agarwala 2015b). Since Indian Americans target both primary and tertiary education, I separate it from poverty alleviation.

Across organizations, education was seen as the key to self-sufficiency and upward economic mobility that Indian Americans exemplify. As one leader said, "Most of our members worked hard and got education and then came here [the United States]. [Our success is] not due to land or political power."[31] Even Indian partner organizations agree that Indian Americans are uniquely focused on education: "They see their own path to success as through education. . . . There is a bit of a feeling that 'we know best, since we went through it. We know what works for success.' "[32]

Beyond individual economic mobility, education was also considered a pathway to larger aims, most of which were supported by elites in India— thereby lending strength to the CEO MDR's elite class pact. For example, improved education was held up as the most important way to ensure the benefits of the Indian government's policies of liberalization and globalization. One leader credited India's private corporations, such as Infosys and Murti, for increasing India's exports to the United States and "eliminating" unemployment in India's technology hubs in just a few years. Like most, this leader enthusiastically embraced liberalization and globalization: "Clearly the neoliberal reforms have been a huge bonus for India, and we need to connect people across the world." But he went onto acknowledge, "But *only* the educated people benefit. So GOI is saying they are going to support higher education more."[33] Leaders also acknowledged the necessity of improving primary education as a necessary pathway to tertiary education, which would enable more Indians to benefit from the reformed economy. As one leader noted, "We all realize that by the time the kids come to the university, they got all the help they needed." As a result, this leader explained, "We plan to expand our programs to include elementary school dropouts."[34]

---

[31] Interview, Organization 14, July 5, 2011.
[32] Interview, Organization 15, March 22, 2011.
[33] Interview, Organization 6, February 17, 2011, emphasis in original.
[34] Interview, Organization 14, July 5, 2011.

Indian Americans' support for education in India was also expressed as support for political parties that promote increased liberalization and globalization. For example, several organizations emerged predominantly to support former chief minister of Andhra Pradesh Chandrababa Naidu because so many elite Indian Americans felt personally indebted to him for fighting for improved tertiary education and globalization in India. As one leader explained, "Even more than creating colleges, he made us aware. He was always talking about IT and opened our eyes to going out and working with foreigners."[35] In 2000, Naidu was a poster child for globalization, named "Person of the Year" by *Time* magazine, prominently featured in Thomas Friedman's famous ode to neoliberalism, *The World Is Flat*, and known as a friend of Bill Clinton and Bill Gates. But Naidu eventually lost electoral power due to the rural vote in India. S. Kannan of the Confederation of Indian Industries in Naidu's home city of Hyderabad explained, "NRIs helped Hyderabad become an IT hub. But we need more government jobs for the rural folks."[36]

Sikh, Christian, and Muslim organizations pointed to education as a way to address human rights at the intersection of class and minority status (Agarwala 2015b).[37] A leader of a Muslim organization that identifies as "nonreligious" said, "Our objective is simple: educate, educate, educate."[38] This organization sees education as the only way to assist religious minorities who are disproportionately represented among the poor in India. The organization raises funds for awards, loans, and scholarships to students in India, and they donate funds to support existing schools (many of them are alumni) and build new new schools, sometimes using property owned by members. This approach is identical to that of the Indian Ministry of Minority Affairs. As Joint Secretary B. P. Sharma explained the work of the relatively new ministry, which was formed in 2006, "We have a small budget and that too must be spent on educational empowerment mostly. We don't have a lot of power to address all issues."[39]

Finally, many leaders credited their interest in investing in education to the rise of return emigrants in leadership positions in Indian institutions, especially the tertiary sector. One leader of a US-based transnational organization pointed to the new director of his old college in India: "In the past, there was lack of enthusiasm, but now people are getting a sense of India's direction . . . and people are getting excited. They see that something of significance is happening. There is a very sharp change in perception that we can detect. The director of

---

[35] Interview, Organization 16, April 21, 2011.

[36] Interview, May 24, 2011.

[37] Hindus are a majority in India, comprising 80% of the population.

[38] Interview, Organization 17, April 19, 2011.

[39] Interview, May 26, 2011.

the college is also very driven. He himself was a graduate of the college, and he has been in the US working for Intel Lab for a couple of years. So he has a big vision."[40] The director of a new public college spoke passionately about his support for American values of entrepreneurship, liberal arts, high merit and reward, and saying no to authority and to government. The director himself had studied and worked in the United States. After returning to India, he worked hard to recruit American-trained PhD students and Indian American faculty. He also set up a transnational organization in the United States to attract tax-exempt donations from diaspora members. Although his college is publicly funded, he was staunchly antigovernment: "I need to raise private funds. Then I don't have to bow down to the government rules. Their power is only their money. I don't ask government permission for anything that is important for my institution."[41]

Education as a Public-Private Partnership

While many leaders expressed their interest in education as indebtedness to the teachers and adults who supported them, and several acknowledged the public funding underlying the quality education they received in India, they did not define education as a public good. Only two organizations in my sample held the Indian government accountable for education. One did so after witnessing the failures of a small, privately funded village school project. The other successfully lobbied the government for funding to support the education of poor seasonal migrant children.

Other than these two examples, Indian American organizations raise private funds for countless scholarships for poor children and children who do not qualify for government funding; assistance to students in networking and finding jobs and internships in the United States; as well as cash or in-kind support for primary schools in poor areas and tertiary institutions. In-kind support for primary schools has included backpacks, books, water facilities, blankets, computer classes, and solar panels for electricity to increase school hours. Support for tertiary institutions has included new lab equipment and other materials, convention centers, schools of management and business, laboratories, hospital wings, pools, and auditoriums. Religious organizations also raise funds to support private religious schools run by ashrams and madrassas. Even when supporting public Indian universities, Indian Americans have tried to impart private American university models of research and teaching techniques, governance structures, differentiated pay structures for staff, incentive systems for

---

[40] Interview, Organization 18, August 1, 2011.
[41] Interview, Organization 19, February 7, 2011.

students, a liberal arts curriculum, and fundraising programs for private donors (Lessinger 2003).

Most organizations worked to shift India's long history of mass public education (supplemented by a small share of elite private schools) to a new "public-private partnership model." One large organization that focuses exclusively on education in India had actively struggled for the 2005 Right to Education Bill that would guarantee education for all in India. But in terms of provision, the organization supports nongovernmental schools. As the leader explained, "I looked at cases where the district magistrate was responsible for primary education and had a lot of control of education money, and we have tried to work with them to improve the government schools. But we support parallel schools . . . in communities where there are no government schools or they are so bad."[42] The organization has also raised money to improve and change existing curriculums.

Another organization began as a supplement to public municipal schools, offering afterschool tutoring, but eventually turned to the US charter school model to start their own schools. Unlike US charter schools, however, they don't take any money from the government. Instead, they raise private funds but operate at the same cost as government schools: "By keeping costs [the] same, we are trying to prove that we can have high-quality schools despite the money."[43] The leader was quick to explain, "We don't want the government out. We want to work with government."[44] But the organization believes government needs guidance from nongovernmental entities. It took credit for convincing the Bombay municipal government to work with consulting firm McKinsey and Company on a school improvement program. "The government wants to work on school improvement programs now, and we think that is because of NGOs' push. . . . We would like to see the government take over our schools with money and pay the bills since we now have twelve schools running at full capacity. And then we want government to replicate them."[45]

Organizations also drew from public education funding, claiming the private and NGO sector was better skilled in using the money. As one leader said, "Every state government has money to use computers in schools. But they don't know how to do that. We train the teachers and integrate the curriculum to use PCs. . . . We have the connections, so we can offer that to people."[46] Even at the tertiary level, which is often publicly funded in India, organizations relied on government funding. Although one organization was committed to running a

[42] Interview, Organization 20, September 30, 2011.
[43] Interview, Organization 21, February 14, 2011.
[44] Interview, Organization 21, February 14, 2011.
[45] Interview, Organization 21, February 14, 2011.
[46] Interview, Organization 8, May 17, 2011.

private college, it relied on the government to buy low-cost land on which to build the school. As the leader explained with pride, "The Rajasthan state government in the end gave us thirty acres of land for the college in my home village. I had to make millions of calls and faxes, and visits. But in the end they gave it and for free, which was a big accomplishment."[47] He lamented, however, that the government did not give him any other funds: "The Indian government doesn't trust people starting private colleges. They see them as *banya* [merchant caste] tribes . . . trying to get money for themselves."[48]

Underlying Indian Americans' education work was a feeling they could upgrade the quality of governmental efforts to emulate higher "Western," private-sector standards. For example, one alumni organization built an oncology center and a maternity ward with an intensive care unit in their medical college, and then gave it to the government to operate. The organization leader spoke proudly of their cooperation with the government: "Once we built it, it is like a gift given. We develop[ed] a budget with charitable donations, and we organized the activities with the dean of the college and head of the hospital."[49] These efforts resulted in an upgraded library and computer facilities in the college and new paint and floors in the hospital, a reduction in the hospital's morbidity and mortality rates and an increase in its delivery rates., But the leader did not trust the government: "We do not give money in cash, so it does not get lost. We personally went there and built it from the ground up. [It is] a new building with high standards . . . elevators of an international brand. Although we also use building materials from India . . . we use newer kind of materials, which will reduce problems."[50]

While private funding was seen as a valid corrective to inefficient and declining government funding for education in the era of liberalization, interviewees in the United States and in India admitted that Indians needed to learn *how* to fundraise from Americans. As one director of an Indian college recounted, "In 1994, GOI was having a financial crunch. So they told [university] directors to raise money from alumni and industries. . . . But the problem with Indian academia is that they never learned fundraising."[51] This director went on a study tour of US campuses (using his personal networks as an alum). "I asked them how they do it. I took furious notes. And then I started asking shamelessly for money. Some people are still upset that I began a beggar mentality. . . . The American schools are training our alumni about philanthropy."[52]

[47] Interview, Organization 6, February 17, 2011.
[48] Interview, Organization 6, February 17, 2011.
[49] Interview, Organization 22, July 26, 2011.
[50] Interview, Organization 22, July 26, 2011.
[51] Interview, Organization 19, February 7, 2011.
[52] Interview, Organization 19, February 7, 2011.

As with all diaspora donations, this director emphasized the lack of corruption involved on the receiving end: "I was very good at communicating and making sure the donors knew there was no corruption. I am not bagging any of it for myself."[53]

Americanizing Indian Education

In addition to raising funds to support Indian education, Indian American transnational organizations seek to transmit their knowledge or social remittances to help *alter* Indian education to emulate American education. As one leader put it, the aim is "to create a change in the culture and expose it to the latest technology in the US."[54] Another organization leader explained why they bring directors of Indian colleges to the United States every year: "We are trying to teach Indian colleges to be more like US colleges."[55] Still another leader stated, "I find knowledge transfer more important than money. GOI gives enough money. Intellectual resource is what is missing. But there is a delicate balance that needs to be maintained. Tenured faculty members [in India] don't take it easily. We can't make it a criticism of India."[56] Several leaders mentioned the delicate balance between supporting Indian educational institutions while simultaneously pushing them to change.

Several organizations extolled American incentive structures for faculty and students as a key to quality education. Such systems contrast with Indian systems that offer equal and public pay structures for university employees. Alumni organizations in the United States raised money to differentiate pay structures by distinguished teaching and student awards in their home colleges. One leader explained, "There has been a lack of focus on recognition of talent in India, and our goal was to put the focus back on that."[57] Another said, "We don't have a mission to help the poor in India, except we have a program to give loans to poor students who are on the campus. . . . But we have a good program to give a signing bonus to new faculty to help with faculty recruitment."[58] One return emigrant who is now a director of a college said, "Equality is the best assurance of mediocrity! . . . [Indians] hate the idea of endowed chairs that create inequality in professors' pay. When a corporation wants to endow a chair, the government

[53] Interview, Organization 19, February 7, 2011.
[54] Interview, Organization 18, August 1, 2011.
[55] Interview, Organization 23, August 5 and 9, 2011.
[56] Interview, Organization 14, July 5, 2011.
[57] Interview, Organization 13, August 1, 2011.
[58] Interview, Organization 24, July 8, 2011.

decreases their pay amount, so the total is the same. I said no to that. I give a proper endowed chair with more money."[59]

Other leaders sought to export the US model of private fundraising, despite Indian institutions' resistance to such a model. One leader explained that Indian institutions "are very proud of the situation where they are generating almost all the operating money for the place. . . . Then they feel they don't need anyone else's help. But if they want to be modern, they need to develop a philanthropic wing to their institution. A lot of what I tried to do during my ten-month stay there is to increase Indian fundraising. I didn't make too much progress. . . . It will come, but it's a struggle."[60] A leader of an India-based organization related that they learned how to use the internet to fundraise from their Indian American partner organization.[61]

Most striking, Indian American transnational organizations have tried to privatize India's top tertiary institutions and have worked closely with India's Ministry of Human Resources to do so. As one leader said, "We learned very quickly to be careful about this. . . . A lot of countries don't want to be told what to do. They are very sensitive to what expats say to them. You have to learn how to not sound like a Westerner trying to tell them what to do."[62] He learned to tell his audience, "You are doing wonderful things, but here are some best practices."

Some Indian American organizations have helped the Indian government "credential" Indian universities in order to improve their reputation in the global/US labor market. Doing so is also expected to improve Indian Americans' standing in the United States. As one leader explained, they wanted to get their old college recognized as a "world-class university" (a term that has become popular in Indian government parlance), so they wrote a detailed report, had it reviewed and validated by the consulting firm McKinsey and Company, shared it with faculty and alumni, and then gave it to their college to publicize.[63] Graduates of the prestigious, publicly funded Indian Institutes of Technology recounted their efforts in 2002, when they gathered in Connecticut with the CEO of McKinsey and Company, Rajat Gupta, to raise awareness about the Institutes in the United States. One alumnus recalled, "We wanted to show how difficult it is to get in, and how much our graduates have done for the US. We have a Joint Entrance Exam, so it is purely based on meritocracy. It is entirely determined by national ranking. For India this is unusual. It is not based on who you know or how much you can pay. The current [human resource development] minister is trying to

[59] Interview, Organization 19, February 7, 2011.
[60] Interview, Organization 12, July 20, 2011.
[61] Interview, Organization 25, March 22, 2011.
[62] Interview, Organization 24, July 8, 2011.
[63] Interview, Organization 26, September 2, 2011.

do away with the joint entrance exam system, and we think he is making a big mistake."[64]

Poverty Alleviation: Justifying the Elite Pact

A large share of Indian American transnational organizations, including religious organizations, work to alleviate income-based poverty in India. To do so, they provide individual-level assistance to those at the bottom of the economic strata. These efforts were expressed in terms of a moral obligation to give back to the community. But almost none advocated for labor rights, systemic changes to India's policy structure, or even redistributive tax systems to ensure greater class-based equality.[65] These poverty-alleviation efforts, therefore, served to justify Indian Americans' own elite status and their class pact with Indian elites rather than altering the structures that created the inequalities in the first place. As in education, poverty-alleviation efforts among Indian Americans avoided the government and expressed more faith in the private provision of services and private funding through organized philanthropy from individuals and corporations.

Indian American transnational organizations have raised funds to launch and implement a range of poverty-alleviation projects. All have followed a tradition of charitable giving. They have been particularly successful in raising funds (from high-net-worth and retail donors) for natural disaster relief, as this was viewed by the community as "nonpolitical" and thus "easy." Organizations have worked with state governments to support basic healthcare projects. Although Indian Americans have not embraced hometown associations to the extent that other diaspora groups have, they have initiated several local poverty-alleviation projects in members' hometowns. Ethnic organizations, in particular, have raised funds to improve infrastructure (such as electricity, water filters, sewage systems, roads, phone lines, irrigation systems, and toilets). Drawing on Indian

---

[64] Interview, Organization 27, July 28, 2011.

[65] In the late 1990s, a few workers' organizations, composed largely of Indian emigrants to the United States, arose to address class-based solidarities and power structures. However, they do not identify along national or ethnic lines (such as "Indian" or "South Asian"), and their efforts focus on the US context. Therefore, they did not qualify as "transnational diaspora organizations" in this study. Moreover, their few and sporadic efforts in India have largely failed. For example, one organization tried to work with Indian consulates in the United States to transport emigrants back to their families in India in cases of death or accident and to support emigrants facing family crises or land disputes in India. The organization leader told me, "I made a lot of contacts, and the idea was good." He traveled to Punjab to set up an office there, but it did not work. It was costly, and it was difficult to instill a radical class solidarity among the members. As the leader explained, "Indian drivers were operating as part of the working class here [in the United States], and going to India to set up a middle-class life there. We wanted to interrupt that... but it was too difficult." Interview, Organization 28, April 2011.

Americans' medical expertise, organizations have funded mobile medical vans, eye camps with free cataract surgery, and medical camps with free assistance with anemia. Some organizations have initiated orphanages and child-rescue centers, where children are provided free education and sometimes employment. A handful of organizations have created income-generation projects for poor women or inhabitants of the poorest states of northeastern India through micro credit for animal husbandry or small business development in rickshaw transport and garbage collection. Organization leaders spoke proudly of "connecting the formal and informal sectors" and "fixing the inefficiencies" in local production of rickshaws and other products.[66]

Religious organizations have been particularly active in poverty-alleviation projects. Some leaders noted that this was more acceptable to Americans than to Indians. One leader said that in the United States, many religious groups were involved in charity, but "the Indian crowd is a different game altogether. They don't like to be associated with religion. They don't even come to us. They want to see themselves as secular. But in our opinion, they don't know what that is. We celebrate religions."[67] Christian organizations pointed to a long tradition of charitable giving to "the needy." Leaders of Hindu organizations said they began their poverty-alleviation projects in the new millennium to counter mounting accusations of Hindus supporting fundamentalist views and violence against religious minorities in India. Muslim organizations identified as nonreligious but worked to improve education levels among poor Muslims. Sikh organizations in the United States displayed the most progressive politics toward poverty alleviation, which may reflect the larger percentage of working-class Indian Americans among Sikhs. Sikh places of worship, or *gurudwaras*, serve as one of the only spaces where elite and working-class Indian Americans gather on a regular basis.

Business Development: Amplifying the Elite Class Pact

A minority of organizations focused their development efforts on increasing India's economic growth through the development of private, globalized businesses. Professional organizations were particularly active in fostering business connections between the United States and India. Unlike others, organization leaders involved in Indian business development expressed their efforts as a rational economic decision, *not* an emotional or cultural one. Leaders pointed to the growing middle-class market in India, which could assist their own small businesses in the United States. One leader asserted, "The more

[66] Interview, Organization 29, July 1, 2011.
[67] Interview, Organization 30, April 15, 2011.

[Indian businesses] can integrate with the global economy, the better."[68] Another even questioned his organization's mobilization around an Indian identity: "We originally were focused on South Asia . . . but we grew beyond our expectations. And now we are global. We want to simply be successful. It is embarrassing that people think they can't join because they are not South Asian. At the same time, we can never deny our history. Our history does come from South Asia."[69] As with education, these leaders emphasized their ability to "teach" Indians the ideals of meritocracy and hard work, as well as the market skills they had learned in the United States. Also like education, private business development is considered an equalizing force for economic mobility that contrasts with the "entitlement approach" common among those many refer to as the "filthy rich."

To assist business development, these organizations arrange for delegations of Indian Americans to meet entrepreneurs, business leaders, and government officials in India. They also use their credibility as "Americans" to help provide skills training and certification to entrepreneurs in India, especially in hospitality, medicine, and IT. Although several organizations expressed disdain for advocacy, they lobby the Indian and US governments to protect the interests of private business. As one organization leader put it, "We believe in a market economy. The government is there to facilitate. But entrepreneurs make the economy. We have started playing a role in policy advocacy. . . . Yes, if we can support the government in policy advocacy, we will do so to revive the entrepreneurial ecosystem."[70] Another leader commented, "We help create jobs, and that is the buzzword with entrepreneurs everywhere."[71]

Geopolitical Power: Building the Global Indian Identity

A minority of organizations aim to improve bilateral relations between India and the United States. Unlike the business development organizations, these universally described their motivation in emotional terms—pointing to a desire to build a global Indian identity. Unlike emigrants' earlier geopolitical efforts that lobbied India to pressure receiving countries to protect the emigrants (as in South Africa and Fiji), these organizations lobbied US officials to improve relations with India. As a prime example of their power in the United States and for India, leaders repeatedly mentioned their involvement in advocating US government officials to sign the Nuclear Non-Proliferation Treaty with India in 2005. Interestingly, organizations of all types (including professional, development,

---

[68] Interview, Organization 31, June 29, 2011.
[69] Interview, Organization 29, July 1, 2011.
[70] Interview, Organization 29, July 1, 2011.
[71] Interview, Organization 29, July 1, 2011.

arts, and ethnic) assisted in this effort.[72] More than any other foreign policy issue, Indian government officials concurred, Indian Americans' involvement in the Indo-US Nuclear Deal cemented India's interest in the diaspora. Leaders also recounted assisting US government officials traveling to India to form agreements with Indian government officials. For example, one leader said they drew on an Indian American delegate from Maryland to pressure that state's governor to accept Andhra Pradesh as a sister state to exchange business.[73]

Entrenching Social Inequalities

Indian Americans' support for individual self-sufficiency, privatization, and voluntarism has forged a development ideology for India that undermines the rights-based empowerment that poor Indian emigrants have long fought for. In the process, elite emigrants in the United States preserve social inequities along lines of gender, caste, and religious community within India, which have also shaped the elite pact of "global Indians."[74]

Gender and Caste

Only a handful of Indian American transnational organizations sought gender or caste equality in India, or even within their organization, as a goal. India-based partner organizations that focus on gender and caste rights noted the US diaspora is more interested in education than gender or caste.[75] Many said the second generation is more likely to address issues of gender and caste, but given the second generation's lack of involvement in transnational organizations, it is unclear whether they will work to address these issues in India.[76] A recent survey of individual Indian Americans' found that, although few consider gender inequality a top challenge facing India, nearly 50% say they support caste-based affirmative action for university admissions, thereby indicating substantive support for caste struggles (Badrinathan, Kapur, and Vaishnav 2020). Nevertheless,

---

[72] Interview, Organization 32, February 8, 2011.

[73] Interview, Organization 3, September 29, 2011.

[74] Scholars have also noted how diaspora giving has re-created the social fragmentation of Indian society in the United States (Khandelwal 2002).

[75] Interview, Organization 4, February 28, 2011.

[76] This statement is supported by the Indian-American Survey, which finds 6% of American-born Indians see gender discrimination as a top challenge facing India, while only 2% of foreign-born Indians agree.

Indian Americans do not appear ready to organize around these issues or pressure the Indian government to address them.

One leader in India said, "My theory is the US diaspora needs India to look good to fight white racism."[77] Indeed, aside from a few Christian organizations that exposed caste injustice as part of their missionary efforts, most transnational organizations avoided caste issues in order to mobilize unity along other identities, including subnational ethnicities and a secular pan-Indian identity. As one Hindu leader said, "We don't believe in talking about caste. Whoever does so, is trying to divide Hindus."[78] Another leader in India who works on gender equity said they have held workshops for Indian Americans to teach them to "think more broadly about Indian identity." Explained the leader, "Clearly I am deeply rooted in my South Asian heritage, but we don't define ourselves as a South Asian organization. I want to push us to think more critically about our identity in a global way . . . beyond just being Indian . . . to thinking about human rights."

The few gender- and caste-empowerment projects that have been launched focused on philanthropic projects that educated poor girls or Dalits or assisted poor or Dalit women to develop small businesses (in dairy farming, husbandry, sewing, and street vending) or attain housing and healthcare. These approaches were consistent with a development ideology that views the market as an equalizing mechanism.

Rather than fighting caste inequalities, several organizations capitalized on caste affiliations to mobilize fellow-caste diaspora members to make financial donations or volunteer time. While most Indian Americans come from middle and upper castes, this was also true among the few lower-caste members in my sample. As with most ascriptive-based identities, caste-based mobilizations fostered trust among Indian Americans. One leader explained that Indian Americans "identify more with organizations of caste or region or language, and that is where their money goes. People always tell me to connect to my own caste group if I want to get anything done."[79] A leader who comes from a farm community in India similarly related, "In the beginning they talked about making the organization caste based. And I was so opposed to it. I became a member of my college alumni association. But I found there were no results with that. It was actually the caste-based organization that I was more able to move."[80] Mobilizing around caste was also described as a way to preserve Indian community, culture, and rituals against a Western-dominated modernity. Interestingly,

[77] Interview, Organization 33, May 26, 2011.
[78] Interview, Organization 34, February 15, 2011.
[79] Interview, Organization 6, February 17, 2011.
[80] Interview, Organization 35, April 22, 2011.

these organizations worked with groups in India to fight such Westernization in the United States *and* in India. In other words, globalization had pushed elite Indians in India and Indian Americans closer together in terms of fears over their children losing their cultural roots.[81]

Some organizations explicitly resist Indian lower-caste movements, especially within higher education. For example, alumni associations have defended their alma maters in India against recent accusations of caste-based discrimination. One organization worked with its home college director to write a paper to prove the rising suicide rates among low-caste students were not due to systemic caste injustices in the college. The leader argued, "I don't buy the Dalit issue at all. The data doesn't support it."[82] Several interviewees attributed the suicides to individual-level pathologies, including ignorance, "broken hearts," "ego issues," inability to handle familial pressures to succeed, technology and social media, and new social norms around gender—all common explanations offered by India's elite as well. Pointing to US programs of individual-level support, one leader offered, "The US has a lot of systems in place to deal with social changes. We need student counselors in every wing of the student hostels."[83]

Only one organization in my sample expressed a desire to overturn caste-based injustices in India. This organization is comprised of Dalits and aims to increase awareness about the symbolic injustices underlying caste. The leader explained, "We do advocacy. Not only about the economically poor, but also emotionally-made poor. You can always tolerate economic poverty. But they [Dalits] are going through mental trauma for centuries."[84] Yet he also emphasized the difficulty in fighting for Dalit rights among elite Dalits in the United States. Elite Dalits often hide their caste identity so their children can marry, so they can form networks with other Indian Americans, and so they can avoid the assumption that their success was due to affirmative action.[85] As a result, even this organization had turned to mainstream service provisions.

Communalism

Unlike with gender and caste, several Indian American transnational organizations addressed religious inequalities in India.

A handful of organizations (Asha, AID, India Literacy Project) that mobilize under a pan-Indian identity said they arose in the mid-1990s specifically to

[81] Interview, Organization 36, April 30, 2011.
[82] Interview, Organization 26, September 2, 2011.
[83] Interview, Organization 26, September 2, 2011.
[84] Interview, Organization 7, April 13, 2011.
[85] Interview, Organization 37, May 12, 2011.

counter the rising popularity of the Hindu right and its attempt to redefine India as a Hindu nation. As one leader clarified, "We have to accept the fact that we [Indians] are diverse. And that cannot happen with BJP.... BJP is popular among rich north Indians. That's it. Not all NRIs!"[86] These organizations extolled liberalization and globalization for their potential to defeat Hindu fundamentalist movements (which they perceived as provincial and "unmodern"). They also credited their own professional status and migration experiences for giving them a "cosmopolitan outlook." One development organization leader expressed it this way: "Our leadership group tends to be in mixed marriages [i.e., from different communities within India] and have lived and studied across Indian states. Therefore, they don't fit into the [subnational] Indian ethnic groups."[87] Another leader described their membership as "the ones that are committed to a larger community in India": "We work well with cosmopolitan Indians, who have come out of the *Guju* [slang for a subnational group] shell."

But religious organizations also address religious inequities in India. To do so, they have built defensive religious identities that underscore the fractious nature of religious communalism in India. Nearly all the religious organizations I interviewed framed their mission as preserving their communal identity against attacks in the United States and in India. This included majority religions in the United States (i.e., Christians) and in India (i.e., Hindus). Christians and Muslims spoke of being under attack by the Hindu right in India, and Hindus and Sikhs spoke about being under attack by "global religions," such as Islam and Christianity, as well as race-based violence in the United States and India (for more on this, see Agarwala 2015a, 2015b).

Muslim, Sikh, and Christian organizations (all minority religious groups in India) placed their efforts to defend their religious community in a human rights framework and were thus unique among Indian American transnational organizations in voicing criticism against the Indian government. However, their critiques were soft. Unlike the anticolonial movement leaders in the early 1900s and the anti-Emergency leaders in the 1970s, these organizations do not try to topple the Indian government. Rather, they try to form bridges with the Indian government and lobby their US government representatives to raise awareness of human rights abuses in India.

This approach was particularly striking among Sikh organizations that had a radical history during the 1980s when they supported the Khalistan secession movement for a separatist Sikh state. Recent and second-generation emigrants, however, eschewed these earlier tactics and suggested economic globalization

---

[86] Interview, Organization 40, May 14, 2011.
[87] Interview, Organization 8, May 17, 2011.

was a more appropriate alternative to ethnic divisions. As one leader explained, "I am trying to push [our organization] to not be as suspicious of the Indian government and snap ties with Punjab politics. I tell them we can't keep looking back to Punjab. We have to think more globally."[88] Said another leader, "[We strive to] protect the Sikh identity and protect minorities globally."[89]

Christian organizations were the most vocal in their critiques of right-wing Hindu movements and politicians in India. One leader said, "Prime Minister Modi makes good roads and he is good for Hindus and agricultural areas. But he is wrong in human rights."[90] Some had supported a fellow alum who had been arrested by the Indian government for helping unions and tribal communities through a Maoist movement. But one leader also added, "In general I don't think this stuff works well in India. It is not really formally done by us. They are very sensitive in India about the West meddling in domestic affairs."[91] Interestingly, Indian American Christian organizations' vocal stance contrasted with Christian organizations in India, who framed Christian Indians as apolitical and divided along class lines.

Muslim Indians were the most vocal in their nationalist struggle for a secular India that many felt is being threatened by the Hindu right. As one leader commented, "When we are trying to raise funds, we explain that a bad neighbor brings down the value of your house price. Similarly, if one section of the community is educated, and another is not, it won't do anything for the country." [92] In some cases, Indian Muslim organizations explicitly noted that, despite their name and membership, they don't identify as a religious organization, but as a cultural and development organization that works to help uplift poor Muslims in India to prevent "people from fighting and bringing the country down."[93] In other words, their identity revolved around developing and strengthening modern India by uplifting those at the bottom, where Muslims are overrepresented. Another leader explained, "There is no right-wing Indian Muslim group in the US, because they would just join an international Muslim group."[94] For Muslims, therefore, the Indian identity serves to temper their religious identity.

In India, 80% of the population is Hindu, making it the country's majority religion. Hindu transnational organizations work to create a global Hindu identity (as a minority world religion) and frame India as the Hindu homeland. More

---

[88] Interview, Organization 38, April 22, 2011.
[89] Interview, Organization 41, March 3, 2011.
[90] Interview, Organization 39, April 26, 2011.
[91] Interview, Organization 12, July 20, 2011.
[92] Interview, Organization 43, April 19, 2011.
[93] Interview, Organization 43, April 19, 2011.
[94] Interview, Organization 42, April 26, 2011.

than other transnational organizations, Hindu groups addressed poverty alleviation in India *and* the United States. This approach has not only underscored
the Hindu global identity; it has attracted second-generation Indian Americans
more than most Indian American transnational organizations.[95] Organizations
have initiated Hindu summer camps for Indian American youth, as well as
competitive service projects in India, where Indian American students work in
Indian NGOs on poverty-alleviation projects. Like ethnic- and caste-based organizations, Hindu American organizations have capitalized on the trust underlying the shared Hindu identity to raise funds for poverty-alleviation projects,
disaster relief, and building Hindu temples. But, as with other groups, Indian
partners expressed their greater interest in Hindu Americans' social remittances.
Vijay Jolly, a former member of the legislative assembly, had actively courted
the US diaspora during the Emergency. Today he is the vice president and
spokesman for BJP Delhi and the All India BJP joint convenor of external affairs.
He explained, "In addition to attracting diaspora connections to India, we want
to consolidate our ideologies among the diaspora. We want to attract them to
our groups."[96]

[95] This strategy was also said to address criticisms and even high-profile lawsuits against earlier
projects that focused only on India and were accused of misrepresenting fundraising claims for poverty rather than religious violence." Interview, SEWA International, April 15, 2011.
[96] Interview, March 11, 2011.

Vulnerabilities in the CEO MDR and a Future Trajectory

Anyone who has had the pleasure of standing in the long customs line in an Indian airport on their way out of the country has witnessed the panoply of people that stand ahead and behind them. Armani suits rub against saris and dhotis; black laptop cases sit on the floor next to red vinyl carriers held together with wrapped cellophane. Across the line, people share brief flickers of empathy with one another. Everyone is exhausted from the last-minute rush of packing and getting to the airport in time; anxious about the line's slow movement forward and, for some, the flight itself; sad about leaving family, loved ones, and experiences behind; but open, even excited, about the next leg of life's journey. But what everyone does *not* share is the costs they incurred to get a spot in that line. For some it involved clicking an app on their phone to purchase a plane ticket. But for the masses of poor Indian workers standing in that line, it required mountains of paperwork, fees, clearance stamps, time, deference to recruiters and government officials, and a lifetime of stress. And that was only the cost of entering the line.

As this book has argued, sending states' emigration practices are complicated. They sometimes reflect northern-imposed neoliberal development ideologies and capital interests. But they also sometimes reflect sending states' own attempts to draw foreign currency or manage domestic political legitimacy. They even sometimes reflect demands from migrants themselves. And they are certainly not new or unique to the contemporary era. This book has tried to expose how this messy web of global and domestic forces, as well as actors with competing interests and power, have shaped Indian emigration over time.

Although receiving states' labor demand and immigration policies, shape the rules of the global migration game, sending states shape how they play within that game—forming what I call a Migration Development Regime. On one

The Migration-Development Regime. Rina Agarwala, Oxford University Press. © Oxford University Press 2022.
DOI: 10.1093/oso/9780197586396.003.0009

hand, MDRs capture the complicated nature of sending states' dynamic emigration practices. Depending on a sending country's size, migrant resource base, and geopolitical power, its MDRs sometimes reproduce, but other times reshape, domestic development ideologies and thus the very rules of the game. MDRs are partly rational, especially for some, but most often yield unintended consequences. While they may appear coherent, they are full of contradictions and contingencies. As a result, MDRs rise and fall and shift over time.

But MDRs also expose what is uncomplicated. As these chapters have shown, India's MDRs have always promoted economic growth and domestic political legitimacy alongside deep class-based inequalities. These class-based inequalities have been cemented and clarified by a crude, legislatively enshrined bifurcation of India's emigrants into two simple categories: the "haves" and the "have nots." The former have the requisite level of formal education to free them of state restrictions on their mobility and (in the contemporary era) deem them worthy of the state's financial incentives, recognition, and power to shape its development agenda. The latter have none of the above.

Despite the clarity of the class inequities undergirding Indian emigration practices, India's MDRs have managed to remain strikingly invisible within Indian politics, media, and debates on development. Indian emigration practices therefore have long served as a quiet but crucial vector through which the state has cemented domestic consent for a development model based on class-based inequalities (both globally and within India).

Contrary to much of the sending-state emigration literature that focuses only on the contemporary era and/or on one class at a time (if it focuses on class at all), this book has used a historical and cross-class lens to show exactly how each of India's MDRs (spanning nearly two centuries) has cemented domestic consent for emigration practices that foster economic growth and political legitimacy, along with class inequality.

This book has also shown, however, that at certain moments, the topic of emigration and emigrants themselves have been instrumental in resisting an MDR and transitioning to a new one. The Coolie MDR (1834–1947) instituted an overtly racialized development model, whereby the state exploited rich and poor Indian emigrants to foster capital accumulation for and through the British Empire. Political legitimacy was attempted through seemingly protective legislations and institutions—most of which continue to guide Indian emigration practices today. But Indian emigrants eventually joined forces with Indian independence leaders to expose the racial exploitation undergirding the Coolie MDR, delegitimizing it, and securing its downfall.

The Nationalist MDR (1947–77) that rose in its place instituted a geographically defined development model that promised domestic accumulation and secured political legitimacy by forbidding poor workers' emigration in the name of the state's "paternalist protection." Rather than applying the same restrictions on elite emigrants, the state permitted elite exit but dismissed them from India's development project thereafter. Although its goals were laudable, the Nationalist MDR failed to deliver domestic employment options to India's poorest workers and created resentment among elites abroad. Indian anti-Emergency leaders therefore mobilized emigrants to fight for global democracy and for India to open its borders to the movement of people (and eventually capital). These movements delegitimized the Nationalist MDR and helped facilitate its eventual fall.

In its place came the CEO MDR (1977–present), which has valorized the private accumulation of wealth and individual (rather than national) self-sufficiency. It has fostered domestic capital accumulation by tapping foreign financial flows from its emigrants, especially its poorest emigrants. As well, it has tapped the social remittances of its elite emigrants in the form of ideas, experiences, business partnerships, and know-how. Underlying the CEO MDR's political legitimacy is a powerful elite class pact between India's domestic elite (state officials and business leaders) and elite Indians abroad. Together, this group of highly celebrated "global Indians" dominates Indian development and has attained significant material wealth and status in the process.

To secure consent from poor emigrants, the CEO MDR appeals to workers' long-held demands for emigration liberalization, retains its paternalist protection through welfare and emigration restrictions, and transmits elite ideals of privatization, self-sufficiency, and entrepreneurship through its new migration institutions. This has de-radicalized poor migrants' organizations, occluded the class differences between poor and elite emigrants, and deflected attention away from the needs of wage labor.

When we expose India's relationship to its elite emigrants against its interactions with poor emigrants, the contrast is not only sharp; it is also embarrassing for the world's largest democracy. But if history can be a guide to our future, we should expect the CEO MDR to eventually fall. The question is: How might this happen? And what can take its place? The findings in this book offer important correctives to our understanding of contemporary emigration and expose some of its underlying vulnerabilities. These insights can provide us with some hints of where to look for our future.

On Poor Emigrants

This book has shown that poor Indian emigrants were instrumental in resisting the Nationalist MDR's restrictions over their mobility and fighting for the CEO MDR's liberalization of emigration. This is an important reminder that liberalized emigration is not simply a result of Northern edicts, but rather enjoys strong support within India. Indeed, in the context of failed domestic employment generation, emigration is one of the only options available to the world's poor workers.

However, the historical roots of India's contemporary MDR detailed in this book also show us that liberalized emigration must take place alongside *rights-based state protection for emigrants* rather than the paternalist protection still being offered by the CEO MDR. India's poor emigrants (like poor domestic workers) have long demanded programmatic support for their efforts to produce and earn enough money to secure their survival and material support for their families to cover their social reproduction needs (in education, health-care, housing, food, and water). But the CEO MDR's response has been woefully inadequate. In the name of state protection, thousands of poor (but not elite) workers *remain* burdened by a dizzying stack of bureaucratic requirements, fees, and paperwork they must submit to the Protector General of Emigrants before they are allowed to emigrate. In addition, the state has offered limp promises of welfare that have failed to protect poor emigrants in all moments of their migration journey: on their way out, in their jobs abroad, and in their return to India. The CEO MDR's paternalist protection effectively humiliates poor emigrants simply for being "vulnerable" and uneducated.

The CEO MDR's failure to adequately protect poor emigrants exposes an important weakness in the regime and may offer a source for change. After all, emigrant welfare programs exist today because the electoral expectation of state protection for poor workers is still deeply embedded in India's mass citizenry. Indeed, this expectation is emblazoned in the nation's Constitution. But they also exist because they secure political legitimacy for India's rulers. The enactments of protection schemes during every electoral cycle and in moments of political crisis are testaments to this fact. In India, state welfare programs thus provide one of the few remaining channels of redistribution that poor workers have some power over. As I have written elsewhere, domestic informal workers in several Indian states have institutionalized welfare programs for extremely vulnerable workers across industries (ranging from construction to domestic work to trash collection) (Agarwala 2013, 2018). Rather than ignoring emigrant welfare programs as useless, therefore, opposition parties, scholars, development practitioners, unions, and emigrants themselves must study these efforts, link them with similar efforts to attain welfare for workers within India, and expose the hollowness of the CEO MDR's promises of state protection through welfare for emigrant workers. Only then will the state be forced to deliver.

In addition to its inadequate welfare delivery, the Indian state will have to rethink its current fascination with entrepreneurship. As with liberalized emigration, entrepreneurship in itself may not be a problem for poor workers.

Among poor women, for example, self-employment has long provided one of the few options they have to carry out their income earning and unpaid household obligations (Agarwala and Saha 2018). And, as I have shown in this book, poor emigrants have embraced entrepreneurship upon their return to India, especially given the dismal job alternatives before them. So long as India's job options remain as limited as they currently are, and gender determines household labor burdens, entrepreneurship should be supported by the state.

But the government's current support is pathetic. As with welfare, the state must be held publicly accountable for its promise to support poor workers' entrepreneurship. As well as supporting rising entrepreneurs with seed capital, the state will need to create new forms of security for entrepreneurs in cases of bankruptcy, old age, and calamity. But more fundamentally, if the Indian government is truly envisioning entrepreneurship as a solution for the nation's mass workforce, India will have to fundamentally rethink its entire accumulation model. Clearly, in a world with large corporations (that require wage labor), everyone cannot be an entrepreneur. This book's findings on the CEO MDR's attack on small and medium-size private recruiters indicate that the Indian government is not, in fact, rethinking its accumulation model, but rather supporting large, corporate businesses over small ones. If exposed explicitly and often enough, these contradictions in the CEO MDR's claims to support entrepreneurship for all can help lead to its demise.

Third, this book's findings underscore the importance of visibility. India's poor emigrants have remained invisible for far too long. The push to improve global data on remittances has shed important light on poor workers' extraordinary financial contribution to India's contemporary economy. But we have a long way still to go. Poor Indian emigrants' working conditions, recruitment processes, family welfare, return cycles, regulatory headaches, and organizations need to be much more thoroughly acknowledged, studied, and counted. Although the CEO MDR relies almost entirely on the circular migration of poor Indian workers, the government keeps no data on return migrants. Increased data will not only help poor migrants become more visible to the state; it will help them become more visible to scholars, journalists, and the public. Again, public pressure to increase collection of this data will help expose the contradictions underlying the CEO MDR and nudge us one step closer to its demise.

But fighting the state for improved welfare, deeper job support (whether in entrepreneurship or wage labor), and better data collection and recognition requires organized pressure from below. This book has exposed the CEO MDR's impressive ability to de-radicalize migrants' organizations. This must change. At present, most Indian social movements do not address the topic of emigration or see emigrants as a source of change. As, noted in this book, trade unions almost never include poor emigrant workers in their membership, and migrant organizations almost never identify as workers' organizations, despite their shared class interests with local workers. Trade unions and migrant organizations must overcome the false divide between domestic and emigrant workers and bring both groups together to fight the class-based exploitation that both suffer. Together, they must not allow attention to be deflected away from the wage labor that the masses of poor Indian workers still rely on for their survival.

In addition to pressure from below, India's migration regime will need new ideals, new visions, and a new *mode* of accumulation that prioritizes the needs of poor emigrants and attacks, rather than relies on, class inequality. This brings us to the vulnerabilities of the state in the CEO MDR.

Sending-State Resistance to Admitting Emigration Craft

The Indian state's position in the CEO MDR's elite class pact screams of insecurity. Throughout the course of my research, government officials at the national and state levels repeatedly expressed variations of the puzzling stance toward emigration that Dr. Singh expressed in the opening lines of this book.

There is little doubt that promoting emigration and tapping emigrants for their financial flows has become a widely celebrated panacea among contemporary development institutions. And, although slow to start, India has clearly joined other sending countries in easing restrictions to facilitate emigration; instituting new technologies, programs, and processes to receive emigrants' financial contributions, especially from poor emigrants; and offering awards and other status currencies to recognize emigrants, especially elites. For India, these efforts have yielded the massive returns they promised, both materially and ideologically.

But throughout my interviews, Indian government officials, even those responsible for managing emigration, never took credit for India's recent emigration "achievements." On the contrary, state officials repeatedly clarified that the government does *not* promote emigration, and that India's investments in emigration are *not* motivated by an expectation of economic return. Rather, Indian emigration was consistently framed as a response to global market demands for India's "high-quality" manual and educated workers.

This sentiment could be seen at the subnational level. As Ooman Chandy, then chief minister of Kerala (INC), said to me, "Kerala is so advanced. English education is very high here. There is no promotion by the government for emigration. We [Malayalis] only go a lot because of our English education. They [Malayali emigrants] go through their own initiative and through their social networks."[1] Minister K. C. Joseph of NORKA similarly stated, "We don't encourage migration anymore. We need workers here [in Kerala]. So migration is a second-best option."[2] As K. Satish Nambudiripad, the second CEO of Norka (2002–5), put it, "It was not a national decision of India to send their citizens abroad. Philippines makes it a state policy. But it is not an official policy of India. . . . Kerala is a quirk of destiny."[3]

This sentiment was also present at the national level. As one senior official in DOIA said to me in 2019, "We view migration as a voluntary and informed choice. We are not in the business of sending them away."[4] Years earlier, under a different ruling party, government officials emphasized only their facilitating role in emigration. G. Gurucharan, CEO of Indian Council of Overseas Employment,[5] underscored that the Indian government "doesn't formally encourage or discourage migration. It is an individual decision. But if you do go, we help with information."[6] Similarly, Alwin Didar Singh, secretary of MOIA, explained, "We recognize migration as a democratic right of every individual. And we will facilitate it to create a framework of transparency."[7]

Although government officials did not take credit for emigration, they did credit the success of elite emigrants in wealthy receiving countries to India's education, booming economy, and geopolitical position. After extolling Indian Americans for being "influential," "successful," and the "ideal diaspora," Gurucharan added, "But Indian Americans are what they are because of their roots in India and the US. . . . In the 1950s to the early 1970s, the science teaching in India was very strong. This Nehruvian legacy is what laid the foundation for the IT revolution."[8] Similarly, Dr. Singh said, "We are very proud of our diaspora. We celebrate their success and [re]ward them. . . . But we believe that the success is a result of their own efforts combined with the global brand of India. . . . As India began to rise and our importance increased, so we got noticed. And all this happened just as the diaspora in the US and UK were doing so well. We have a much-respected brand. It is completely different from what it was twenty years ago. No one now thinks of snake charmers and treehouses with India now. They'll just ask you to fix their laptop!"[9]

---

[1] Interview, March 22, 2012.

[2] Interview, March 22, 2012.

[3] Interview, January 11, 2017, emphasis in original.

[4] Interview, January 4, 2019.

[5] A think-tank within MOIA that aimed to examine how India should address issues of migration.

[6] Interview, March 20, 2012.

[7] Interview, January 19, 2011.

[8] Interview, January 25, 2011.

[9] Interview, January 25, 2011.

As well, national government officials downplayed emigrants' emotional motivation to interact with India's development. This was striking given the Indian government's investments in appealing to ethnic solidarity bonds with elite emigrants (as detailed in Chapter 5). Government officials framed elite emigrants' contributions to India as a *rational* (as opposed to emotional) decision to invest in the country's booming economy. Yogeshwar Sangwan, director of Diaspora Services at MOIA, reiterated, "We need to connect to the diaspora, learn from them, maybe they will come and invest, form partnerships, maybe business links . . . but it should be a mutual benefit."[10] Similarly, Shefali Chaturvedi, CEO of OIFC, asserted, "NRIs don't give money on emotional grounds. It's a logical act. They give because they believe India is a good safe place to put their money. . . . In our world it is the economy and money that matters . . . During the [global] economic crisis, India was a safe haven. The banks are secure here. And people can invest in real estate."[11] J. C. Sharma, secretary of the High-Level Committee of Indian Diaspora and former secretary of the Ministry of External Affairs, similarly said, "The diaspora's attitude changes with India's stature in the world. When [India] is down, they [elite emigrants] are hypercritical. Now they want to contribute. But they invest not on emotion but on hard calculations . . . not a love for India . . . [but] a return. Indians are hardheaded investors. They invested because the interest rate was three percent higher than in the US."[12] Dr. Singh repeated several times to me, "People are investing in India because it's the only good, safe, logical place to invest. We believe we have a tremendous economy. So we will showcase our growth and opportunities, and we will facilitate and welcome any investments that come in."[13]

A similar frame emanated from the subnational level. Gujarat government officials, for example, separated their pioneering efforts to forge cultural bonds with emigrants from any desire to attract emigrant investments. As Ravi Saxena, Additional Chief Secretary in Gujarat's Department of Science and Technology, noted, "No Indian diaspora wants to invest in India for the love of their country. They are more business oriented—looking for cheap costs and large markets. We don't find investments due to emotional bonds."[14] Throughout all the symbolic performances the government invested in to build emigrants' emotional attachments to Gujarat, Director K. H. Patel of the NRG Center emphasized, "We *never* ask for investment." Patel is also the chairman of the NRG Committee and a former Indian high commissioner to Uganda and ambassador to Rwanda

[10] Interview, January 19, 2011.
[11] Interview, January 20, 2011.
[12] Interview, March 15, 2011.
[13] Interview, January 19, 2011.
[14] Interview, March 12, 2011.

and Burundi. He spoke proudly of the NRG Centers he helped start throughout the state: "The idea for our Centers is that we can assist the NRIs. We never talk about investing. They will invest if they think there is a profit."[15]

As this book has shown, however, India's emigration practices have never been a random quirk or passive response to global labor markets. They have long been an important and deliberate state subject. And migration states have always created local labor supplies *and* controlled its mobility abroad. What, then, explains Indian government officials' refusal to admit statecraft in emigration?

At first glance, we may interpret this stance as a display of India's adherence to the neoliberal ideals of free markets with minimal state intervention. But the market ideal explanation would not explain why the Indian state has *always* refused to admit statecraft in emigration, long before it embraced neoliberal ideals. An alternative explanation for India's refusal to admit emigration as a part of its deliberate development agenda is that, despite international celebrations of the migration-for-development agenda, the Indian state is humiliated by its emigration practices. As it should be. And herein lies another vulnerability in the CEO MDR.

The CEO MDR's class-differentiated emigration practices expose the fallacy of India's democracy, where some citizens are more equal than others. Moreover, its export of poor emigrants and its massive flood of financial remittances from wages earned abroad exposes the state's inability to meet its poor citizens' material interests within India; indeed, India risks being once again seen as a "Coolie nation." As one emigration official candidly admitted to me, "India is a superpower . . . that is [at least] their perception. They can't be seen as sending their workers abroad."[16] China, for example, does not have a high level of remittances. Finally, the CEO MDR's partnerships with elite emigrants in wealthy receiving countries risk exposing India's inferior structural location in the geopolitical hierarchy. As the Gujarat government wrote in its *Directory for Non-Resident Gujaratis*, "In this relationship [between the government of Gujarat and the Gujarati diaspora], center-periphery models for relations between the government of Homeland and the Diaspora should be avoided. . . . [T]he Homeland and the Diaspora should act as equal partners, full of respect for one another and the relationship should be project-oriented and partnership based" (Government of Gujarat, 2013).

The Indian state should be forced to admit its role in, and reliance on, India's contemporary emigration. Doing so may help transition India to a new MDR. To this end, scholars of Indian development *and* scholars of immigration in

---

[15] Interview, March 24, 2011.
[16] Interview, January 11, 2017.

receiving countries must pay more attention to the role that sending countries play in the global migration game. Whether the Indian government wants to admit it or not, India's emigration practices are a function of India's failed domestic development efforts. And the state is making India interdependent with powerful, wealthy receiving countries. So, if the Indian state is feeling defensive about its global image and its sovereignty, it would be in its geopolitical interest to increase quality job opportunities for its poor and its elite *within* India. But pushing the Indian state in this way will require pressure from elites.

On India's Domestic and Emigrant Elites

This book has shown that India's MDRs have fallen when Indian resistance movements address the topic of emigration *and* mobilize elite emigrants abroad. Doing so not only gives Indian resisters material support and safe havens; it raises the resistance movement's global visibility and legitimacy. The Coolie MDR crumbled under the weight of a powerful antiracist movement that had a global reach. And the Nationalist MDR crumbled under the weight of a globally organized pro-democracy movement. Both movements greatly benefited from the involvement of elite Indians residing abroad.

But as this book has also shown, the CEO MDR has complicated this path to resistance by folding elite Indian emigrants into an elite class pact *with* the Indian state and domestic businesses. Elite Indian emigrants, especially those residing in the United States, have thus been instrumental in shaping and benefiting from, rather than critiquing, the CEO MDR. In 2021, Indians comprised 30% of the CEOs of Fortune 500 companies (including Google, Microsoft, IBM, Adobe Systems, Pepsi, MasterCard, and Nokia), and all (but one) were born and educated in India (the remaining one was born in Nairobi). At present, therefore, elite Indian emigrants do not appear poised to resist the CEO MDR.

But an important vulnerability in the CEO MDR might soon become the relative power India's elite emigrants hold in India's elite pact, particularly because their interests align so well with those of the powerful North. This could be plainly seen during the spring of 2021, when COVID-19 ravaged the Indian population, and the Indian government stood by incapacitated and unwilling to address the catastrophic human tragedy that was taking place. Indian Americans drew on their powerful positions in the United States to mobilize medical supplies, financial support, oxygen tanks, and US government aid to send to India. This formed what has been called the "perfect trifecta," where the interests of the US government, US business, and Indian elites (within India and abroad) were aligned (Kapur 2021). This alignment was the result of the Indian government's decades-long investments in building partnerships with

Indian emigrants to make India a service support provider for the world (akin to China's role as the world's manufacturer). But this powerful trifecta might not feel so "perfect" if it joins forces against the Indian state.

What, if anything, might mobilize elite Indian emigrants to resist the CEO MDR? One option worth exploring is social organizations in India. These are usually led by middle- and upper-class, educated Indian elites who often share personal ties with elite emigrants and have forged countless partnerships through their social work. And relative to Indian American transnational organizations, Indian partner organizations are far more critical of the persisting class inequities in India.

At present, however, my interviews with Indian social organizations indicate that there are several tensions between them and elite emigrants. For example, many viewed elite emigrants' philanthropy as a last resort in the context of dwindling state funds for development aid within liberalizing India. As one leader in India explained, "We are definitely swimming upstream in the present context of liberalization and globalization. Sure, in some ways we have benefited, because there is more wealth and prosperity among rich and middle-class donors. But the negative effects have been far worse than these benefits. . . . Perhaps if the negative effects had not been there, we wouldn't *need* the increased donations from the new wealthy!"[17] Similarly, another organization leader in India noted, "Since 1991, the number of [private] donors has increased [in India and abroad]. . . . But the giving motivations have changed since 1991. Now there is a strong growth in individualism . . . and more guilt. . . . 'How good do I feel about myself when I give?' It is entirely *not* about the cause."[18]

Indian social organization leaders also complained that elite emigrants channel private funding to do the development work of the government, rather than advocate for policy change or hold the government accountable for doing the work itself. One leader of a network of 370 development NGOs in India spoke about the need to retain NGOs' role as critics of government actions: "The arrogance of [the government of India] is coming from the money numbers in the [Indian] corporate sector. In this situation, the government thinks that everything it does is good and correct."[19]

In other words, Indian NGOs do not yet share Indian Americans' lack of faith in the Indian government as the responsible implementer of development. As one activist and scholar of NGOs exclaimed, "Love them or hate them, development will happen in India through the government. . . . Vote bank politics in India will always make sure that the government remains present for social

---

[17] Interview, Organization 25, March 22, 2011.

[18] Interview, Organization 25, March 22, 2011, emphasis in original.

[19] Interview, Organization 45, March 17, 2011.

benefits."[20] Another Indian organization leader noted, "We don't need [diaspora] money to run a health service, the government of India has that money."[21]

Most Indian Americans acknowledged the tension in their partnerships with Indian social organizations. One leader explained, "It is sensitive, and we make sure that the Indian body is in charge."[22] Another said, "We do not tell them how to run things. Just because we bring money does not mean we are the bosses. We have listening ears. Whatever they ask, we are willing to help. We don't control them. But they are accountable to us, we want to know where the money goes."[23] And several Indian American organizations admitted their lack of trust in Indian organizations made them want greater control over the use of their donations.

But if we are to transition to a new MDR, these tensions between India's social organizations and Indian American transnational organizations must be bridged—as they were during previous MDR transitions (through India's independence movement and its anti-Emergency movement). Indian social organizations should share and persuade their partners in the United States of their critical insights into India's class inequities and their intentions to hold the Indian state accountable, rather than quietly accepting emigrants' funding.

And Indian social organizations should try to build global partnerships with elite Indian emigrants who are equally critical of India's present economic policies. While such critics are a minority in the Indian American population, they do exist. As I have shown in this book, this minority have tended not to organize through transnational diaspora organizations; rather, they have tended to focus on fighting inequities within the United States. The streets and halls of Washington, DC, are teeming with social movements (from the left and the right) protesting the material failures of neoliberal globalization and the invisibility of marginalized populations. And Indian Americans are increasingly participating in these movements (on the streets and in the halls of government). Indian social movements should more actively mobilize alongside these critical elite Indian Americans so together we can make these social movements global, addressing class inequities in the United States *and* in India; after all, as this book has demonstrated, these structures have become worryingly interconnected.

Ironically, however, while Washington itself is debating a new New Deal, the Washington Consensus is still enjoying a heyday in New Delhi, and the CEO MDR is still holding strong, backstage and outside public debate. But the COVID-19 pandemic has pushed India's economy to an embarrassing and materially devastating sputter, and the streets of India are ready for action. As

[20] Interview, Organization 11, March 18, 2011.
[21] Interview, Org 45, March 17, 2011.
[22] Interview, Org 12, July 20, 2011.
[23] Interview, Org 44, April 18, 2011.

Antonio Gramsci (1971: 184) famously wrote, economic crises may not produce historical events, but they can certainly "create a terrain more favourable to the dissemination of certain modes of thought." Perhaps the time is now ripe for Indians to join forces across classes and with the critical members of the diaspora to attain a safe haven for critique, financial support for an alternative, and a moral compass with global legitimacy. Perhaps now it is time for a Humane MDR.

REFERENCES

Abella, Manolo I. 2004. "The Role of Recruiters in Labor Migration." In *International Migration: Prospects and Policies in a Global Market*, edited by Douglas Massey and Edward Taylor, 201–11. New York: Oxford University Press.

Abercrombie, Nicholas, Stephen Hill, and Bryan Turner. 1980. *The Dominant Ideology Thesis.* London: George Allen and Unwin.

AccountAid. 2011. "NGO Regulation." In *Accountable*. New Delhi.

Adelman, C. 2009. "Global Philanthropy and Remittances: Reinventing Foreign Aid." *Brown Journal of World Affairs* 15(2): 23–33.

Agarwala, Rina. 2013. *Informal Labor, Formal Politics and Dignified Discontent in India.* New York: Cambridge University Press.

Agarwala, Rina. 2015a. "Divine Development: Transnational Religious Organizations in the US and India." *International Migration Review* 50(4): 910–950.

Agarwala, Rina. 2015b. "Tapping the Indian Diaspora for Indian Development." In *The State and the Grassroots: Immigrant Transnational Organizations in Four Continents*, edited by Alejandro Portes and Patricia Fernandez-Kelly, 84–110. New York: Berghahn Press.

Agarwala, Rina. 2018. "From Theory to Praxis and Back to Theory: Informal Workers' Struggles against Capitalism and Patriarchy in India." *Political Power and Social Theory.* 35: 29–57.

Agarwala, Rina. 2019. "The Politics of India's Reformed Labor Model." In *Business and Politics in India*, edited by Christophe Jaffrelot, Atul Kohli, and Kanta Murali, 95–123. New York: Oxford University Press.

Agarwala, Rina, and Shiny Saha. 2018. "The Employment Relationship and Movement Strategies among Domestic Workers in India." *Critical Sociology* 44(7/8): 1207–23.

Agnew, J., and S. Corbridge. 1995. *Mastering Space: Hegemony, Territory and International Political Economy.* London: Routledge.

Al-Ali, N., R. Black, and K. Koser. 2001. "The Limits to 'Transnationalism': Bosnian and Eritrean Refugees in Europe as Emerging Transnational Communities." *Ethnic and Racial Studies* 24(4): 578–600.

Al-Assaf, Ghazi, and Abdullah M. Al-Malki. 2014. "Modelling the Macroeconomic Determinants of Workers' Remittances: The Case of Jordan." *International Journal of Economics and Financial Issues* 4(3): 514–26.

American Community Survey. 2019. Washington, DC: US Census Bureau. https://www.census.gov/programs-surveys/acs/data.html.

Amjad, Rashid. 1989. "Economic Impact of Migration to the Middle East on the Major Asian Labour Sending Countries: An Overview." Munich Personal RePEc Archive, University Library of Munich, Germany. https://mpra.ub.uni-muenchen.de/38134/

Amrith, Sunil. 2013. *Crossing the Bay of Bengal: The Furies of Nature and the Fortunes of Migrants.* Cambridge, MA: Harvard University Press.

Anderson, Clare, ed. 2018. *A Global History of Convicts and Penal Colonies.* London: Bloomsbury Academic.

Anderson, Edward, and Patrick Clibbens. 2018. "'Smugglers of Truth': The Indian Diaspora, Hindu Nationalism, and the Emergency (1975–77)." *Modern Asian Studies* 52(5): 1729–73.

Assar, Nandini Narain. 2000. "Gender Hierarchy among Gujarati Immigrants: Linking Immigration Rules and Ethnic Norms." Unpublished paper. Blacksburg: Virginia Polytechnic Institute and State University.

Badrinathan, Sumitra, Devesh Kapur, and Milan Vaishnav. 2020. "How Will Indian Americans Vote? Results from the 2020 Indian American Attitudes Survey." Washington, DC: Carnegie Endowment for International Peace, Johns Hopkins School of Advanced International Studies, and University of Pennsylvania.

Bakewell, Oliver. 2007. "Perspectives from Governments of Countries of Origin and Migrant Associations." In *Migration and Development: Perspectives from the South*, edited by Manuel Castells and Raúl Delgado Wise, 285–304. Geneva: International Organization of Migration.

Bakker, Matt. 2007. "The Remittances-to-Development Discourse and the Political Agency of the Collective Migrant." *Migración y Desarrollo* (Second Semester): 41–63.

Bakker, Matt. 2015a. "Discursive Representations and Policy Mobility: How Migrant Remittances Became a 'Development Tool.'" *Global Networks* 15(1): 21–42.

Bakker, Matt. 2015b. *Migrating into Financial Markets: How Remittances Became a Development Tool.* Berkeley: University of California Press.

Bald, Vivek. 2013. *Bengali Harlem and the Lost Histories of South Asian America.* Cambridge, MA: Harvard University Press.

Bardhan, Pranab K. 1984. *The Political Economy of Development in India.* Oxford: Blackwell.

Bartlett, Thomas. 2010. *Ireland: A History.* Cambridge: Cambridge University Press.

Bauböck, Rainer 2003. "Reinventing Urban Citizenship." *Citizenship Studies* 7(2): 139–60.

Betts, Alexander. 2015. "Human Migration Will Be a Defining Issue of This Century. How Best to Cope?" *The Guardian.* September 20.

Bornstein, Erica. 2012. *Disquieting Gifts: Humanitarianism in New Delhi.* Stanford, CA: Stanford University Press.

Bose, P. S. 2008. "Home and Away: Diasporas, Developments and Displacements in a Globalising World." *Journal of Intercultural Studies* 29(1): 111–31.

Breman, Jan. 2016. *On Pauperism in Present and Past.* New Delhi: Oxford University Press.

Buckley, Michelle. 2012. "From Kerala to Dubai and Back Again: Construction Migrants and the Global Economic Crisis." *Geoforum* 43: 250–59.

Burawoy, Michael. 1985. *The Politics of Production: Factory Regimes under Capitalism and Socialism.* London: Verso.

Burawoy, Michael. 1991. *Ethnography Unbound: Power and Resistance in the Modern Metropolis.* Berkeley: University of California Press.

Castells, Manuel. 2010. *The Information Age: Economy, Society, and Culture.* Vol. 2: *Power of Identity.* Malden and Oxford: Wiley-Blackwell.

Castles, Stephen, and Mark J. Miller. 2009. *The Age of Migration: International Population Movements in the Modern World.* 4th edition. Hampshire, UK: Palgrave Macmillan.

Castles, Stephen, and Raul Delgado Wise, eds. 2007. *Migration and Development: Perspectives from the South.* Geneva: International Organization for Migration.

Chakravorty, Sanjoy, Devesh Kapur, and Nirvikar Singh. 2017. *The Other One Percent: Indians in America.* New York: Oxford University Press.

Chand, Masud. 2009. "Leveraging Diaspora Human Capital: Brain Circulation of the Indian Diaspora." Paper presented at the Annual Conference of the Administrative Sciences Association of Canada.

Charities Aid Foundation. 2010. "Dimensions of Voluntary Sector in India." Report. New Delhi: Charities Aid Foundation.

Chibber, Vivek. 2003. *Locked in Place: State-Building and Late Industrialization in India*. Princeton, NJ: Princeton University Press.

Chidambaram, Palaniappan. 2002. "Commanding Heights: The Battle for the World Economy." PBS. www.pbs.org/wgbh/commandingheights/shared/pdf/int_palaniappanchidamba ram.pdf.

Chishti, Muzaffar. 2007. "The Rise in Remittances to India: A Closer Look." *Migration Information Source*. Migration Policy Institute. February 1. https://www.migrationpolicy.org/article/rise-remittances-india-closer-look.

Chitkara, M. G. 2004. *Rashtriya Swayamsevak Sangh: National Upsurge*. New Delhi: S. B. Nangia.

Cohen, J. H., and L. Rodriguez. 2005. "Remittance Outcomes in Rural Oaxaca, Mexico: Challenges, Options and Opportunitites for Migrant Households." *Population, Space and Place* 11(1): 49–63.

Cohen, Robin. 2006. *Migration and Its Enemies: Global Capital, Migrant Labour and the Nation-State*. Aldershot, UK: Ashgate.

de Haas, Hein. 2010. "Migration and Development: A Theoretical Perspective." *International Migration Review* 44(1): 227–64.

de la Garza, R. O., H. P. Panchon, M. Orozco, and A. D. Pantoja. 2000. "Family Ties and Ethnic Lobbies." In *Latinos and U.S. Foreign Policy: Representing the Homeland?*, edited by R. O. de la Garza and H. P. Pachon, 43–101. Oxford: Rowman and Littlefield.

Delgado Wise, Raúl, and Héctor Rodríguez Ramírez. 2001. "The Emergence of Collective Migrants and Their Role in Mexico's Local and Regional Development." *Canadian Journal of Development Studies* 22(3): 747–64.

Desai, Mihir A., Devesh Kapur, John McHale, and Keith Rogers. 2009. "The Fiscal Impact of High-Skilled Emigration: Flows of Indians to the U.S." *Journal of Development Economics* 88: 32–44.

Dimaggio, Paul, and Walter Powell. 1983. "The Iron Cage Revisited: Institutional Isomorphism and Collective Rationality in Organizational Fields." *American Sociological Review* 48: 147–60.

Dimock, Michael. 2016. "Global Migration's Rapid Rise." *Trend Magazine of PEW Research Trust* 1 (Summer). https://www.pewtrusts.org/en/trend/archive/summer-2016/global-migrati ons-rapid-rise.

D'Souza, Eugene J. 2000. "Indian Indentured Labour in Fiji." *Proceedings of the Indian History Congress* 61: 1071–80.

Dugger, Celia W. 2000. "Web Moghuls' Return Passage to India." *New York Times*. February 29.

Durand, Jorge, William Kandel, Emilio Parrado, and Douglas Massey. 1996. "International Migration and Development in Mexican Communities." *Demography* 33: 249–64.

Eckstein, Susan. 2010. "Remittances and Their Unintended Consequences in Cuba." *World Development* 38(7): 1047–55.

Fischer-Tine, Harald. 2007. "Indian Nationalism and the 'World Forces': Transnational and Diasporic Dimensions of the Indian Freedom Movement on the Eve of the First World War." *Journal of Global History* 3: 325–44.

Fisher, Maxine. 1980. *The Indians of New York City*. Columbia, MO: South Asia Books.

Freeman, Gary P. 1995. "Modes of Immigration Politics in Liberal Democratic States." *International Migration Review* 29(4): 881–902.

Free Press Journal. 2019. "Modi Ignored Indian Workers in the Gulf." May 30. http://www.freep ressjournal.in/analysis/modi-ignored-indian-workers-in-the-gulf/1224923.

Georgi, Fabian. 2010. "For the Benefit of Some: The International Organization for Migration and Its Global Migration Management." In *The Politics of International Migration Management*, edited by Martin Geiger and Antoine Pécoud, 45–72. New York: Palgrave Macmillan.

Gereffi, Gary. 1994. "Rethinking Development Theory: Insights from East Asia and Latin America." In *Comparative National Development: Society and Economy in the New Global Order*, edited by A. D. Kinkaid and A. Portes, 26–56. Chapel Hill: University of North Carolina Press.

Ghose, Ajit K. 2016. "India Employment Report 2016: Challenges and Imperative of Manufacturing-Led Growth." New Delhi: Institute of Human Development (IHD) and Oxford University Press.

Ghosh, Bimal. 1995. "Movement of People: The Search for a New International Regime." In *Issues in Global Governance*, edited by The Commission of Global Governance and Kluwer Law International, 405–24. London.

Gibson, Campbell J., and Kay Jung. 2006. "Historical Census Statistics on the Foreign-Born Population of the United States: 1850–2000." Working Paper no. 81. Washington, DC: US Census Bureau.

Glick Schiller, Nina. 2012. "Unravelling the Migration and Development Web: Research and Policy Implications." *International Migration Review* 50(3): 92–97.

Gobierno de México, Secretaría de Bienestar. 2017. "Programa 3x1 para Migrantes." March 28. https://www.gob.mx/bienestar/acciones-y-programas/programa-3x1-para-migrantes.

Goldring, L. 1998. "The Power of Status in Transnational Social Spaces." In *Transnationalism from Below: Comparative Urban and Community Research*, vol. 6, edited by L. Guarnizo and M. P. Smith, 162–86. Livingston, NJ: Transaction Press.

Goldring, Luin. 2001. "The Gender and Geography of Citizenship in Mexico-U.S. Transnational Spaces." *Identities* 7(4): 501–37.

Gordon, Jennifer. 2017. "Regulating the Human Supply Chain." *Iowa Law Review* 102: 445–504.

Government of Gujarat. 2013. *Non-Resident Gujaratis' Contributions to Gujarat*. Gandhinagar: Non-Resident Gujarat Foundation and Times of India.

Government of India. 2002. Inaugural Address of Prime Minister Shri Atal Bihari Vajpayee at the 8th General Conference of the Third World Academy of Sciences. October 21. https://arc hivepmo.nic.in/abv/speech-details.php?nodeid=9068.

Gramsci, Antonio. 1971. *Selections from the Prison Notebooks*. New York: International Publishers.

Grasmuck, Sherri, and Patricia Pessar. 1991. *Between Two Islands: Dominican International Migration*. Berkeley: University of California Press.

Guarnizo, Luis Eduardo. 1998. "The Rise of Transnational Social Formations: Mexican and Dominican State Responses to Transnational Migration." *Political Power and Social Theory* 12: 45–94.

Guha, Ashok, and Amit Ray. 2000. "Multinational versus Expatriate FDI: A Comparative Analysis of the Chinese and Indian Experience." Working Paper No. 58. New Delhi: Indian Council for Research on International Economic Relations.

Heller, Patrick. 1999. *The Labor of Development: Workers and the Transformation of Capitalism in Kerala, India*. Ithaca, NY: Cornell University Press.

Henning, C. G., Jagat K. Motwani, and Jyoti Barot-Motwani, eds. 1989. *Global Migration of Indians: Saga of Adventure, Enterprise, Identity and Integration*. New York: National Federation of Indian-American Associations.

Hirschman, Albert. 1968. "The Political Economy of Import-Substituting Industrialization in Latin America." *Quarterly Journal of Economics* 82: 2–32.

Hobsbawm, Eric. 1975. *The Age of Capital: 1948–1875*. London: Weidenfeld & Nicolson.

Hollifield, James F. 2004. "The Emerging Migration State." *International Migration Review* 38(3): 885–912.

Hoye, J. Matthew. 2020. "Sanctuary Cities and Republican Liberty." *Politics & Society* 48(1): 67–97.

India Abroad. 1974. "Indian Scientists in US Discuss Ways to Help India Meet Her Needs." November 15.

International Organization for Migration. 2020. "World Migration Report 2020." Geneva: International Organization for Migration.

Iskander, Natasha. 2010. *Creative State: Forty Years of Migration and Development Policy in Morocco and Mexico*. Ithaca, NY: Cornell University Press.

Iskander, Natasha. 2021. *Does Skill Make Us Human? Migrant Workers in 21st Century Qatar and Beyond*. Princeton, NJ: Princeton University Press.

Itzigsohn, J. 2000. "Immigration and the Boundaries of Citizenship: The Institutions of Immigrants' Political Transnationalism." *International Migration Review* 34(4): 1126–55.

Jacobs, Elizabeth. 2020. "Work Visas and Return Migration: How Migration Policy Shapes Global Talent." *Journal of Ethnic and Migration Studies* 48(7): 1647–1668.

Jaiswal, Ritesh Kumar. 2018. "Ephemeral Mobility: Critical Appraisal of the Facets of Indian Migration and the Maistry Meditations in Burma (c. 1880–1940)." *Almanack* 19: 80–118.

Jessop, Bob. 1982. *The Capitalist State: Marxist Theories and Methods.* Oxford: Martin Robertson.

Jones-Correa, Michael. 1998. *Between Two Nations: The Political Predicament of Latinos in New York City.* Ithaca, NY: Cornell University Press.

Juergensmeyer, M., and D. M. McMahon. 1998. "Hindu Philanthropy and Civil Society." In *Philanthropy in the World's Traditions,* edited by W. Ilchman, S. Katz, and E. L. Queen, 263–78. Bloomington: Indiana University Press.

Kamat, Anjali. 2015. "The Men in the Middle." *Dissent,* Spring. http://www.dissentmagazine.org/article/men-in-the-middle-gulf-states-kafala-migrant-workers.

Kapur, Devesh. 2005. "Remittances: The New Development Mantra?" In *Remittances: Development Impact and Future Prospects,* edited by S. M. Maimbo and Dilip Ratha, 331–60. Washington, DC: World Bank.

Kapur, Devesh. 2010. *Diaspora, Development, and Democracy: The Domestic Impact of International Migration from India.* Princeton, NJ: Princeton University Press.

Kapur, Devesh. 2018. "International Migration from India and Its Economic Effects." P. R. Brahmanananda Memorial Lecture presented to Reserve Bank of India, New Delhi.

Kapur, Devesh. 2021. "The Power of Indians Abroad." *Foreign Policy,* May 13. https://foreignpolicy.com/2021/05/13/the-power-of-indians-abroad/.

Kapur, Devesh, and John McHale. 2005. "The Global War for Talent: Implications and Policy Responses for Developing Countries." Report. Washington, DC: Center for Global Development.

Kapur, Devesh, Ajay Mehta, and Moon R. Dutt. 2004. "Indian Diasporic Philanthropy." In *Diaspora Philanthropy and Equitable Development: Perspectives on China and India,* edited by Peter Geithner, Lincoln Chen, and Paula D. Johnson. Cambridge, MA: Harvard University Press.

Kearney, Michael. 1991. "Borders and Boundaries of the State and Self at the End of Empire." *Journal of Historical Sociology* 4(1): 52–74.

Keck, Margaret, and Kathryn Sikkink. 1998. *Activists beyond Borders: Advocacy Networks in International Politics.* Ithaca, NY: Cornell University Press.

Keely, C., and B. N. Tran. 1989. "Remittances from Labor Migration: Evaluations, Performance, and Implications." *International Migration Review* 23(3): 500–525.

Kessinger, T. G. 1974. *Vilayatpur 1848–1968: Social and Economic Change in a North Indian Village.* Berkeley: University of California Press.

Ketkar, Suhas L., and Ratha Dilip. 2007. "Development Finance via Diaspora Bonds: Track Record and Potential." Working Paper presented at Migration and Development Conference. Geneva: World Bank Policy Research, 2–21.

Khadria, Binod. 2007. "India: Skilled Migration to Developed Countries, Labor Migration to the Gulf." In *Migration and Development: Perspectives from the South,* edited by Stephen Castles and Raul Delgado Wise, 79–112. Geneva: International Organization for Migration.

Khadria, Binod. 2009. "Bridging the Binaries of Skilled and Unskilled Migraiton from India." *IMDS Working Paper Series,* 23–44. New Delhi: International Migration and Diaspora Studies Project, JNU.

Khandelwal, Madhulika S. 2002. *Becoming American, Being Indian: An Immigrant Community in New York City.* Ithaca, NY: Cornell University Press.

Khatkhate, Deena. 1971. "Brain Drain as a Social Safety Valve." *Finance and Development* 18(1): 34–39.

Kohli, Atul. 2012. *Poverty amid Plenty in the New India.* Cambridge: Cambridge University Press.

Korzeniewicz, Roberto Patricio, and Timothy P. Moran. 2009. *Unveiling Inequality: A World-Historical Perspective.* New York: Russell Sage Foundation.

Koshy, Susan, and R. Radhakrishnan, eds. 2008. *Transnational South Asians: The Making of a Neo-Diaspora.* New Delhi: Oxford University Press.

Krishnamurty, V. 1994. "National Study of Investment Preferences of Expatriates from India." Report. New Delhi: Council of Applied Economic Research.

Kudaisya, Gyanesh. 2006. *Region, Nation, "Heartland": Uttar Pradesh in India's Body-Politic.* Thousand Oaks, CA: Sage.

Kumar, Kedar Nath. 1978. "The Ideology of the Janata Party." *Indian Journal of Political Science* 39(4): 587–98.

Kumar, S. Krishna, and S. Irudaya Rajan. 2014. *Emigration in 21st-Century India Governance, Legislation, Institutions.* London: Routledge.

Kumari, Kamini. 2010. "Interview with Dr. Vivek Wadhwa, Founding President of Carolinas Chapter of the IndUS Entrepeneurs (TiE)." In *Pravasi Bharatiya*, 30–33. New Delhi: Ministry of Overseas Indians.

Kuruvilla, Sarosh, and Aruna Ranganathan. 2008. "Economic Development Strategies and Macro and Micro-Level Human Resource Policies: The Case of India's 'Outsourcing' Industry." *Industrial and Labor Relations Review* 62(1): 39–72.

Lal, Brij V., ed. 2006. *The Encyclopaedia of the Indian Diaspora.* Singapore: National University of Singapore.

Lal, V. 1999. "Establishing Roots, Engendering Awareness: A Political History of Asian Indians in the United Sattes." In *Live Like the Banyan Tree: Images of the Indian Amerian Experience*, edited by L. Prasad, 42–48. Philadelphia, PA: Philadephia Balch Institute for Ethnic Studies.

Larson, Erik, and Ron Aminzade. 2007. "Neoliberalism and Racial Redress: Indigenization and Politics in Tanzania and Fiji." In *Politics and Neoliberalism: Structure, Process, and Outcome*, edited by Harland Prechel, 121–66. Oxford: Elsevier.

Lenin, V. I. 1956. *The Development of Capitalism inRussia.* Moscow: Progress Publishers.

Leonard, Karen. 2007. "Transnationalism, Diaspora, Translation: Punjabis and Hyderabadis Abroad." *Sikh Formations* 3(1): 51–66.

Lessinger, J. 1992. "Investing or Going Home? A Transnational Strategy among Indian Immigrants in the United States." *Annals of the New York Academy of Sciences* 645: 53–80.

Lessinger, J. 2003. "Indian Immigrants in the United States: The Emergence of a Transnational Population." In *Culture and Economy in the Indian Diaspora*, edited by Bhikhu C. Parekh, Gurharpal Singh, and Steven Vertovec, 165–82. London: Routledge.

Levien, Michael. 2018. *Dispossession without Development: Land Grabs in Neoliberal India* New York: Oxford University Press.

Levitt, Peggy. 1999. "Social Remittances: A Local-Level, Migration-Driven Form of Cultural Diffusion." *International Migration Review* 32: 926–49.

Levitt, Peggy 2001. *The Transnational Villagers.* Berkeley: University of California Press.

Levitt, Peggy, and Rafael de la Dehesa. 2003. "Transnational Migration and the Redefinition of the State: Variations and Explanations." *Ethnic and Racial Studies* 26(4): 587–611.

Linebough, P., and M. Rediker. 2000. *The Many Headed Hydra.* London: Verso.

Lipton, M. 1980. "Migration from the Rural Areas of Poor Countries: The Impact on Rural Productivity and Income Distribution." *World Development* 8: 1–24.

Louie, A. 2000. "Re-Territorializing Transnationalism: Chinese Americans and the Chinese Motherland." *American Ethnologist* 27(3): 645–69.

Lucas, Robert E. B. 2005. *International Migration and Economic Development: Lessons from Low-Income Countries.* Cheltenham, UK: Edward Elgar.

Madhavan, M. C. 1985. "Indian Emigrants: Numbers, Characteristics, and Economic Impact." *Population and Development Review* 11: 457–81.

Mahler, S. J. 2000. "Constructing International Relations: The Role of Transnational Migrants and Other Non-State Actors." *Identities* 7(2): 197–232.

Malkani, Rohini. 2009. "Economic and Market Analysis: India." Report. Mumbai: Citigroup Global Markets.

Mann, Jatinder. 2012. "The Evolution of Commonwealth Citizenship, 1945–1948 in Canada, Britain and Australia." *Commonwealth & Comparative Politics* 50: 293–313.

Martin, Philip, and Edward Taylor. 2001. "Managing Migration: The Role of Economic Policies." In *Global Migrants Global Refugees: Problems and Solutions*, edited by Aristide Zolberg and Peter Benda, 95–120. Oxford: Berghahn Books.

Marx, Karl. 1976. *Capital: Volume I.* London: Penguin Books.

Marx, Karl, and Fredreich Engels. 1965. *German Ideology.* London: Lawrence and Wishart.

Massey, Douglas. 1988. "Economic Development and International Migration in Comparative Perspective." *Population and Development Review* 14(3): 383–413.

Massey, Douglas S., Joaquin Arango, Graeme Hugo, Ali Kouaouci, Adela Pellegrino, and J. Edward Taylor. 1993. "Theories of International Migration: A Review and Appraisal." *Population and Development Review* 19(3): 431–66.

Massey, Douglas, Joaquin Arango, Graeme Hugo, Ali Kouaouci, Adela Pellegrino, and J. Edward Taylor. 2008. *Worlds in Motion: Understanding International Migration at the End of the Millenium.* Oxford: Clarendon Press.

Mawdsley, Emma 2015. "DFID, the Private Sector and the Re-centring of an Economic Growth Agenda in International Development." *Global Society* 29(3): 339–58.

Meyer, John W., and Brian Rowan. 1977. "Institutionalized Organizations: Formal Structure as Myth and Ceremony." *American Journal of Sociology* 83(2): 340–63.

Milkman, Ruth. 2018. "Low-Wage Worker Organizing and Advocacy in the US: Comparing Domestic Workers and Day Laborers." *Political Power and Social Theory* 35: 57–73.

Milkman, Ruth, Deepak Bhargava, and Penny Lewis, eds. 2021. *Immigration Matters: Movements, Visions, and Strategies for a Progressive Future.* New York: New Press.

Ministry of External Affairs. 2001. "Annual Report 2000–2001." New Delhi: Ministry of External Affairs.

Ministry of External Affairs. 2004. "Annual Report 2003–2004." New Delhi: Ministry of External Affairs.

Ministry of External Affairs. 2016. "Annual Report 2015–16." New Delhi: Ministry of External Affairs.

Ministry of External Affairs. 2018. "Annual Report 2017–18." New Delhi: Ministry of External Affairs. https://www.mea.gov.in/annual-reports.htm?57/Annual_Reports.

Ministry of External Affairs. 2020. "Population of Overseas Indians." New Delhi. https://mea.gov.in/images/pdf/3-population-overseas-indian.pdf.

Ministry of External Affairs. 2021. "Annual Report 2020–21." . New Delhi: Ministry of External Affairs.

Ministry of External Affairs, Non Resident Indians and Persons of Indian Origin Division. 2000. "Report of the High Level Committee on the Indian Diaspora." New Delhi. https://mea.gov.in/oia-publications.htm.

Ministry of Overseas Indian Affairs. 2015. "Ministry of Overseas Indian Affairs Annual Report (2014–2015)." New Delhi. https://www.mea.gov.in/annual-reports.htm?57/Annual_Reports.

Monbiot, George. 2004. "This Is What We Paid For." *Outlook India.* May 18.

Mongia, Radhika Viyas. 1999. "Race, Nationality, Mobility: A History of the Passport." *Public Culture* 11(3): 527–56.

Moyo, D. 2009. *Dead Aid: Why Aid Is Not Working and How There Is a Better Way for Africa.* New York: Farrar, Straus and Giroux.

Naidis, Mark. 1951. "Propaganda of the Gadar Party." *Pacific Historical Review* 20(3): 251–60.

Nair, Gopinathan P. R. 1991. "Asian Migration to the Arab World: Kerala (India)." In *Migration to the Arab World: Experience of Returning Migrants,* edited by Godfrey Gunatilleke, 19–55. Tokyo: United Nations University Press.

Naujoks, Daniel. 2013. *Migration, Citizenship, and Development: Diasporic Membership Policies and Overseas Indians in the United States.* New Delhi: Oxford University Press.

Nayyar, Deepak. 1989. "International Labour Migration from India: A Macro-Ecnomic Analysis." In *To the Gulf and Back,* edited by Rashid Amjad, 344–64. New Delhi: International Labor Organization.

Nayyar, Deepak. 1994. *Migration, Remittances and Captial Flows: Yhe Indian Experience.* Delhi: Oxford University Press.

NDTV. 2007. "Invest in New India: PM to Diaspora." January 7.

Nehru, Jawaharlal. 1972. *Selected Works of Jawaharlal Nehru.* New Delhi: Orient Longman.

Neuman, W. 2011. *Social Research Methods: Qualitative and Quantitative Approaches.* Boston: Allyn & Bacon.

Ngai, Mae M. 2014. *Impossible Subjects: Illegal Aliens and the Making of Modern America.* Princeton, NJ: Princeton University Press.

Nyblade, Benjamin, and Angela O'Mahony. 2014. "Migrants' Remittances and Home Country Elections: Cross-National and Subnational Evidence." *Studies in Comparative International Development* 49: 44–66.

Ong, Aihwa. 2006. *Neoliberalism as Exception: Mutations in Citizenship and Sovereignty.* Durham, NC: Duke University Press.

Orozco, M. 2006. "International Flows of Remittances: Cost, Competition and Financial Access in Latin America and the Caribbean-Toward an Industry Scorecard." Report. Washington, DC: Inter-American Development Bank.

Osella, Caroline, and Filippos Osella. 2008. "Nuancing the Migrant Experience: Perspectives from Kerala, South India." In *Transnational South Asians: The Making of a Neo-Diaspora,* edited by S. Koshy and R. Radhakrishnan, 146–78. New Delhi: Oxford University Press.

Osella, F., and C. Osella. 2000. *Social Mobility in Kerala: Modernity and Identity in Conflict.* London: Pluto.

Østergaard-Nielsen, Eva. 2003. "The Politics of Migrants' Transnational Political Practices." *International Migration Review* 37(3): 760–86.

Overseas Indian Facilitation Centre. 2009. "Remittances from Indian Diaspora: A Report." New Delhi: Overseas Indian Facilitation Centre.

Park, Jeanne. 2015. "Europe's Migration Crisis: An Escalating Migration Crisis Is Testing the European Union's Commitment to Human Rights and Open Borders." Council on Foreign Relations. https://www.cfr.org/backgrounder/europes-migration-crisis.

Parrenas, Rachel. 2004. "The Care Crisis in the Phillipines." In *Global Women,* edited by Barbara Ehrinreich and Arlie Hochschild, 39–54. New York: Henry Holt.

Pearlman, Wendy. 2014. "Competing for Lebanon's Diaspora: Transnationalism and Domestic Struggles in a Weak State." *International Migration Review* 48(1): 34–75.

Pérez-Armendáriz, Clarisa. 2014. "Cross-Border Discussions and Political Behavior in Migrant-Sending Countries." *Studies of Comparative International Development* 49: 67–88.

Pessar, Patricia R., and Sarah J. Mahler. 2003. "Transnational Migration: Bringing Gender In." *International Migration Review* 37(3): 812–46.

Portes, Alejandro. 2001. "Introduction: The Debates and Significance of Immigrant Transnationalism." *Global Networks* 1(3): 181–94.

Portes, Alejandro. 2003. "Conclusion: Theoretical Convergencies and Empirical Evidence in the Study of Immigrant Transnationalism." *International Migration Review* 37(3): 874–92.

Portes, Alejandro, Cristina Escobar, and Alexandria Walton Radford. 2007. "Immigrant Transnational Organizations and Development: A Comparative Study." *International Migration Review* 41(Spring): 242–81.

Portes, Alejandro, and Patricia Fernandez-Kelly, eds. 2015. *The State and the Grassroots: Immigrant Transnational Organizations in Four Continents.* New York: Berghahn Press.

Portes, Alejandro, William Haller, and Luis Eduardo Guarnizo. 2002. "Transnational Entrepreneurs: The Emergence and Determinants of an Alternative Form of Immigrant Economic Adaptation." *American Sociological Review* 67: 278–98.

Portes, Alejandro, and Min Zhou. 2012. "Transnationalism and Development: Mexican and Chinese Immigrant Organizations in the United States." *Population and Development Review* 38: 191–220.

Prasad, Birendra. 1979. *Indian Nationalism and Asia (1900–1947).* New Delhi: B. R. Publishing.

Raghuram, Parvati. 2008. "Conceptualising Indian Emigration: The Development Story." In *Global Migration and Development,* edited by Ton Van Naerssen, Ernst Spaan, and Annelies Zoomers, 309–25. New York: Routledge.

Rajan, S. Irudaya, V. J. Varghese, and M. S. Jayakumar. 2011. *Dreaming Mobility and Buying Vulnerability*. New York: Routledge.

Ramji, H. 2006. "British Indians 'Returning Home': An Exploration of Transnational Belongings." *Sociology* 40: 645–62.

Ramnath, Maia. 2005. "Two Revolutions: The Ghadar Movement and India's Radical Diaspora, 1913–1918." *Radical History Review* 92(Spring): 7–30.

Ratha, Dilip. 2019. "Remittances on Track to Become the Largest Source of External Financing in Developing Countries." Report. Geneva: World Bank.

Reichert, J. S. 1981. "The Migrant Syndrome: Seasonal U.S. Labor Migration and Rural Development in Central Mexico." *Human Organization* 40: 56–66.

Reserve Bank of India. 1991. "Annual Report 1990–1991." New Delhi.

Reserve Bank of India. 2006. "Invisibles in India's Balance of Payments." *Reserve Bank of India Monthly Bulletin*. November, 1339–74. https://rbidocs.rbi.org.in/rdocs/Bulletin/PDFs/74250.pdf.

Reserve Bank of India. 2013. Notifications, September 6. https://www.rbi.org.in/scripts/NotificationUser.aspx?Id=8388&Mode=0.

Reserve Bank of India. 2018. "India's Inward Remittances Survey 2016–17." New Delhi.

Reserve Bank of India. 2021. "Annual Report 2020–2021." New Delhi.

Rodriguez, Robyn. 2010. *Migrants for Export: How the Philippine State Brokers Labor to the World*. Minneapolis: University of Minnesota Press.

Rubenstein, H. 1992. "Migration. Development and Remittances in Rural Mexico." *International Migration* 30(2): 127–53.

Rutten, Mario, and Pravin Patel. 2007. "Contested Family Relations and Government Policy: Links between Patel Migrants in Britain and India." In *Global Indian Diasporas: Exploring Trajectories of Migration and Theory*, edited by Gijsbert Oonk, 167–94. Amsterdam: International Institute of Asian Studies/Amsterdam University Press.

Sassen, Saskia. 1988. *The Mobility of Labor and Capital: A Study in International Investment and Capital Flow*. New York: Cambridge University Press.

Saxenian, Annalee. 2002. "The Silicon Valley Connection: Transnational Networks and Regional Development in Taiwan, China and India." *Science Technology & Society* 7(1): 117–49.

Saxenian, Annalee. 2005. "From Brain Drain to Brain Circulation: Transnational Communities and Regional Upgrading in India and China." *Studies in Comparative International Development* 40(2): 35–61.

Securities and Exchange Board of India. 2000. "Amendments to Securities and Exchange Board of India (Disclosure and Investor Protection) Guidelines, 2000."Mumbai: Primary Market Department.

Seshadri, R. K. 1993. *From Crisis to Convertibility: The External Value of the Rupee*. Bombay: Orient Longman.

Shah, Nasra M., and Indu Menon. 1999. "Chain Migration through the Social Network: Experience of Labour Migrants in Kuwait1." *International Migration* 3(2): 361–82.

Shastri, Varnita. 1997. "The Politics of Economic Liberalization in India." *Contemporary South Asia* 6(1): 27–56.

Sheth, Arpan. 2010. "An Overview of Philanthropy in India." Bain. March 19. https://media.bain.com/Images/India_Sheth_Speech.pdf.

Shukla, Sandhya. 1999. "New Immigrants, New Forms of Transnational community: Post-1965 Indian Migrations." *Amerasia Journal* 25(3): 17–38.

Shukla, Sandhya Rajendra. 2003. *India Abroad: Diasporic Cultures of Postwar America and England*. Princeton, NJ: Princeton University Press.

Sidel, Mark. 2005. "Diaspora Philanthropy to India: A Perspective from the United States." In *Diaspora Philanthropy and Equitable Development in China and India*, edited by Johnson Geithner, Lincoln Chen, and Paula D. Johnson, 215–57. Cambridge, MA: Global Equity Initiative, Harvard University.

Sidel, Mark. 2008. "A Decade of Research and Practice of Diaspora Philanthropy in the Asia Pacific Region: The State of the Field." University of Iowa, Legal Studies Research Paper. Ames: University of Iowa, College of Law.

Singh, Amit. 2014. *India's Diaspora Policy: A Case Study of Indians in Malaysia.* Doctoral Dissertation. New Delhi: Jawaharlal Nehru University. https://shodhganga.inflibnet.ac.in/handle/10603/18346?mode=full.

Singh, Jagadip N. 2011. "NGR's Contributions to Gujarat." Report. Edited by Government of Gujarat Non-Resident Gujaratis Foundation. Gandhinagar: National Media Foundation and Times of India.

Singh, Manmohan. 1999. "South Asian of the Year: Chandrababu Naidu." *Time Asia,* December 30. http://articles.cnn.com/1999-12-30/world/9912_30_sd_1_andhra-pradesh-reforms-indias?_s=PM:ASIANOW.

Singha, Radhika. 2013. "The Great War and a 'Proper' Passport for the Colony: Border-Crossing in British India, c. 1882–1922." *Indian Economic and Social History Review* 50(3): 289–315.

Sirkeci, Ibrahim, Jeffrey H. Cohen, and Dilip Ratha, eds. 2012. *Migration and Remittances during the Global Financial Crisis and Beyond.* Washington, DC: World Bank.

Slezkine, Yuri. 2006. *The Jewish Century.* Princeton, NJ: Princeton University Press.

Smith, R. 1998. "Reflections on Migration, the State and the Construction, Durability, and Newness of Transnational Life." *Soziale Welt Sonderband 12 Trannationale Migration NOMOS Verlagsgesellschaft, Baden-Baden, Germany* 12.

Sohi, Seema. 2011. "Race, Surveillance, and Indian Anticolonialism in the Transnational Western U.S.-Canadian Borderlands." *Journal of American History* 98(2) (September): 420–36.

Somers, M. 1993. "Citizenship and the Place of the Public Sphere: Law, Community, and Political Culture in the Transition to Democracy." *American Sociohgical Review* 58(5): 587–620.

Sørensen, Ninna Nyberg. 2012. "Revisiting the Migration-Development Nexus: From Social Networks and Remittances to Markets for Migration Control." *International Migration Review* 50(3): 61–76.

Stark, Oded. 1991. *The Migration of Labor.* Cambridge: Basil Blackwell.

Subramanian, Ajantha. 2015. "Making Merit: The Indian Institutes of Technology and the Social Life of Caste." *Comparative Studies in Society and History* 57(2): 291–322.

Taylor, J. E. 1999. "The New Economics of Labour Migration and the Role of Remittances in the Migration Process." *International Migration* 37(1): 63–88.

Taylor, Steve, Manjit Singh, and Deborah Booth. 2007. "Migration, Development and Inequality: Eastern Punjabi Transnationalism." *Global Networks* 7(3): 328–47.

Terrazas, Aaron, and Cristina Batog. 2010. "Indian Immigrants in the United States." Report. Migration Policy Institute. June 9. https://www.migrationpolicy.org/article/indian-imm igrants-united-states-2008.

Thompson, Derek. 2018. "How Immigration Became So Controversial: Does the Hot-Button Issue of 2018 Really Split the Country? Or Just the Republican Party?" *The Atlantic.* February 2. https://www.theatlantic.com/politics/archive/2018/02/why-immigration-divides/552125/.

Tsai, Kellee S. 2010. "Friends, Family or Foreigners? The Political Economy of Diasporic FDI and Remittances in China and India." *China Report* 46(4): 387–429.

Tsourapas, G. 2019. "The Long Arm of the Arab State." *Ethnic & Racial Studies* 43(2): 351–70.

Turcu, Anca, and R. Urbatsch. 2015. "Diffusion of Diaspora Enfranchisement Norms: A Multinational Study." *Comparative Political Studies* 48(4): 407–37.

United Nations, 2010. "Technical Group Support on the Movement of Persons: Mode 4." https://unstats.un.org/unsd/tradeserv/tfsits/subgroup.htm.

United Nations, Department of Economic and Social Affairs, Population Division. 2019. "International Migrant Stock 2019." https://www.un.org/en/development/desa/populat ion/migration/data/estimates2/estimates19.asp.

US Citizenship and Immigration Services. 2007–17. "Number of H-1B Petition Filings Applications and Approvals, Country, Age, Occupation, Industry, Annual Compensation

($), and Education." https://www.uscis.gov/sites/default/files/document/data/h-1b-2007-2017-trend-tables.pdf.

US Citizenship and Immigration Services. 2018. "H-1B Petitions by Gender and Country of Birth." https://www.uscis.gov/sites/default/files/document/reports/h-1b-petitions-by-gender-country-of-birth-fy2018.pdf.

US Citizenship and Immigration Services. 2019. "H-1B Petitions by Gender and Country of Birth." https://www.uscis.gov/sites/default/files/document/data/h-1b-petitions-by-gender-country-of-birth-fy2019.pdf.

US Department of State, Bureau of Consular Affairs. n.d. "Non-Immigrant Visa Statistics. Accessed March 5, 2022. https://travel.state.gov/content/travel/en/legal/visa-law0/visa-statistics/nonimmigrant-visa-statistics.html.

Valiani, Salimah. 2012. *Rethinking Unequal Exchange: The Global Integration of Nursing Labour Markets.* Toronto: University of Toronto Press.

Varsanyi, Monica W. 2006. "Interrogating 'Urban Citizenship' vis-à-vis Undocumented Migration." *Citizenship Studies* 10(2): 229–49.

Vigdor, Jacob L. 2008. "Measuring Immigrant Assimilation in the United States." In *Civic Report.* New York: Manhattan Institute. May 1. https://www.manhattan-institute.org/html/measuring-immigrant-assimilation-united-states-5835.html.

Viswanath, Priya. 2000. "Rejuvenating the Spriit of India: Diaspora Philanthropy and Non Resident Indians in the US." Report. New Delhi: Charities Aid Foundation.

Vora, Neha. 2013. *Impossible Citizens: Dubai's Indian Diaspora.* Durham, NC: Duke University Press.

Waldinger, Roger D., and David Fitzgerald. 2004. "Transnationalism in Question." *American Journal of Sociology* 109(5): 1177–95.

Walton-Roberts, Margaret. 2004. "Returning, Remitting, and Reshaping: Non-resident Indians and the Transformation of Society and Space in Punjab, India." In *Transnational Spaces*, edited by Peter Jackson, Phil Crang, and Claire Dwyer, 78–103. London: Routledge.

Walton-Roberts, Margaret. 2012. "Contextualizing the Global Nursing Care Chain: International Migration and the Status of Nursing in Kerala, India." *Global Networks* 12(2): 175–94.

Walton-Roberts, Margaret. 2014. "Diasporas and Divergent Development in Kerala and Punjab: Querying the Migration-Development Discourse." In *Global Diasporas and Development: Socio-Economic, Cultural, and Policy Perspectives*, edited by Sadananda Sahoo and B. K. Pattanaik, 69–86. New Delhi: Springer.

Wang, Zheng. 2016. *Finding Women in the State: A Socialist Feminist Revolution in the People's Republic of China, 1949–1964* Berkeley: University of California Press.

Wei, Wenhui. 2005. "China and India: Any Differences in Their FDI Performances?" *Journal of Asian Economics* 16(4): 719–36.

Weiner, Myron. 1982. "International Migration and Development: Indians in the Persian Gulf." *Population and Development Review* 8(1): 1–36.

Wimmer, Andreas, and Nina Glick Schiller. 2002. "Methodological Nationalism and Beyond: Nation-State Building, Migration and the Social Sciences." *Global Networks* 2(4): 301–34.

World Bank. n.d. World Development Indicators. Accessed July 2021. https://databank.worldbank.org/data/reports.aspx?source=world-development-indicators.

World Bank. 2015. "India Receives Top Remittance of US$ 70 Billion in 2014." In *Capital Market.* Washington, DC.

World Bank. 2016. *Migration and Remittances Factbook 2016.* 3rd edition. Washington, DC: World Bank.

Xiang, Bao. 2002. "Ethnic Transnational Middle Classes in Formation: A Case Study of Indian Information Technology Professionals." Paper presented at Conference "Making Politics Count," University of Aberdeen, 3–21.

Xiang, Biao. 2011. *Global "Body Shopping."* Princeton, NJ: Princeton University Press.

Yang, Jia Lynn. 2020. *One Mighty and Irresistible Tide.* New York: W. W. Norton.

Yatsko, P. 1995. "Call Home." *Far Eastern Economic Review* 158(4): 50–52.

Ye, Min. 2014. *Diasporas and Foreign Direct Investment in China and India*. New York: Cambridge University Press.

Ye, Min. 2016. "Utility and Conditions of Diffusion by Diasporas: Examining Foreign Direct Investment Liberalization in China and India." *Journal of East Asian Studies* 16: 261–80.

Ye, Min. 2020. *The Belt, Road and Beyond: State-Mobilized Globalization in China, 1998–2018*. New York,: Cambridge University Press.

Zachariah, K. C., K. P. Kannan, and Irudaya S. Rajan. 2002. *Kerala's Gulf Connection: CDS Studies on International Labour Migration from Kerala State in India*. Thiruvananthapuram: Center for Development Studies.

Zachariah, K. C., and Irudaya S. Rajan. 2009. *Migration and Development: The Kerala Experience*. New Delhi: Daanish Books.

Zhou, Min, and Rennie Lee. 2015. "Traversing Ancestral and New Homelands: Chinese Immigrant Transnational Organizations in the United States." In *The State and the Grassroots: Immigrant Transnational Organizations in Four Continents*, edited by Alejandro Portes and Patricia Fernandez-Kelly. Chapter 1. New York: Berghahn Press.

INDEX

For the benefit of digital users, indexed terms that span two pages (e.g., 52–53) may, on occasion, appear on only one of those pages.

recruiters/recruiting agencies, 21, 157
  cultural capital, 199–200
  demanding recognition as economic
    heroes, 200–1
  Emigration Act of 1983 and, 193–94
  increased invisibility of, 198
  interviews with, 48
  overview, 190
  reframing as emigrant representatives, 198–99
  view of government regulations, 194–97
  villification of, 190–92
Reddy, N. V. Ramana, 149
Rediker, Marcus, 29–30
regime, 40. *See also* MDRs
Rejuvenate India movement, 147
Rekhi, Kanwal, 147
Reliance Industries, 135n.2
religious/religious combination organizations,
    49n.20, 204, 205t. *See also* transnational
    organizations
  addressing religious inequities, 230–32
  Christian, 218, 225, 228, 230, 231
  education initiatives and, 218, 219–20
  Hindu, 99–100, 225, 230, 231–32
  Indian Union Muslim League, 176, 176n.19
  Kerala Muslim Cultural Center, 170–71, 172–
    73, 176–77, 181–82, 188–89
  poverty-alleviation initiatives, 225, 231–32,
    232n.95
  Sikh, 218, 225, 230–31
remittances
  China, 2n.2, 241
  defined, 1–2
  development institutions' promotion of, 24–26
  ethnic direct investment vs., 128–31
  financial, 2, 33, 173–74
  foreign direct investment vs., 1–2, 116
  foreign investments, 34–35
  foreign portfolio investments vs., 2, 116
  global, in 2019, 2n.2
  from Gulf countries, 117–18
  ideational, 30–31, 36
  ideological, 16–17, 33–34, 132, 133–34, 149
  India 2018, 1–2
  India 2019, 2
  Mexico, 2n.2
  NRI deposits, 2
  overseas development aid vs., 1–2, 116
  Philippines, 2n.2
  political, 33
  recognizing value of, 114–16
  Russia, 2n.2
  social, 21, 33, 35–36, 106, 202–3, 222,
    231–32
  success of, 116–18
  wage-based, 34–35
Reserve Bank of India

Foreign Currency Non-Resident (External)
    Ordinary Account, 125
  liberalization of capital accounts, 127
  Non-Resident (External) Rupee Account, 125
retail philanthropy, 213. *See also* private sector
returnee organizations
  asserting emigrant dignity, 173–75
  close relationship to political parties, 186–87
  cross-class membership and leadership, 188–90
  demands for welfare assistance, 170–72
  deregulation efforts, 170
  formation of, 167–69
  framing of poor emigrants as economic
    heroes, 178–80
  lack of government data on poor emigrants,
    172–73, 172n.9
  promoting entrepreneurial identity, 180–84
  role in instituting government welfare
    programs, 184–86
  supporting emigrants' citizenship
    power, 175–78
  targeting government for help, 169–75
Right to Education Bill of 2005, 220
rights-based protection, 17, 21, 107, 111–12, 236
right-wing politics. *See also* BJP
  influence on emigration policies, 28–29
  transnational organizations and, 210–12,
    210n.13
Rodriguez, Robyn, 30–31
Roy, Jayanta, 142n.18
rule of truth (*satyagraha*) campaign, 69–70
Russia
  remittances in 2019, 2n.2
  Russian Revolution of 1905, 70

Sampradan organization, 148
"sanctuary cities," 43
Sangwan, Yogeshwar, 240
Sarma, B. N., 74
Sarvodaya movement, 144n.22
satyagraha (rule of truth) campaign, 69–70
Saudi Arabia, 121n.40
Saund, Dilip Alwin, 95
Saxena, Ravi, 150, 151, 240–41
Schumacher, E. F., 98–99
self-sufficiency ideal, 215–16
sending states
  "brain drain," 90–91, 95, 96
    circular migration and, 27, 121–22
    defined, 3
  "brawn drain," 3
  "care drain," 25–26
  CEO MDR's resistance to admitting emigration
    craft, 238–42
  class-based emigration practices, 6–9
  cost of emigration, 25–26
  emigrant education requirements, 6, 6n.5